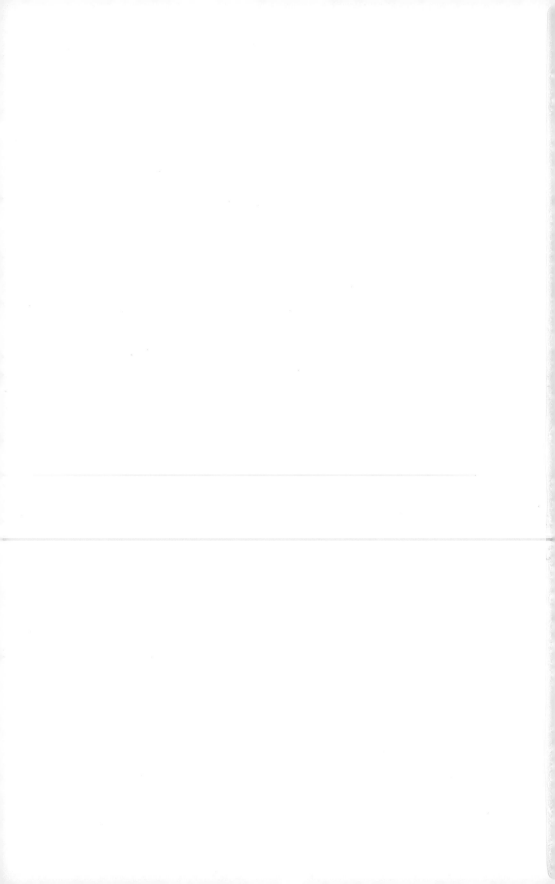

Twenty-First-Century Children's Gothic

From the Wanderer to Nomadic Subject

Chloé Germaine Buckley

EDINBURGH
University Press

Edinburgh University Press is one of the leading university presses in the UK. We publish academic books and journals in our selected subject areas across the humanities and social sciences, combining cutting-edge scholarship with high editorial and production values to produce academic works of lasting importance. For more information visit our website: edinburghuniversitypress.com

Edinburgh University Press Ltd
The Tun – Holyrood Road,
12(2f) Jackson's Entry,
Edinburgh EH8 8PJ

Typeset in 11/13 Adobe Sabon by
IDSUK (DataConnection) Ltd, and
printed and bound in Great Britain by
CPI Group (UK) Ltd, Croydon CR0 4YY

A CIP record for this book is available from the British Library

ISBN 978 1 4744 3017 3 (hardback)
ISBN 978 1 4744 3019 7 (webready PDF)
ISBN 978 1 4744 3020 3 (epub)

Contents

Acknowledgements

There are many people whose support, friendship and expertise made this book possible. I am deeply obligated to the scholarly community of the Department of English and Creative Writing at Lancaster University where I completed my PhD. Thanks to the 'Lancaster Gothic Crew' and its various affiliates. I would like to thank Stephen Curtis, Alan Gregory and Sarah Ilott for the coffee, the chat and their wealth of expertise. Many thanks, too, to the various members of the Contemporary Gothic Reading Group (especially, Xavier, David, Sunday, Ellie, Rhianon, Gosia, Enrique, Sarah, Alan, Neal, Steven, Kerry and Jo). So many of my ideas germinated during our wonderful and far-reaching discussions. Deepest and heartfelt thanks to Catherine Spooner for her expertise and generous support. Without her, this book would not exist. I would also like to thank Kamilla Elliott, Brian Baker, Lynne Pearce, David Punter and Andrew Tate for their kind attention to my work at various stages of its development. Thanks also to Uta Papen for supporting my writing during some difficult times. Writing retreats were my lifeline!

I want to thank the organisers of various conferences for providing such wonderful spaces for academic discussion and exchange. In particular, to the various organisers of The International Gothic Association conferences at the University of Surrey (2013), at John Fraser University, Vancouver (2015) and at Universidad de las Américas Puebla (UDLAP), Cholula, Mexico. Thanks, too, to the teams behind the annual conferences, Fantastika and Current Research in Speculative Fiction at Lancaster and Liverpool universities. I would also like to thank the staff and students of the Centre for Gothic Studies at Manchester Metropolitan University. It has been wonderful to be part of such a vibrant research community. Thanks also to my students at Manchester Metropolitan University in Cheshire, for their enthusiasm for the study of children's fiction, which helped me keep the faith during the writing of this book!

A version of Chapter 1 was originally published as 'Psychoanalysis, "Gothic" Children's Literature and the canonization of *Coraline*'. This article appeared in *Children's Literature Association Quarterly* (Volume 40, Issue 1, Spring 2015), copyright © 2015 Children's Literature Association. Portions of Chapter 5 were originally published under the title, 'Do Panic. They're Coming: Remaking the Weird in contemporary children's fiction' in *New Directions in Children's Gothic: Debatable Lands*, copyright © 2017. Reproduced by permission of Taylor and Francis Group, LLC. Thanks to reviewers and editors for their comments and kind attention to my work for these publications.

Finally, I want to thank my family. Joanne, Mike, June and Mark: thanks for the innumerable ways you supported my family after I gave up my sensible job to become an academic. Thanks also to Laura Mitchell, Louise Stewart, Michael Williamson and Sam West for the friendship (and all the gin!). Neal Kirk: I hope you know how important your support and friendship has been to me. Last, but by no means least, Jon Buckley: Thank you for your many sacrifices, for your support, and for reassuring me that it would all be worth it. I like to think I helped you in return . . . You can recite Chris Baldick's definition of the Gothic by heart, which is a pretty good party trick, right? Love you.

For Lucas

From Gothic Wanderer to Nomadic Subject

Twenty-First-Century Children's Gothic: The Bad Beginning

Twenty-first-century children's Gothic fiction begins with a violent act of *un-homing*. Three children lose their parents and their home, set adrift to wander an expansive, treacherous, Gothic landscape on a journey spanning the thirteen books that comprise Lemony Snicket's *A Series of Unfortunate Events* (1999–2007). In the opening pages of the first book of this series, titled *The Bad Beginning*, a 'mysterious figure' approaches three children playing alone on a 'grey' and 'misty' beach. The figure is revealed to be a family lawyer, Mr Poe, who promptly informs the children that their parents have 'perished' in a fire, a fire that has 'engulfed' and 'destroyed' their 'entire house' (Snicket [1999] 2007: 4, 9). With sparse directness, Snicket renders the children – Violet, Klaus and Sunny – homeless. The un-homing of the Baudelaire orphans in *The Bad Beginning* inaugurates a theme of homelessness that becomes a central concern in many Gothic fictions written for children in the twenty-first century. However, the wide-ranging narrative of *A Series of Unfortunate Events* reconfigures this state of homelessness as nomadism. It is this idea of homelessness as nomadism that I want to trace through a range of Gothic fictions produced for children, in print and on the screen, between 2000 and 2015.

The Bad Beginning figures homelessness as both catastrophic loss *and* call to adventure. The Baudelaire fire precipitates a journey and acts as the catalyst for a host of exciting and transformative encounters. Violet observes that Mr Poe is both the children's executor and executioner: he had 'simply walked down to the beach and changed their lives forever' (Snicket [1999] 2007: 10). Yet, Violet's gloomy assessment contains within it positive possibilities. Snicket suggests such possibilities when he describes Poe leading the Baudelaires 'away from the beach and from their previous lives' (Snicket [1999] 2007: 10). Though acknowledging the loss of the children's previous life, this moment also looks forward to new lives, to a prolonged state of nomadism that allows the children to inhabit a multiplicity of locations and identities. The fire causes the death of their parents and passes to the children a Gothic inheritance that prompts the disintegration of home and identity. For Chris Baldick, disintegration is the quintessential Gothic effect (1992: xix). Yet, in *A Series of Unfortunate Events*, this Gothic disintegration does not lead to despair, nor to the aporia – or black hole – of subjectivity as it is imagined by deconstructive psychoanalytic theories so often applied to contemporary Gothic works. Out of the ashes of their home, the Baudelaires construct a new, nomadic existence. Each book relocates the children from one place to another, pursued by the Gothic tyrant, Count Olaf. However, the children's escape from Olaf is, to borrow a term from Deleuze and Guattari, a 'line of flight', a 'line of becoming', and it affords all the positive possibilities suggested by nomadic philosophy (Deleuze and Guattari [1987] 2013: 342). *A Series of Unfortunate Events* exemplifies a new form of writing for children that reconfigures homelessness as nomadism.

A Series of Unfortunate Events is a landmark text because it inaugurates a new form of Gothic writing for children in the postmillennial period that challenges assumptions about Gothic and children's literature alike. *A Series* positively reconfigures Gothic exile, but also resists the cosy restitution associated with children's literature. The mystery of the fire remains impervious to hermeneutics; neither the Baudelaires nor the readers find any answers about the unexplained deaths that precipitate the adventure. As the names 'Baudelaire' and 'Poe' suggest, the series also typifies the explicitly intertextual character of this new mode of Gothic writing. Though the name 'Poe' recalls the dissolution of the family and its residence in 'The Fall of the House of Usher' (1839), the name 'Baudelaire' evokes the figure of the *flâneur*, whose ambulatory motion is suggestive of nomadic existence. This is a mode of writing that rejects destructive disintegration and instead esteems the creative figure of the nomad. Just as it takes its characters on journeys far from home, it asks readers to follow its narrative threads outwards to a variety of Gothic locations beyond the bounds of the individual book.

In twenty-first-century children's Gothic fiction, homelessness as nomadism functions thematically and structurally to resolve contradictions at the heart of the project of writing for children. Dominant critical discourses about children's literature anchor their readings of texts in the idea of a real child, who is identified through the fiction, but exists outside of it. On behalf of this child, critics seek to draw out a unifying meaning from the text so that its effects can be accounted for and its value assessed. Critics typically conceive of these effects in pedagogical and maturational terms. That is, they assess the value of the book in relation to its instrumental use in children's social, literary, or emotional education and/or in relation to a linear maturational narrative with a fixed beginning and end point. In its rejection of home, typified in *A Series of Unfortunate Events*, twenty-first-century children's Gothic prompts multiple 'lines of flight' from restrictive notions of singular identity (in Deleuze and Guattari's terms, 'being') to multiple possible iterations of a self that is continually in the process of becoming. In so doing, it proffers a multiplicity of subject positions and reading locations, offering a figuration of the child not yet conceived of in children's literature criticism.

Echoing the political dimension of Deleuze and Guattari's formulation of nomadism, the nomadic subject constructed in twenty-first-century children's literature offers an alternative ethical vision of writing for children to the widespread pedagogical view expressed by children's writers, critics and other commentators. In its relatively short history, children's literature has prompted much debate about what children's books are for and what they should do. On the one hand, liberal humanism and left-wing politics in the academy regard children's literature as a pedagogical project aimed at producing a critically engaged reader. On the other hand, the reader constructed in this pedagogy is typically passive; it is an implicitly teachable child. Gothic has a paradoxical allure for this pedagogical project. It has been identified as radical, subversive and excessive by critics who situate Gothic on the margins of hegemonic culture. For example, Clive Bloom describes Gothic as a 'refusal of bourgeois consciousness'; Susanne Becker claims its principal strategy is one of excess; and Fred Botting claims that Gothic's engagement with 'darker issues' and 'disturbing energies' marks it as a mode fascinated with transgression and taboo (Bloom 1996: 14; Becker 1999: 1; Botting 2008a: 14). At the same time, Gothic has also been read as a deeply conservative mode, implicated in the reproduction of bourgeois, nationalist and imperialist ideologies and social structures throughout its history. Thus, as Jacqueline Howard argues, 'we find strong, mutually exclusive political claims being made for the Gothic. For one theorist it is a subversive genre while for another it is conservative' (Howard 1994: 4). Cast as a transgressive mode, Gothic might be used by the writer of children's books to inculcate a questioning and rebellious subjectivity; while in its conservative figuration, Gothic might provide the children's writer with a tool to inculcate normative and compliant subjectivity.

Twenty-first-century children's Gothic inherits a contradiction between the pedagogical function of children's literature as it has been traditionally conceived on the one hand and the supposedly transgressive nature of Gothic on the other hand. In the years following the millennium, there has emerged a critical discourse (in the academy and the wider media) championing the value of children's Gothic in the postmillennial period. Yet, this discourse sustains paradoxical oppositions and contradictory ideas about Gothic writing for children. I stand apart from these critics in my desire to address such contradictions head on. I suggest that the project of writing for children in the twenty-first century forges a productive dialogue out of opposing ideas (about the Gothic and about children's literature), and is thus able to locate a model of subjectivity that lies beyond the humanist-inflected (and often conservative) pedagogies of children's literature without disappearing into the aporia of a fragmented and disintegrating selfhood offered by modernist-inflected Gothic criticism. In other words, children's Gothic imagines nomadic subjects.

Twenty-first-century children's Gothic poses a number of challenges to Gothic critics. Foremost, it counters the claim that Gothic has become pervasive and diffuse in contemporary culture such that it is no longer able to offer radical challenges to social and cultural norms as it once did. Particularly invested in Gothic's 'darker' and 'disturbing' figuration, Fred Botting asks, 'with its darkness dragged into the light, how does the genre stand up to scrutiny?' (Botting 2008a: 4). The question suggests a rather gloomy view of the contemporary Gothic. Botting argues that late twentieth- and early twenty-first-century 'Gothic times' produce a Gothic form emptied of its affective power, 'shedding the allure of darkness, danger and mystery', 'incapable of shocking anew' (Botting 2008b: 37, 40; Botting 2002: 298). For Botting, this is because Gothic has become a norm of cultural production, rather than remaining at the cultural 'margins' (2008b: 37). Botting is most concerned with the fact that Gothic has become a staple of consumer culture: 'Clothes, puppets, masks, lifestyles, dolls, sweets, locate Gothic images in a thoroughly commodified context in which horror is rendered familiar' (2008b: 9). In this description of 'thoroughly commodified' Gothic, many of the offending objects are those typically associated with children, pejoratively denoted as 'dolls' and 'sweets'. The suggestion is both that consumer culture is infantile and that the diffusion of Gothic into cultural objects associated with children is a clear indicator of the dire situation of contemporary Gothic. Botting's view of Gothic has been influential, prompting other critics to shore up Gothic against its supposed cultural diffusion by defining its limits. For example, Maria Beville claims that Gothic still retains its power to disturb and terrify, but only if its definition is limited to certain kinds of texts. For Beville, the problem of twenty-first-century Gothic is solved by ensuring that its borders are more vigorously policed. Under this regime, *American Psycho* is designated Gothic, but *Buffy the Vampire Slayer* is not (Beville 2009: 9). Beville's argument discounts mass-market Gothic, particularly those texts aimed at children rather than adults.

This discourse within Gothic Studies dismisses 'mainstream' cultural production according to the logic of subcultural capital. The arguments of Botting and Beville echo the mournful narratives told by subcultures about the appropriation of their practices by mainstream audiences. Botting's insistence that Gothic belongs on the margins rather than in the mainstream contains the same 'veiled elitism and separatism' that Sarah Thornton identifies in subcultural identity practices (Botting 2008b: 37, 9; Thornton 1995: 5). For Thornton, narratives employed by subcultures to shore up their identity and practices from appropriation by the mainstream work to 'reaffirm binary oppositions such as the alternative and the straight, the diverse and the homogenous, the radical and the conformist, the distinguished and the common' (1995: 5). Botting and Beville's arguments, in different ways, imply that the mainstream Gothic literature and culture represented by 'dolls' and *Buffy the Vampire Slayer* are straight, homogenous and conformist. The reiteration of such value-laden binaries have become commonplace in Gothic criticism's rejection of mass-cultural and mainstream iterations of the form. Many of my students echo such value judgements in class when, for example, discussing (and dismissing) the 'sparkly vampires' of *Twilight*.

Twenty-first-century children's Gothic counters such elitist evaluations with a reminder that the Gothic has its roots in popular culture, in consumption and in fakery. Children's Gothic fiction delights in the form's 'inauthentic' elements, combining these alongside Gothic's excessive energies to challenge traditional pedagogical ideas about children's reading. In so doing, children's fiction announces Gothic's continued power to unsettle totalising narratives offered on both the left and the right of politics. Furthermore, the use by children's fiction of Gothic techniques to unsettle limiting pedagogical narratives challenges 'social anxiety' readings of the Gothic. That is, children's fiction suggests a positive function for the Gothic in contrast to the idea that the form functions symbolically as a barometer of social and cultural anxieties. This reading of Gothic is particularly apparent in the academic study of zombies, as I shall explore in Chapter 2, but may be found throughout contemporary Gothic criticism, particularly since 2001. The social anxiety reading is evidenced in claims, such as Johan Höglund's, that the predominant Gothic genre of the post-9/11 period casts the 'other' as a Gothic and monstrous creature (Höglund 2014: 85). The nomadism of twenty-first-century children's Gothic alternatively offers an affirmative account of subjectivity that undoes the othering often initiated by a discourse that reads Gothic monstrosity through the lens of social and cultural anxiety. Nomadic children's Gothic affirms a positive function for the Gothic, while at the same time acknowledging the continuing effects of oppressive discourses and uneven power relations. Whether they are uncanny children, grotesque zombies, romance heroines, horror nerds, or troubled teens battling Lovecraftian monsters, the child protagonists of twenty-first-century children's Gothic offer a variety of affirmative, if sometimes precarious, subject positions.

Becoming Nomad

A *Series of Unfortunate Events* recontextualises the figure of the 'wanderer', typified in Gothic novels such as Mary Shelley's *Frankenstein* (1818) and Charles Maturin's *Melmoth the Wanderer* (1820). Gothic criticism tends to proffer tragic readings of the wanderer, drawing on a model of subjectivity that is pathologised or othered. Marie Mulvey-Roberts describes the wanderer as 'the ultimate embodiment of the other . . . always on the edge and at the edge, a monster of the in-between and as such, the supreme outsider' (Tichelaar and Mulvey-Roberts 2012: vii). Likewise, Kate Ferguson Ellis posits the wanderer as central to a 'masculine' Gothic tradition, in which the protagonist becomes exiled from the refuge of the home (1989: xiii). This image of the Gothic wanderer suggests a model of subjectivity that is structured around loss. The Gothic wanderer is the self in exile, forever estranged from the wholeness seemingly offered in the idealised fantasy of the home, a place that is also riven along gender lines.

Lemony Snicket offers an alternative figuration of the Gothic wanderer, placing Gothic in dialogue with other modes of writing, notably the picaresque. In the picaresque novel, the *picaro* is explicitly nomadic, remaking themselves over and over in different encounters and different locations in response to a corrupt society that has no place for them. This form of mobility is affirmatory and often empowering for characters such as Daniel Defoe's *Moll Flanders* (1772). Moreover, unlike the Gothic wanderer, which is associated with a 'masculine' Gothic tradition, the *picaro* has from its inception been a female as well as male occupation. Snicket's dastardly antagonist, Count Olaf, is equal parts Gothic villain and roguish *picaro*. In each encounter with the Baudelaire orphans, Olaf remakes himself anew, his tactics a bricolage of conmanship, disguise and dubious charm. Initially, the loss of their home places the Baudelaire orphans in flight from Olaf, but increasingly the children remake themselves in his image. Like Olaf, the children never rest in one place, but must always mobilise to face the challenges of an irredeemably corrupt world. They must also learn the tactics of bricolage, forging new and temporary identities in an immanent field of collaboration and interaction. Violet is the engineer of this makeshift 'war machine' of metamorphosis, while Klaus's love of books allows him to make rhizomatic connections and offer solutions to the children's most immediate problems (Deleuze and Guattari 2013: 420). Through Olaf and the Baudelaire orphans, Snicket constructs an adaptable nomadism, reworking Gothic's concern with exile from the home as an opportunity for deterritorialisation and self-fashioning. Reducing the Gothic castle to ashes, Snicket imagines nomadism not as a desperate flight from the world, but as an empowering mobility. This is not exile, but a 'line of flight' from hierarchical, or otherwise restrictively organised territories.

The final book of *A Series of Unfortunate Events*, deceptively titled *The End* (2006), concludes with an image of nomadism as a hopeful engagement with the world. The orphans are living as castaways on an island far from the rest of the world. At first they imagine staying on the island so as to escape the corruption they have everywhere else encountered. However, the children find a note from their parents (who once also sheltered on the island). The note declares: 'We cannot truly shelter our children, here or anywhere else, so it might be best for us . . . to immerse ourselves in the world' (Snicket 2012: 1–2).[1] Violet takes the note as a sign that the children must move on and when Klaus asks where they will go, she simply replies, 'anywhere' (Snicket 2012: 3). The children repair their tiny sailing boat, aptly named 'Count Olaf', and make ready to depart. The series concludes, leaving the children drifting out onto 'the open sea', an evocative image of a boundless territory (Snicket 2012: 12). For Deleuze and Guattari the sea represents 'an open space', or 'smooth' space, because it is not 'striated' by hierarchical power structures or fixed territories of being (2013: 423, 451). The sea is a space of contact, not exile. Becoming adrift on the sea does not suggest a linear movement 'from one point to another', but a 'vector of deterritorialisation in perpetual motion' (Deleuze and Guattari 2013: 451). In its deliberate frustration of closure, *The End* offers an equally tantalising image of homelessness as a kind of seafaring nomadism. Despite its famously gloomy opening, the book locates its characters in a hopeful subject position that offers active engagement with the world even as it recognises the corruption, restrictions and violence at large in that world. Many of the mysteries inaugurated by the house fire in *The Bad Beginning* remain unsolved and a secure home is not restored. Yet, mystery and loss are reconstituted as possibility and transformation.

The story of the Baudelaire children offers one figuration of what Rosi Braidotti, building on philosophical concepts proposed by Deleuze and Guattari, formulates as 'nomadic subjectivity'. In Braidotti's work, the nomadic subject is the self in process, a perpetually multiple and dynamic being. The nomad is embodied in concrete power and social relations, but occupies an affirmatory rather than oppressed position. Nomadic subjectivity is Braidotti's 'project of redesigning subjectivity as a process of becoming nomad . . . an image of the subject in terms of a non-unitary and multi-layered vision, as a dynamic and changing entity' (Braidotti 2011a: 5). This non-unitary model of subjectivity incorporates postmodern and post-structuralist notions of the subject as fluid and partly determined by social formations and other structures, but rejects a pessimistic structuralism and a tragic image of the fragmented subject found in linguistic and deconstructive theories. Nomadism accounts for the 'present condition of mobility' in a contradictory, complex global context (Braidotti 2011a: 4). It is a method for mapping subject positions and for creatively imagining alternative spaces of becoming from which to challenge and 'destabilize dogmatic, hegemonic, exclusionary power at the very heart of the identity structures of the dominant subject' (Braidotti 2011a: 3, 7, 9). I want to draw on Braidotti's evocative conception of nomadic subjectivity because it seems to be an eminently practical and ethical critical concept. My view of children's literature and culture is that it provides one potential creative space in which writers, readers and critics can explore other ways of becoming.

Nomadic subjectivity is not simply a utopian fantasy, but accounts for and actively engages with power differentials and processes of othering at work in our current social and political moment. Braidotti recognises that the 'bodies of women, youth, and others who are racialized or marked off by age, gender, sexuality and income, reduced to marginality, come to be inscribed with a particular violence' and offers nomadism as a tool to refigure these experiences of 'enforced eviction' (2011a: 6). Though the idea of the child is often universalised (often, implicitly white and middle class) in discussions of children's literature and culture, children's fiction itself is crowded with figures and bodies located in variously marginal positions, implicated in very different power struggles. *A Series of Unfortunate Events* focuses on orphaned aristocrats fighting to make their voices heard; Darren Shan's *Zom-B* (2012) features a working-class 'thug' negotiating the demands of macho culture; and *Paranorman* (2012) highlights the plight of the social outcast. Nomadic subjectivity offers contingent solutions to the problems faced by these characters, figuring productive, positive and affirmative selves. These entities are 'fully immersed in processes of becoming, in productive relations of power, knowledge and desire' and so offer 'a positive vision of the subject as an affective, productive and dynamic structure' (Braidotti 2011a: 17). I find Braidotti's account of nomadic subjectivity compelling politically and ethically since it provides a model of subjectivity that is inclusive and multiple. I also find it useful as a methodology because it allows me to engage in critique and interrogation of cultural products, imaginative texts and critical discourse, without the weight of literary or aesthetic values that might lead me to dismiss certain texts as unworthy of study. Nomadic subjectivity also resists the aporia of deconstruction, which is something of a trend in recent children's literature criticism as well as Gothic Studies. Thus, Nomadism seems to me to be a concept particularly suited to the reading of twenty-first-century children's Gothic, and, in turn, twenty-first-century children's Gothic provides an exemplary creative space in which nomadism can be imagined.

Nomadic subjectivity offers an alternative to prevailing conceptions of the child in children's literature criticism. Two main approaches currently dominate. The first advances an essentialist and universalising image of the child built on the theories of psychoanalysis. Critics that evoke this notion of the child in discussions of children's literature and culture tend to produce totalising readings of texts that echo narratives of maturation and mastery found in principle texts of ego-relational psychology, such as Bruno Bettelheim's *The Uses of Enchantment* (1976). This psychological reading is particularly problematic when directed at Gothic children's fiction because the child and the Gothic end up being subordinated to a 'master' discourse of psychoanalysis, against which they are constructed as symptoms. The totalising tendency of psychoanalytic criticism also suppresses other readings available in a text and, moreover, pathologises the child it claims to elucidate. In contrast, nomadic subjectivity replaces the fixed idea of 'being' with 'becoming'. Since the process of becoming is never complete and has no particular destination, the child cannot be constructed as an inferior and incomplete subject. For Deleuze and Guattari, 'a line of becoming has neither beginning nor end, departure nor arrival . . . A line of becoming has only a middle' (2013: 342). I want to emphasise that nomadic subjectivity is not, then, simply a synonym for maturation. Becoming is not linear; it is vortical. Becoming is not contained; it is open-ended. Becoming is not singular; it suggests that subjectivity is formed through mingling and combining with others.

One response to the essentialism of children's literature criticism has been to declare that the child 'does not exist' and, through deconstruction, reveal the futility of critical attempts to locate the child inside a book. This other approach to children's fiction might be termed 'constructivist', simply meaning that it takes as its central tenet the fact that the child is a discursive construct. I find constructivist criticism immensely helpful because it articulates a convincing critique of psychoanalysis and dispenses with the idea that children's literature must have a pedagogical function. If there is no real child, there is little point in assessing a book based on what effects it might have on a child reader. However, this approach can lead swiftly to the aporia of deconstruction, evident in the method's founding statement: 'the child does not exist'.[2] Though this is a useful refrain in reminding critics that the child – the one residing inside the book and the one produced in critical writing – is always a construction, it is in danger of becoming a dogmatic mantra that might prevent critics from saying anything productive about how we write about – and what we write for – children.

Nomadism, both as a figuration of subjectivity *and* a critical methodology, recognises the dangers of such aporia in (de)constructivist criticism, and provides some routes beyond it. As Braidotti claims (of the linguistic turn in post-structuralist thought more generally), a 'social constructivist grid leaves little room for negotiation and instils loss and melancholia at the heart of the subject' (2011b: 5). In other words, (de)constructivist approaches are in danger of concluding (rather unhelpfully) that there is no real self, only the master codes of language or discourse. Following Kant (whose transcendental idealism inaugurated a split between the perceiving subject and the world), through the linguistic theories of Lacan and Derrida, the 'linguistic turn' in Western thought is responsible for 'a negative form of social constructivism' in which 'matter is conceived of being formatted and regulated by a master code' (Braidotti 2011b: 3). In contrast, I employ nomadism to develop an intertextual concept of subjectivity that leads not to the aporia of deconstruction, which formulates the 'I' as an empty signifier, but to 'an opening out toward an empowering connection to others' (Braidotti 2011b: 3). Although the child constructed within the text and by the critic is fictional, a discursive and textual figuration, it provides a creative space for exploring the different ways subjectivity is constructed, narrated and experienced. Reading such constructions – or figurations – intertextually, which means placing them in dialogue with other texts and critical discourses, allows me to read the child of Gothic fiction as dynamic, productive and multiple. Conceiving of the child as a nomadic subject offers a myriad of alternative visions of the child and so can begin to counter hegemonic and limiting narratives of the child and of childhood without ending up in the black hole of the non-existent child. Rather than dismissing what we say about children as empty discourse and constructions, nomadic criticism allows for an engagement with real politics and issues of representation in fiction.

I want to use nomadic subjectivity to extricate the image of the child from an ethical dilemma that plagues children's literature criticism. This criticism paradoxically constructs children as passive even as it seeks to read them as active. Critics' limiting focus on the pedagogical value of the book produces a paradox whereby the 'good' book is one that will produce an active reader, but it can only do this work because the reader has been constructed a priori as passive. The child must submit to the pedagogy of the text in order *to be produced as* active. Echoes of this paradox appear in some Gothic criticism, particularly in discussions that dismiss 'trashy' Gothic texts, such as *Twilight*, because of the negative messages they transmit to a child reader (imagined as gullible, naïve and, usually, female). In contrast, nomadism suggests that the subject positions constructed within texts and cultures may be passive, or restricted in some way, but that space exists nonetheless within such locations for agency and empowerment. In many of the works I consider, authors make claims about the kinds of readers they wish to produce, but the writing itself throws up a number of alternative subject positions counter to this authorial intent. In other words, the texts imagine 'lines of flight' from potentially limiting or repressive figurations of subjectivity. Such 'lines of flight' emerge through the theme of homelessness, which demands that children learn to become adaptable, confident, fluid subjects. This becoming-subject is motivated by a vital and dynamic desire, which further counters the dominant psychoanalytic construction of the child in children's literature criticism. Psychoanalysis tells a melancholy story of a self driven by 'repression and the negative definition of desire as lack' (Braidotti 2011b: 2). In contrast, nomadism affirms what Braidotti terms the 'potentia' of the subject (2011a: 12). This hopeful and future directed concept of subjectivity is particularly suited to reading children's literature.

Post-structuralist literary criticism, particularly as it manifests in some readings of the Gothic, also tends to cynicism and melancholy even as it asserts the value of the Gothic as a disruption of political hegemony and cultural norms. Braidotti specifically conceives of nomadic thought as a counter to this 'dominant cynicism and melancholy' in order to stress the 'affirmative force of a political imagination that is not tied to the present in an oppositional mode of negation' (2011a: 13). In other words, criticism must offer something more than a critique. As Braidotti contends, 'more theoretical effort is needed to bring about the conceptual leap across inertia, nostalgia, aporia and other forms of critical stasis' (2011a: 13). This inertia is present in Gothic Studies' assessment of children's literature and culture, which has been little considered despite its long-standing relationship with the wider Gothic form. Most often, critics only mention children's literature and culture as an example of the contemporary pervasion of Gothic. Else, they view it as nostalgic, lacking the affective or political punch of adult Gothic. These evaluations of children's Gothic appear in the work of Botting and Beville, discussed above, but also in critical works ostensibly exploring the cultural value of children's texts. Jeffrey Weinstock's analysis of Tim Burton's children's animation, *Frankenweenie* (2012), for example, considers the film fundamentally 'inauthentic' (Weinstock 2013: 26). Drawing on the category of authenticity, Weinstock implicitly evokes Botting's assertion that contemporary Gothic empties out into commodification and simulacra, unable to provide real transgression or meaning as an 'authentic' Gothic once did. Exploring the nomadic themes and structures of Gothic children's fiction allows me to challenge these value judgements and reveal the productive relationship between Gothic and children's fiction. The latter is not merely a nostalgic pastiche of the former. Nomadism also allows me to explore the oppositional spaces forged within children's texts, and thus to read them as productive figurations of subjectivity rather than empty simulacra.

Nomadism is a reading strategy that can account for the conflictual nature of twenty-first-century children's Gothic and explore what its internal conflicts produce. Just as children's Gothic un-homes its protagonists, it unhouses its critics from the sheltered edifices and certainties of established critical narratives. Children's Gothic asks readers to explore pathways leading away from dominant formulations of literary form and of subjectivity. In turn, I employ nomadic thought as an alternative to critical methods that seek to subordinate the creative work to a totalising or unifying critical reading, or that reject meaning altogether for the seductive aporia of deconstruction.

'Fibers' and Threads: Nomadic Intertextuality

A Series of Unfortunate Events seems to invite a deconstructive reading by frustrating resolution and rejecting final meanings. However, though its central mysteries remain unsolved, *A Series of Unfortunate Events* refuses deconstruction by opening out into a positive intertextuality, represented by the ocean that frames the beginning and ending of the series. The smooth space of the sea is a virtual plane containing different possible 'fibers' of becoming (Deleuze and Guattari 2013: 291) that are here figured as the threads of different possible stories. The opening of last book, *The End* seems at first nihilistic, offering the onion as a metaphor for the text. As the reader peels away each thin, papery layer, they simply reveal yet 'another thin, papery layer'; their final 'reward' is only one misfortune 'after another, and another' (Snicket 2012: 1, 2). However, the final pages of the book refute this seeming disappearance of meaning into a textual *mise en abyme*. Though Snicket's investigation 'is over' he allows the story to stay mobile, leaving the Baudelaire children adrift on the ocean. He asserts that even though *he* has reached the last chapter of *his* story, 'the Baudelaires had not' yet finished their story (Snicket 2012: 10). Reading the nameplate of the boat, the new baby, adopted by the Baudelaire orphans during their stay on the secluded island, whispers a new secret. This is 'baby's first secret, joining the secrets the Baudelaires were keeping from the baby, and all the other secrets immersed in the world' (Snicket 2012: 12). Stories are secrets, and the open sea symbolises their continuing circulation. Snicket echoes the central metaphor of Rushdie's novel, *Haroun and the Sea of Stories* (1990), in which an ocean of stories is composed of multiple coloured strands: 'all the stories that had ever been told and many that were in the process of being invented could be found here' (Rushdie 1990: 72). In Rushdie's novel, the Sea of Stories constantly transforms as stories recombine to form new tales. *A Series of Unfortunate Events* makes a similar gesture, offering intertextuality as a creative and mobilising force that keeps stories and meanings fluid and vital. Though intertextuality does not offer a grand narrative or a unifying meaning, meaning is still available in provisional and dynamic ways.

Snicket's use of intertextual references and metafictional play in *A Series of Unfortunate Events* maintains a long-standing Gothic tradition. The first Gothic tales stitched together medieval and historical romance, with the novel of manners and supernatural and sensationalist tales from chapbooks and ballad sheets. Eighteenth-century Gothic was a new literary vogue, but it was also a reconstitution of past forms and old stories. Since the eighteenth century, the Gothic has continued to incorporate older works and a variety of narrative forms. For example, *Frankenstein* and *Dracula* anticipate postmodern metafiction in their use of textual fragments and multiple narrative structures. Fred Botting notes that *Frankenstein* is 'fragmented, disunified, assembled from bits and pieces; the novel is like the monster itself' (1996: 94). Likewise figuring intertextuality through Gothic tropes, Catherine Spooner notes that while many forms of literature might be said to be intertextual and self-reflexive, 'Gothic has a greater degree of self-consciousness about its nature, cannibalistically consuming the dead body of its own tradition' (2006: 10). *A Series of Unfortunate Events* continues this cannibalistic tradition in the way it draws on characters, tropes and threads from earlier Gothic works, and calls its reader's attention to this process with repeated authorial interventions reflecting upon the structure of the story.

Jacqueline Howard gives this aspect of Gothic attention in her explicitly Bakhtinian approach to the form (1994). Howard argues that plural and contradictory interpretations of Gothic are generated not only at the time of publication, but that interpretations of Gothic change over time with readers' changing perceptions and contexts (1994: 4). Thus, Gothic cannot be accounted for through one critical reading, nor does it serve one political narrative. Rather, Howard contends that Gothic is a 'plural form . . . in which the propensity for multiple discourse is highly developed and that it is dialogic because of its indeterminacy or its open structure' (1994: 16).

Twenty-first-century children's Gothic is likewise multiple, open and inherently (as well as often explicitly) dialogic and intertextual. Moreover, it also inherits particularly contradictory and paradoxical ideas about writing for children. An intertextual approach to children's Gothic can account for these contradictions and paradoxes, while leaving the texts open for further readings.

Twenty-first-century children's Gothic exemplifies Barthes's assertion that 'the metaphor of the Text is that of the network; if the text extends itself, it is as a result of a combinatory systematic' (1977: 161). Drawing on Bakhtin, Barthes rejects the idea of the text as a closed object emanating from one source (such as the author, a particular society or a moment in history). 'The Death of the Author' (1967) describes the text as 'not a line of words releasing a single "theological" meaning . . . but a multi-dimensional space in which a variety of writings, none of them original, blend and clash' (Barthes [1967] 1977: 146). In accord with Barthes, I envisage the field of children's Gothic, as well as the individual works within it, as a network comprised of multiple echoes, citations and retorts. There is no one particular 'originary' or foundational text, nor a core meaning, at the centre of this network, and critics should avoid suggesting where its limits or borders may lie. Each text in the network refers in part to each other text, whether this be a literary fiction, a film, a cultural idea about the child, or a critical narrative. Even where the texts are not explicitly referential or metafictional (though many are), they extrude 'fibers', or threads, outward, leading to other works and locations. The metaphor of text as network has the added advantage of promoting an inclusive rather than exclusive approach to reading, working against entrenched (and often unarticulated) notions of value in literary criticism that would hold some types of texts as more important and worthy than others.

Intertextuality asks critics to resist the temptation to read inwards, towards a central meaning. Intertextuality pulls readers outward, drawing them to yet more texts and ideas. Intertextuality declines to accept authorial intent as the final word. Throughout this book I include the commentary of various authors and give those voices fair hearing, but I do not allot the author a primary role in assigning meaning. Barthes's assertion that the writer's 'only power is to mix writings, to counter the ones with the others, in such a way as never to rest on any one of them' runs through this book because it leaves room for multiple and competing interpretations of texts to emerge (Barthes [1967] 1977: 146). Barthes argues that writing is always rewriting, offering an image of a text with porous borders and of reading as 'ventures' beyond these borders (1974: 4, 5, 8, 20). This image of the text accords with Deleuze and Guattari's image of subjectivity. The threads of the text work in a similar way to fibers of becoming, those 'continuous line[s] of borderlines (fiber) following which the multiplicity changes . . . A fiber strung across borderlines constitutes a line of flight or of deterritorialization' (Deleuze and Guattari 2013: 291). Developing the idea of becoming, Braidotti also echoes Barthes in her insistence that intersubjective connections do not 'plung[e] us inward toward a mythical "inner" reservoir of truth. On the contrary, they are better thought of as propelling us outward along the multiple directions of extratextual collective connections and experiences' (2011a: 19). Just as there is no unified being for the nomadic subject; there is no final or totalising meaning of a text. I want to follow the multiple threads of the works explored herein even as they work against one another, producing meanings that disrupt the narrative or that lead into territories outside the story.

In concert with this intertextual approach, I want to examine fiction alongside existing critical interpretations, including readings from Gothic Studies and children's literature criticism, as well as commentary from popular culture. I place the texts discussed in this books in dialogue with one another and trace links between popular commentary and critical discourse, examine where the texts themselves invite or anticipate particular critical interpretations, and consider how fictional texts offer a response to ideas about the child circulating in criticism and popular culture. In this way I hope to encourage critical dialogue that can resist the monologising tendency of some modes of literary criticism, which seek to put fiction in the service of one reading, or assign it one social function. It is possible to find meaning through literary criticism, but this meaning is always relational, multiple and open to further dialogue. As well as considering theories of intertextuality, originating in the work of Barthes and Bakhtin, this book also adopts other theoretical positions. I draw variously on theories of the grotesque, on Spinoza's formulation of desire, on theories of parody, on de Certeau's formulation of the reader as poacher, and on the philosophical writings of speculative materialism as I consider different manifestations of children's Gothic. None of these theories offers a unifying or overarching solution to the problems I identify in current literary criticism of children's literature and Gothic. Rather they serve, in particular locations, to elucidate the multiple points of connections, resonances and possible meanings generated by children's Gothic fiction that criticism has thus far ignored.

The works discussed in this book form an intertextual network that is also historically specific, and incorporates the intertwined histories of Gothic fiction and children's literature, as well as a history of debate about the function and value of these two forms. Gothic fiction and children's literature coalesced at the same historical moment in the eighteenth century. Later, in the late nineteenth century, both were bound up with the development of psychoanalysis. The concerns, direction and interpretation of Gothic and children's writing were influenced by the predominance of psychoanalytical thought in criticism and wider culture. As clinical practice and, later, as a literary theory, psychoanalysis borrows from and takes both children's literature and the Gothic as its object of analysis. Gothic narratives inform psychoanalytic theory and psychoanalytic theory has in turn been used to explain Gothic narratives. Likewise, psychoanalysis has drawn upon fairy tale and other forms of writing for children, just as writing for children has itself often drawn on psychoanalytic ideas. We have, then, three forms of writing (psychoanalysis, Gothic and children's literature) bound up together in a particularly fraught intertextual relationship in which one form cannot assert interpretive authority over any other. One key aim of this book is to explore this relationship and in so doing counter two trends in discussions of children's Gothic. First, I want to refute the truth claims often made through psychoanalysis about Gothic children's literature. Second, I want to show how Gothic and children's literature share a history and that children's literature is thus not a degraded or imitative form of Gothic cultural production.

Uneasy Exchange: A History of Gothic Children's Fiction

Gothic and children's fiction comprise a mutually constitutive intertextual network, their histories connected since their inception. Gothic and children's literature emerge as distinct forms of writing at the same historical moment and in the same literary and social context: Walpole's *The Castle of Otranto* (the first Gothic novel) and John Newbery's *The History of Little Goody Two-Shoes* (the first children's novel) were published in 1764. Both Gothic and children's fiction, inaugurated by these two books, are the result of developments in print culture in the eighteenth century, which saw the increased production of moderately priced print fiction for a growing middle-class audience. The development, readership, reception and criticism of both Gothic and children's literature evolved in tandem and in relation to similar cultural and social conditions. Though there has been a marked proliferation of explicitly Gothic fiction produced for children since 2000, the Gothic has always been present as a strand within children's literature and culture. Likewise, children's literature and culture have always been a significant location for the development of the Gothic form. Accordingly, the postmillennial proliferation of Gothic works for children represents a significant moment in the shared histories of the two modes of writing. What has shifted since 2000 is the status of children's Gothic fiction in both popular culture and academic criticism. Increasingly, commentators value the Gothic for its perceived pedagogical and maturational value: the Gothic helps children grow up.

When I embarked upon the research for this book, Gothic seemed to dominate children's publishing across a number of genres. Since the success of J. K. Rowling's *Harry Potter* novels (the first published in 1997) and Philip Pullman's *His Dark Materials* (first published in 1995), children's fantasy has favoured gothically inflected modes sometimes called 'dark' or 'urban'. Recent examples include Joseph Delaney's *The Spook's Apprentice* series (2004–14), which was adapted for film by Universal; Derek Landy's *Skulduggery Pleasant* series (2007–14); F. E. Higgins's *Tales from the Sinister City* (2007–10) and Philip Reeves's *Mortal Engines* quartet (2001–6). Paranormal Romance has also proliferated since the publication of Meyer's *Twilight* in 2004. A number of novels employing romance narratives and supernatural beings have since been marketed at teens in the UK and the US, including P. C. Cast's *House of Night* series (2007–14), *The Wolves of Mercy Falls* series by Maggie Stiefvater (2009–14), Cassandra Clare's *The Mortal Instruments* series (2007–14), Becca Fitzpatrick's *Hush, Hush* (2009–12) and Paula Morris's *Ruined* series (2009–13). Beyond this, a number of books have been published since 2000 that overtly engage with a literary Gothic tradition, rewriting classic and canonical Gothic works of the eighteenth and nineteenth centuries. Notable examples include novels and short story collections by Chris Priestley, such as the *Tales of Terror* series published between 2007 and 2011, the *Goth Girl* series by Chris Riddell (2013–15), various novels by Marcus Sedgwick, including *My Swordhand is Singing* (2006) and *Midwinterblood* (2011), and ghost stories by Anne Fine, *The Devil Walks* (2012), and Jonathan Stroud, *Lockwood and Co* (2014). Overtly 'psychological' Gothic fiction has also emerged in this period, offering gothicised narratives of trauma. These include the now canonical *Coraline* by Neil Gaiman (2002) and *A Monster Calls* by Patrick Ness (2011), both of which gained multiple awards and have been adapted into critically acclaimed films. Pulp horror also remains popular, exemplified by the gory zombie serials by Darren Shan (*Zom-B*, published between 2012 and 2016) and Charlie Higson (*The Enemy*, published between 2009 and 2015). As in adult pulp horror, these works attempt to exceed previous limits of acceptability in terms of gross-out aesthetics and violent content. Finally, 'Weird' fiction inspired by the writings of H. P. Lovecraft from the 1920s has also begun to appear in children's books, notably in Anthony Horowitz's *Power of Five* series (2005–12) and Celia Rees's novel, *The Stone Testament* (2007).

As these examples indicate, adaptation of children's Gothic print fiction for film and television is increasingly common. *A Series of Unfortunate Events* was adapted for film by director Brad Siberling and comic actor Jim Carrey in 2004 and has, very recently (in 2017), been re-adapted as a series for Netflix by Daniel Handler (the man behind 'Lemony Snicket') and actor, Neil Patrick Harris. A Gothic visual aesthetic notable in the *Harry Potter* films marks the adaptation of markedly non-Gothic children's golden-age classics, too, from John Stevenson's *5 Children and It* (2004) to Tim Burton's *Alice in Wonderland* (2010). In the midst of this flurry of Gothic and gothicised adaptations, producers are also making original content for children's television and film. Examples abound, from the BBC's paranormal children series *Wolf Blood* (2012–present) to feature-length animations such as Tim Burton's *Frankenweenie* (2012), Genndy Tartakovsky's *Hotel Transylvania* (2012) and its sequel (2015) and Chris Butler and Sam Fell's *Paranorman* (2012).

It is tempting to see this proliferation of Gothic in children's fiction as evidence that the recent millennium represents a watershed moment in cultural production for children, but such a claim belies the complexity of the relationship between Gothic and children's fiction. Though drastic changes have occurred since the 'golden age' of children's literature in the nineteenth and early twentieth centuries, and traditional fantasy 'backlist' favourites have been swept aside for new Gothic works, the Gothic has always been present in children's literature. In the eighteenth century, Gothic circulated in the form of chapbooks, read by adults and children alike, and elements of the new Gothic novels appeared in the very first children's books, published by John Newbery; in the nineteenth century, Gothic themes were threaded in 'golden age' texts produced for the middle classes, and abounded in the popular penny dreadfuls read by the working classes; *fin de siècle* Imperial Gothic influenced the juvenile adventure novels of Haggard and Stevenson, who in turn influenced writing for boys well into the twentieth century; from here, Gothic finds its way into children's fiction of the interwar period and on into the late twentieth century. In the eighteenth and nineteenth century, Maria Edgeworth, Mary Wollstonecraft, William Godwin, John Harris and Charles Dickens draw on the Gothic in their works for children. In the early and mid-twentieth century, Frances Hodgson Burnett, Philippa Pearce, John Masefield, Susan Cooper, Alan Garner and Roald Dahl continue a Gothic tradition, and many of their books remain in print to the present day. Later in the twentieth century, Gillian Cross, Robert Swindells and Christopher Pike are just a few of the writers for children explicitly working in a Gothic mode. This cursory glance over the history of children's literature demonstrates the continued presence of the Gothic. Matthew Grenby argues that even during periods of children's literature history in which writers explicitly stated their intentions to expel the Gothic, it continued to persist (2014: 243). Though Grenby cautions against placing too much significance on the coincidental date of 1764, he shows that the two forms communicate throughout their respective histories (2014: 252).

Given their shared material and social contexts, it is not surprising that borrowings occur between the Gothic and children's literature. However, some critics insist that the relationship between the two forms is the result of a marked sympathy and that Gothic is ideally suited to child readers in particular. In their introduction to *The Gothic in Children's Literature* (2008), Anna Jackson, Karen Coats and Roderick McGillis argue that the postmillennial proliferation of Gothic works for children is the reinstatement of a vital and natural relationship that dates back to *beyond* 1764. In their analysis, this date marks a regrettable break in the elemental synchronicity between Gothic and child readers:

> Children today would be more likely to enjoy the chapbook romances children used to read *before* a literature *specifically created* for children was developed, stories such as 'Jack the Giant Killer', 'Robin Hood', 'Children in the Wood', or 'Whuppity Storie'. Indeed, it is the stories that Enlightenment philosophers warned children against reading, such as the stories of Raw Head and Bloody Bones, that are likely to be the ones that children today would pick up first . . . Children, it seems, *have always had a predilection for* what we now categorize as the Gothic, for ghosts and goblins, hauntings and horrors, fear and the pretence of fear . . . Perhaps the really strange development of the eighteenth century was the transformation of the Gothic narrative into an adult genre, when it had *really belonged to children's literature all along.* (Jackson, Coats and McGillis 2008: 2; my emphasis)

In this history of Gothic and children's literature, Gothic is expunged from children's literature in the eighteenth century, to make a triumphant return in the twenty-first century, when children need it most. Concerned with establishing the authenticity of the current popularity of Gothic, Jackson, Coats and McGillis backdate children's Gothic to *before* the beginning of an established history of children's literature, to a period *before* the establishment of Romantic and Victorian ideas of childhood that informed that literature. This is an attempt to locate children's Gothic outside material histories of childhood, in a past location existing outside of cultural constructions and social institutions, claiming that Gothic is natural and essential. This naturalising of Gothic as intrinsically *belonging* to childhood is then linked to the appetites and desires of a child who is also constructed here to exist outside of discourse and history. This essential child's delight in Gothic, which has been historically denied and only now being recognised, further legitimises the texts Jackson, Coats and McGillis wish to explore through a model of children's literature that evaluates texts based on their ethical and pedagogical effects upon a real child reader.

The claim that children's Gothic has a renewed significance since the millennium is coupled to a narrative of resurgence common in histories of Gothic. For Jackson, Coats and McGillis postmillennial Gothic is significant precisely because it is a resurgence, the reappearance of a form previously suppressed into the 'byways' of children's literature (2008: 3). They argue that after a long period of suppression, 'by the late twentieth and early twenty-first centuries, the books children are reading are . . . haunted once again' (2008: 4). This narrative of demise and resurgence is something of a critical commonplace in histories of the Gothic. Spooner explains that Gothic 'has throughout its history taken the form of a series of revivals', continually reconstituting itself even as elsewhere its demise is announced (2006: 10). Likewise, Alexandra Warwick warns that the 'obiturally-minded critic' should be wary of announcing the death of Gothic since it can always be shown to have returned or been resuscitated (2007: 5).

This Gothic narrative of death and resurgence has been articulated a number of times in relation to the history of Gothic children's fiction, though which periods are marked as revivals, and which as periods of suppression vary from critic to critic. Neil Gaiman, whose psychological Gothic tale *Coraline* (2002) has been given a special significance by children's critics, echoes Jackson, Coats and McGillis, positing the millennium as the watershed moment. Gaiman claims that publishers declined *Coraline* when he approached them in 1990, in favour of realistic novels 'about a kid in a tower block whose brother has heroin problems' (Gaiman in Ouzounian 2009). Gaiman here references the success of various realist novels in the 1990s, such as Melvin Burgess's *Junk* (1996), which won the Carnegie Medal and The Guardian Children's Fiction Award. Yet, Gaiman's complaint that he could not get a publisher for *Coraline* until after 2000 seems disingenuous considering that throughout the 1990s Scholastic's horror labels, *Point Horror* and *Goosebumps*, dominated the popular fiction market in the UK and the US. In fact, in a survey of horror fiction for children published in 2001, Kimberley Reynolds identifies 'the last two decades' as a period of proliferation for Gothic (Reynolds 2001: 1). Reynolds's assessment contradicts Gaiman's claim of a dearth of Gothic fiction in the 1990s, dating the boom in horror fiction for children back to the 1980s.

As well as being dependent on point of view, narratives of death and resurgence inevitably fail to be comprehensive and do not account for the complex interactions between Gothic and children's literature, which have been both complementary and antagonistic. Children's Gothic is not a mode marked by sympathy or synchronicity, but by contestation and conflict. Depending on the point of view of the critic weighing in on the debate, contradictory claims have been made about the function of Gothic in children's literature. There is no evidence of a particular suppression, nor of a particular affinity that can be definitely proved in relation to any particular period. Instead, critics offer different assessments of the relationship, often during the same historical moment. Accordingly, Grenby is sceptical of a 'straightforward account of a steadily growing acceptance of Gothic in children's culture' for, even as he finds evidence of Gothic in children's fiction throughout the eighteenth and nineteenth centuries, he finds an equal number of critics and writers continuing to decry the mode as unsuitable. This back-and-forth leads Grenby to argue that the relationship between the two forms is 'uneasy' (2014: 251). Dale Townshend likewise traces a continual critical back-and-forth about the ethics, effects and value of including Gothic in children's literature throughout this early period (2008). As I have argued elsewhere, a linear narrative of children's literature and Gothic offers too much of a temptation to retroactively 'gothicise' texts from the history of children's literature, backwardly projecting contemporary concepts of the Gothic onto texts that would have been read very differently in their original context (Buckley 2014: 257).

A conflictual relationship between Gothic and children's literature is evident from the eighteenth century to the present. On one side of the debate, critics bemoan the sad decline of Gothic affect in the face of what they decry as the sanitising effects of literature produced for children, while, on the other side, critics rail against the continuing pernicious influence of Gothic and gory tales on child readers. Early children's literature set itself the task of instilling bourgeois values such as 'integrity, reliability, and level-headedness', countering a working-class oral tradition that included gory, Gothic tales (Grenby 2014: 245, 246). At the same time, Romantic writers praised Gothic affect as a vital component of childhood experience. In 1805, Wordsworth nostalgically calls for the gory chapbook tales of his youth: 'Oh! Give us once again the wishing cap . . . Jack the Giant Killer, Robin Hood and Sabra in the forest with George' (Wordsworth quoted in Townshend 2008: 29). Whereas, in 1829, the Society for the Diffusion of Useful Knowledge promoted the didactic fiction of Barbauld and Edgeworth as a much needed antidote to the tales of terror that were still 'so constantly taught' (Townshend 2008: 33). These contradictory positions about Gothic affect and child readers continued to circulate through the nineteenth century. For example, Dickens's 'Frauds on the Fairies', an attack on Cruikshank's bowdlerised versions of fairy tales for children, warned that 'we must soon become disgusted with the old stories into which modern personages so obtruded themselves, and the stories themselves must soon be lost' (Dickens 1853: n. p). Paradoxically, though Dickens disliked censorship in retellings of fairy tales, his own foray into Gothic writing for children allotted the ghosts a firmly 'moralizing' role, rather than indulging in terror for terror's sake (Grenby 2014: 251). So, just as children's literature was never wholly didactic to the exclusion of Gothic, nor did it ever fully embrace an easy and sympathetic relationship with Gothic affect and the sublime pleasures of terror. Contrary views suggest a long-standing conflict over the function of children's Gothic, and over the ethical dimensions of its affectivity. Romantic nostalgia for a 'haunted boyhood', informed by an image of childhood influenced by Rousseau (Townshend 2008: 30), echoes in current writing about Gothic fiction. Jackson, Coats and McGillis return to the very same chapbook titles included in Wordsworth's 'Prelude' to make their authentication of Gothic as a children's mode (Jackson, Coats and McGillis 2008: 2). At the same time, concerns about the negative effects of Gothic fictions on young readers, seen for example in the moral panic of the 1870s surrounding juvenile delinquency and the 'penny dreadful' (see Springhall 1994), continue to be voiced in relation to video nasties in the UK in the 1980s and, more recently, in concerns about the effects of teenage girls reading *Twilight* in the 2000s. That conflictual discussions of this nature continue to circulate in popular and critical discourses suggests that competing and often paradoxical desires for, and anxieties about, childhood remain unresolved. This ambivalence lies at the heart of twenty-first-century children's Gothic and the critical response to it.

I present this interrogation of the historical relationship between children's fiction and the Gothic as the springboard for my critique of narratives emerging in the postmillennial moment about the value of Gothic for the child reader. I agree with Jackson, Coats and McGillis that there has been a significant proliferation of Gothic fiction for children since 2000, but I question their reading of this significance. Instead of basing my analysis on a child reader who uses Gothic fiction to 'court their dark side and own it as an aspect of the self' (Jackson, Coats and McGillis 2008: 8), I argue that it is in adult-produced discourse and criticism that Gothic for children finds unprecedented acceptance in the twenty-first century. Children's Gothic fiction has gained unprecedented status in economic, pop-cultural *and* literary terms since 2000. The factors contributing to this status are multiple and include economically motivated interests on the part of publishing companies, who have promoted Gothic fiction for children, particularly in series form and across multimedia platforms. At the same time, critical interest and mass popularity have converged in an unusual way, particularly given that children's literature criticism has long been suspicious of mass-market forms of fiction. As recently as 2001, for example, Jack Zipes implicates mass-market publishing for children in the 'cultural homogenization' of American children (2002: 3). There is, generally, throughout children's literature, a focus on the 'literary' book to the detriment of popular fiction and visual media. As in Gothic Studies, a modernist aesthetic often surfaces in children's literature criticism, which values subversive art over mainstream culture, in an attempt to defend the field against its many detractors by arguing for the literary value of its objects of study. This suspicion of mass culture also originates in children's literature criticism's liberal humanist assumptions about the value of art. The discipline 'keeps faith with the fundamental assumption that literature (as opposed to books as a whole) will affect and therefore influence – and, with a bit of luck influence in desirable ways' (Lesnik-Oberstein 1994: 126). Nonetheless, since the publication of Jackson, Coats and McGillis's *The Gothic in Children's Literature: Haunting the Borders* (2008), children's literature critics are beginning to embrace contemporary children's Gothic, much of which could be characterised as mass-market popular fiction of the culture industry. As Victoria Carrington argues in her study of Gothic for children, 'toys are . . . a reminder of the very strong ties that the Gothic has always had with popular culture and mass consumption (with young children increasingly positioned as a large market)' (2012: 301). Increasingly, such products of mass-consumption are applauded. Carrington's study, for example, argues that mass cultural forms of Gothic are valuable in literacy education. Such readings suggest a marked critical shift in line with a proliferation of Gothic in popular and literary culture since 2000 that has occurred more generally, beyond the boundaries of children's fiction. This critical shift constitutes a decided swing away from a critical back and forth about Gothic affectivity and its positive or pernicious effects, towards a wider acceptance of the Gothic as an exemplary mode for children.

Eat Up, Children: Pedagogies of the Gothic

Though concerns about the effects of frightening fiction have arisen as recently as the 1990s, a noticeable shift has since occurred in academic and popular discourse toward the idea that Gothic is not only suitable for children but, moreover, that it is actually good for them. Writing in 2001, Reynolds notes that critical responses to horror in children's literature are still 'mixed', with anxieties frequently voiced 'about the potentially harmful effects on young people of getting the horror habit' (Reynolds 2001: 1, 2). Reynolds surveys newspaper articles and material released by educational groups that brand books, like those in the *Point Horror* series, 'vile and truly pernicious'. Reynolds likens the concerns raised over the *Point Horror* books to the moral panic in the US in the 1950s over horror comics, though they are most likely the consequence of the British 'video nasty' moral panic, intensified by the killing of James Bulger in 1993 by two children supposedly influenced by *Child's Play 3*. However, such damning commentary does seem to be in retreat by 2001, a shift due in part to the *Harry Potter* phenomenon. J. K. Rowling's work rapidly gained popularity from the beginning of the millennium, signalling and contributing to a transformation in the way children's fiction is valued. Nick Hunter notes that by the time all seven of Rowling's *Harry Potter* titles had been published in 2008, the series had sold more than 375 million copies in 63 languages. In response, the *New York Times* introduced a children's bestsellers list in 2001 after *Harry Potter* titles had filled the first three spots on their regular bestseller list for over a year (Hunter 2013: 46). As a cursory search of Amazon sales data indicates, *Harry Potter* continues to top bestseller lists even today. Though arguably not Gothic, the use of 'dark' fantasy in the *Harry Potter* novels appeals to adult readers and critics. Its popularity with the gatekeepers of children's fiction has led to the fantastic becoming more culturally valuable. In particular, darkly fantastical fictions crafted for children are now often hailed by critics as a valuable means of promoting reading and encouraging literacy, particularly amongst boys (see, for example, D. Smith 2005).

This shift in critical opinion can be seen in newspaper reviews, indicators of taste and value in children's literature where popular consumption and critical opinion converge. For example, *The Telegraph*, which branded *Point Horror* 'vile and truly pernicious' during the 1990s, featured many Gothic titles in their article on 'Adventures to Enchanting Worlds' in 2009. The piece contains recommendations by contemporary writers and critics, including a series of novels set in the 'dark, dark fairy tale world of the Brothers Grimm', *The Hunger Games*, Philip Reeve's *Mortal Engines*, China Mieville's Weird novel, *Un Lun Dun*, Marcus Sedgwick's *Blood Red Snow White*, and Chris Priestley's *Tales of Terror* collection, this latter described as 'wonderfully macabre and beautifully crafted horror stories' (*The Telegraph* 2009). *The Telegraph* has also favourably reviewed Darren Shan's pulp horror series, *Zom-B*, calling it 'a clever mix of horror, fantasy and realism' (Chilton 2012). Reviewers across the news media praise children's Gothic as 'deliciously scary', 'deliciously dark and satisfying', 'deliciously spine-tingling', 'chilling, creepy and utterly compelling' and 'marvellously strange and scary' (Merritt 2008; *Stirling Observer* 2010; Seymenliyska 2011; Lewis 2012; Pullman 2002).

Children's book award shortlists also demonstrate Gothic's new-found status. *Coraline* gained a series of accolades in the UK and the US, including the Hugo Award for Best Novella, the SFWA Nebula Award for Best Novella, a Bram Stoker Award for Best Work for Young Readers, a *Publishers Weekly* Best Book award, the *School Library Journal* Best Book award, and a *Guardian* Best of 2002 selection, among others. In the UK, *A Monster Calls* won both the prestigious Carnegie Medal and the Kate Greenaway medal in 2012. Critics have also recognised more playful texts, and Chris Riddell's pastiche of Romantic and Gothic fiction, *Goth Girl and the Ghost of a Mouse* won the Costa Children's Book Award in 2013. *Goth Girl* is an unlikely winner; in previous years the award was given to markedly more serious works. The triumph of *Goth Girl* is indicative of a change in perceptions of literary value, and shows a willingness in critical circles to value parody and humour alongside 'serious' psychological Gothic novels, like *Coraline*. Recently, Frances Hardinge's children's novel, *The Lie Tree* (2015) was awarded the title of Costa Book of the Year (a title usually awarded to adult fiction). The range of Gothic fictions now being recognised is not simply an indication of the mass popularity of the form, but shows that this popularity is accompanied by a positive critical reception.

A shift in critical discourse is also evident in the different academic evaluations of children's Gothic made by Reynolds in 2001 and by Jackson, Coats and McGillis in 2008. In the introduction to *Frightening Fiction*, Reynolds dismisses many texts labelled 'horror' (2001: 1). For Reynolds, most 'horror' texts marketed at children do not deserve the descriptor: 'Overall, horror fiction directed at young teenage readers backs away from the uncertain endings or all-pervasive sense of fear and ghastly transgression which characterises true horror' (2001: 3). For Reynolds, 'true horror' must be transgressive, a feature sadly lacking in mainstream writing for children. Her comments echo a point of view in Gothic Studies that requires horror and Gothic texts to be radical and subversive as opposed to conservative and mainstream. A concern with authenticity is seen here in Reynolds's use of quotation marks around 'horror', and also in her comment that many of the texts the volume surveys merely 'masquerade' as horror, when they in fact constitute a commercial genre that 'makes use of none of the traditional features of horror fiction' (2001: 3, 4).

In contrast, Jackson, Coats and McGillis dispense with genre boundary policing and do not question the authenticity of the texts under consideration. The shift from the label 'horror' to the term Gothic is also significant since it brings the study of children's fiction within a recognisable *literary* field. The label 'Gothic' links the texts to a historical literary period that suggests that popular and contemporary works have a legitimate heritage. Their evaluative language is markedly more positive and does not make a distinction between commercial or mass-market fiction and 'authentic' Gothic literature. The editors are keen to

> assess children's Gothic *on its own terms*, as a *pure* form destined for a profoundly knowing audience, who hears its parody and excess as a call to know more about what *really* haunts us. (Jackson, Coats and McGillis 2008: 9; my emphasis)

The editors stress the legitimacy and authenticity of children's fiction in the context of wider Gothic literature, valued here as a form of excess. For them, this 'pure irruption of the Gothic in children's literature' has a 'cultural and personal importance for contemporary child readers' (2008: 9). Here, children's Gothic is assimilated into a long Gothic tradition of a literature of excess. Thus, it is valuable in itself as an object of academic study as opposed to Reynolds's assessment which posits children's horror fiction as largely suspect in itself, but interesting in terms of the uses child readers might make of it.

Critics and reviewers of children's Gothic since 2000 embrace the form as authentic, often legitimising it through a language of desire and appetite. This language can be seen in many of the newspaper reviews mentioned above, which describe children's Gothic as 'deliciously' scary. The word connotes a gleeful delight in Gothic for its own sake, but also suggests that the books satisfy a deep desire in the child reader. The construction of the child reader as possessing a rapacious appetite for Gothic is repeated in academic and popular discourse. One newspaper reviewer claims that 'there is nothing most kids like more in their literary diet than a good helping of gruesome', while Jackson, Coats and McGillis refer to the child reader's 'appetite' for and delight in 'the more piquant pleasures of a good shiver' (*Stirling Observer* 2010; Jackson, Coats and McGillis 2008: 2). In statements such as these, critics assume that Gothic fiction satisfies an innate desire, which originates in the child itself.

The language of appetite evokes the idea of 'diet', and, specifically, what a healthy reading diet for children consists of. Thus, even as they imagine and construct a child reader with active desires and Gothic tastes, critics position themselves as arbiters of what is *good* and *nourishing* for children. The logic at work here is pedagogical at root, and a pedagogical framework is being established in which Gothic fiction is increasingly valued for its role in maturation and identity formation. Thus, an uneasy conflict emerges between the idea of Gothic originating in the child's unconscious desires, and the idea that Gothic must serve a pedagogical function. The conflict is neatly demonstrated in the success of Neil Gaiman's *Coraline*. Though claiming to write on behalf of a child whose dark desires unlock the doorway to an uncanny Gothic space, critics invariably read *Coraline* and its eponymous character as a fable of maturation, a moral tale with the message: be careful what you wish for.

The conflict between imagining children's Gothic as satisfying deep pleasures and needing it to serve a pedagogical function is not new. Neil Gaiman's claim that he wrote *Coraline* for his daughter because there was a dearth of Gothic stories for children in the 1990s echoes the claims of nineteenth-century writer, Heinrich Hoffmann. In 1848, the self-styled 'kinderlieb' (meaning lover of children) published the now infamous *Struwwelpeter: Merry Stories and Funny Pictures* in English. In this gruesome volume, naughty children are violently punished for various misdeeds. Now widely regarded as moral didacticism at its most severe, *Struwwelpeter* was intended by its author as humorous entertainment. He claimed that the child's appetites and tastes were not catered for by other writers of the time. Similarly, Neil Gaiman claims that his daughter Holly couldn't find any of the scary stories she loved on the shelves of the bookshop, 'so I thought I'd write one for her' (Gaiman, quoted in Ouzounian 2009). Gaiman and Hoffmann make recourse to the appetites of their own children and so duck accusations that they write to instruct. Other contemporary writers make similar claims. Charlie Higson claims to write for his son, Stanley, and explains that each instalment in his gory zombie series (*The Enemy*) represents an attempt to provoke a response in his horror-loving son (Flood 2014). Time and again, authors offer commentaries on their work that construct a real child whose appetites their work satisfies in ways that traditionally (pedagogical) children's literature does not.

Nonetheless, these writers cannot escape the pedagogical logic of children's literature criticism. As Lesnik-Oberstein points out:

> Children's books are written by adults for children. The subsequent criticism of this fiction is then produced by adults on behalf of children who are supposed to be reading the books. There are thus multiple layers of adults writing, and then selecting and analysing, children's fiction. (2000: 222)

As Zipes further argues, Hoffmann's book 'was never really conceived or created for children . . . *Struwwelpeter* had to appeal to the tastes and values of adults' (2002: 153). So, just as Hoffmann's book became an incredibly popular instructional text, found on nursery shelves throughout Europe and the United States, so *Coraline* has come to be lauded as an important Gothic tale of maturation that parents ought to share with their children.

The pedagogical logic behind the new praise for Gothic is exemplified by Sam Leith in a *Guardian* article aptly invoking Hoffmann's infamous book: 'Do you know what today's kids need? Thumb amputation, that's what'. Leith proclaims that 'art for children should be scary. It needs to be scary' (2009). A similar tone is adopted by Higson in his assertion that horror is '*good* for kids': 'Kids *should* have night-mares, they *should* be scared of things.' For Higson, nightmares help children learn 'how to cope with things' (Higson quoted in Flood 2014; my emphasis). Praise for Gothic horror as vital in children's social and psychological maturation is increasingly common. More recently, in a blog titled 'Why Horror is Good for You (And Even Better for Your Kids)', writer Greg Ruth states that now more than ever is the time to 'scare the hell out of kids and teach them to love it'. For Ruth, horror 'teaches' children to 'cope' and helps them 'grow' (Ruth 2014). Thus, the 'appetites' imagined to originate in the child authorise an adult dis-course about what how the child should be guided, through its read-ing, to grow and mature. It seems that there is no escaping children's fiction's association with instruction and education.

For critics now turning their attention to Gothic children's fiction, the form aids social maturation, psychological growth and encourages vital literacy skills. For Reynolds, frightening fiction is attractive to child readers since it promises 'agency [and] the acquisition of power that will enable them to make decisions and operate effectively in the world' (2001: 8). Likewise, Jackson, Coats and McGillis suggest that children's Gothic not only 'stretches children's literary competencies' but it pro-vides a space in which strong, active identities can be forged (2008: 4). Jackson, Coats and McGillis claim that Gothic produces a child reader who is responsible and empowered: '[they] acknowledge [their] respon-sibility for bringing the evil into the world and assert [their] agency in the face of it' (2008: 8). Jackson, Coats and McGillis suggest that chil-dren's Gothic serves the child reader's needs as a growing and develop-ing subject. Reading Gothic is here constructed as therapy in which the child's identity is shaped and matured through the positive interventions of the text.

The agency of the child reader continues to be a focus in Victoria Carrington's work, which identifies a new and radically subversive literacy available through Gothic toys. Unlike Coats and Reynolds, Carrington is less squeamish about explicitly labelling Gothic as 'ped-agogic' and so illuminates clearly the pedagogical logic at work behind the critical claims that Gothic is good for children (Carrington 2012: 304). Carrington argues that the Gothic provides vital resources in the process of identity construction: 'skill sets and attitudes that allow the young to construct coherent resilient bespoke identities' (2012: 304, 305). A twenty-first century Gothic resurgence demands and promotes literacy skills that

will ensure that young citizens are equipped with the critical skills to analyse, unpack, repackage and redeploy texts . . . Children learning to be literate in Gothic times must have opportunities to become aware of the rights and responsibilities that go with citizenship and engagement in communities . . . To this end, their practices with text creation and deployment should always be authentic and in the world and sometimes subversive so that they learn the power of text in relation to civic engagement. (Carrington 2012: 305–6)

Carrington's claim that contemporary Gothic can produce a new form of literacy ideally suited to the contemporary moment echoes children's literature criticism, which read texts in light of their role in producing active, questioning, critical and literate child subjects (see, for example, Nikolajeva 2010; Stephens 1992). This pedagogy is increasingly linked to Gothic texts, with writers themselves echoing critical discourse to claim that their works aid in producing a critical literacy broadly aligned with liberal humanist politics.

The emergent critical narrative about children's Gothic is thus both pedagogical and politically liberal, identifying with a subversive and critical child reader. This active pedagogy constitutes a shift from previous understandings of the function and value of scary stories for children, a shift that can be expressed in a move from being eat*en* to eat*ing*. In their analysis of a children's poem, 'The Ghoul', Jackson, Coats and McGillis express this shift:

The Gothic releases forces usually repressed . . . Our enjoyment is visceral: the cracking of bones and the snapping of backs. Parts of the body are delicious morsels, tasty tarts and candy snacks. (2008: 11)

Typically, the ghoul is a cannibalistic nursery bogey who poses a threat to the child, rather than offering a site of identification. In her study of fairy tale, myth and children's stories, Marina Warner argues that cannibal giants are typical nursery bogeymen throughout history (2000: 33). Cannibal bogeys represent a physical threat expressed through their desire to consume the child: 'they are ravenous, and ravenous for the wrong food' (Warner 2000: 36). In modern times, Warner argues, the threat the cannibal bogey represents may no longer be physical, but stand in for sexual threats, such as the abuser or paedophile (Warner 2000: 38). Warner's study focuses on the appetite of the bogeyman and what anxieties this appetite represents – in particular adult anxieties about childhood. In contrast, the emergent critical discourse of contemporary children's Gothic focuses on the appetite of the *reader*, and posits this appetite as the source of the Gothic irruption. Jackson, Coats and McGillis note contemporary Gothic's link to the 'cautionary tale', but argue that contemporary writers have made a knowing and ethical progression forward from these older tales, suggesting that the text is a therapeutic space for identity formation (2008: 12). Whereas in Warner's analysis, it is the staging of the defeat of the bogeyman that provides this function, for Jackson, Coats and McGillis, it is in the act of identifying with the bogey and its appetites that the child's identity is formed (Warner 2000: 46, 329; Jackson, Coats and McGillis 2008: 11, 13).

This evaluation of children's Gothic premised upon the child's appetite is deeply paradoxical. The child reader is both the source of the Gothic and the object upon which it acts, in a pedagogical model that aims at an active, empowered reader, but nonetheless requires that reader to be passive so it can do its work. As Lesnik-Oberstein argues, children's literature criticism is still rooted in didacticism even as it tells a story of moving away from didacticism:

> The narratives adults attempt to convey to children are controlled and formed, implicitly and explicitly, by the didactic impulse . . . the roots of allocating books (that is, criticism) to, and producing them for, children, lie in the effort to *educate*. This is in contrast to the generally accepted view that children's fiction is a category defined by, and originating from, a *move away* from didacticism, instruction, or education. (Lesnik-Oberstein 1994: 38)

This deeply paradoxical pedagogy is exposed when it intersects with Gothic. Gothic has come to be valued for its subversive and transgressive nature, ideally suited for this ethical progression of children's fiction away from didacticism and instruction. Paradoxically, Gothic is put to work to serve a pedagogy that claims to create freedom for children, but continues to rely on 'an all-knowing, all-controlling adult' (Lesnik-Oberstein 1994: 63).

The exhortation for the child to be exposed to Gothic is also informed by a construction of childhood as itself inherently Gothic. The picture book author Maurice Sendak has been widely praised for acknowledging 'the terrors of childhood' and refusing to 'cater to the bullshit of innocence' (Brockes 2011). Drawing on Sendak as inspiration, Greg Ruth claims that Gothic is good because it accurately reflects the fact that 'childhood is scary'. Describing childhood as a 'terrifying ordeal' that the Gothic author can 'help children survive', Ruth argues that Gothic is pertinent to the postmillennial moment, with its economic crises, terrorist threats and ecological disasters: 'It's a spooky time to be a kid . . . let's give them some tools to cope with it' (Ruth 2014). The idea that childhood is traumatic sits uneasily with the claim that Gothic emerges in response to children's innate appetites, and so empowers them. Moreover, Ruth's explanations of why Gothic is good cannot do without the idea of 'guardians and guides' helping children through the trauma (Ruth 2014). Jackson, Coats and McGillis are also unable to resolve this tension, arguing that Gothic for children 'warns of dangers . . . close to even the most familiar of places. It reminds us that the world is not safe. It challenges the pastoral myths of childhood, replacing these with myths of darkness drawing down' (2008: 12). Likewise, for all Carrington's appraisal of Gothic as producing subversive literacy, she also claims that 'the contemporary Gothic revival is a marker of anxiety around identity, trust, authenticity, and, to some extent, childhood itself' (2012: 298). Thus, as well as a conflict between activity and passivity within the underlying pedagogy of children's Gothic, gothicised narratives of childhood sit in uneasy tension with an image of an empowered and delighted reading child.

To summarise, the pedagogical logic of the emergent critical discourse praising children's Gothic originates in the fundamental and paradoxical assumptions of children's literature criticism. The valuation of Gothic as transgressive and subversive adds a further tension to this paradoxical pedagogy, since Gothic is ultimately valued for its pedagogical effects upon a passive child reader. Another conflict has also emerged here in the construction of twenty-first century childhood itself as Gothic, a site of trauma, but also the privileged space of imaginative engagement with the liberating energies of the Gothic.

Multiple Territories: A Note on the Chapters

The following chapters offer my response to the problems I have identified in the current analysis and evaluation of children's Gothic fiction. Acknowledging the lessons of (de)constructivist challenges to notions of the child reader, I reject an analysis of Gothic reliant on a 'real child' reader or viewer. However, I wish to avoid the aporia tempted by the mantra, 'the child does not exist'. Instead, I propose to explore the multiple locations in children's Gothic fiction across which subjectivity is constructed. Following Braidotti, I seek to reveal a 'diversity of possible subject positions' that children's Gothic offers (2011a: 16). Child characters and implied child readers are conceptual personae, practical experiments in the virtual plane that explore various different methods of self-organisation and ways of becoming. Rather than submit children's fiction to critical readings, I want to engage productively with them, offering my analysis up to the processes of deterritorialisation initiated within the fiction. These books and films reconfigure both the child reader and the adult critic as nomadic subjects, un-homed from familiar and enclosed locations, adrift in an expansive intertextual terrain, and open to productive dialogue.

Throughout the book, I draw on a broad definition of Gothic that aims at revealing the multiplicity of twenty-first-century children's fiction in print and visual culture. I take Chris Baldick's assertion that the Gothic effect is attained through a combination of 'a fearful sense of inheritance in time with a claustrophobic sense of enclosure in space, these two dimensions reinforcing one another to produce an impression of sickening descent into disintegration' (1992: xix). This definition allows me to include a broad array of fiction, while also differentiating Gothic to some extent from the related mode, horror. That said, the two traditions are interrelated (as my analysis of zombie fiction acknowledges). For me, the Gothic denotes any text that uses recognisably Gothic tropes or characters, or that draws and makes reference to a history of Gothic in its multiple forms. I include works that draw on and explore popular and cultural ideas about the Gothic or that provide a pastiche or parody of past works. The texts I examine are part of a varied body of work that remains very much open and in process, and I have no interest in policing its borders or marking out firm boundaries. Overall, I am most interested in those texts critical discourse has marked as Gothic within children's literature, and those it has not. Unpacking the implicit valuations in these demarcations allows me to reveal blind spots within existing criticism.

Likewise, my definition of what constitutes 'children's' fiction is deliberately broad and includes teen or adolescent fiction, as well as works suggested for readers as young as eight or nine. Works marketed at children aged between eight and sixteen are sometimes labelled 'Young Adult' or 'teen' fiction. This category is not helpful since it denotes marketing strategies, rather than suggesting anything about real readers. Different bookshops shelve works differently, and one publisher might suggest a work is for young adult readers, while a comparable work from another publisher (in terms of theme, length and content) might be suggested as a '9+' work. For example, on its *Booktalk* website, Scholastic suggests its romance range, *Point*, for readers aged 12–18. However, elsewhere on Scholastic's website, individual titles in the *Point* series are suggested for readers in Grade 5 and Grade 6 (ages 10–12). Elsewhere, an academic study of 'teen' romance suggests its readers are aged between ten and fifteen (Kutzer 1986: 94). The children's Gothic novel, *Coram Boy*, is included in the UK curriculum for Key Stage 3 (ages 11–13), even though the book includes typically 'Young Adult' content, such as sex and violence. Categorisations within children's literature publishing are thus too loose to provide any evidence that the texts are written for, or read by, a specifically 'adolescent' child rather than just a 'child'. Similarly, film classifications are not useful indicators of audience age. *Frankenweenie* and *Paranorman* were given a 'PG' rating by the British Board of Film Classification and *Hotel Transylvania* received a 'U'. Yet, the potential audience for all three films ranges from young accompanied children all the way through to adults, like myself. The various works I look at through this book, then, might be suitable for readers and viewers under twelve years old, but may also appeal to readers above this age. Since my analysis is not anchored upon a real, concrete child outside the text, I have jettisoned the various categorisations of children's fiction that draw lines between age groups (e.g. 5–8, 9–12, 'Young Adult') and I focus instead on what image of the child, what nomadic conceptual persona, the texts construct. After all, this conceptual persona, or reading position, may be adopted by readers of any age.

My reading of *Coraline* in Chapter 1 undercuts the truth claims psychoanalytic criticism makes about the Gothic and the child, revealing such criticism as just another story that adults tell about children. I explore the recent 'canonisation' of Neil Gaiman's 2002 novel, *Coraline*, one of the most discussed works of twenty-first-century children's Gothic. Popular commentary and academic criticism present *Coraline* as exemplary in its field and the various analyses of the novel represent the culmination of a trend in children's literature criticism to subordinate creative fiction, particularly the Gothic, to the master narrative of psychoanalysis. The novel seems to invite a psychoanalytic reading, drawing explicitly on Freud's essay 'The uncanny' (1919). However, the novel's self-awareness also confounds a psychoanalytic reading. In its doubling of Coraline's home with a mirror image, the book also invokes Lewis Carroll's famous *Alice* books as a further intertext and so asks its reader to interrogate the shared histories of children's literature and psychoanalysis. Reading the intertextual connections of *Coraline*, this chapter suggests that the psychoanalytic child often invoked in existing critical accounts of this book, and children's Gothic more generally (see Coats 2008; Rudd 2008; Gooding 2008), is an illusion. In the place of this illusion, I offer the image of the nomadic, intertextual child, constructed at the intersection of Gothic, psychoanalysis and children's literature.

Chapter 2 continues with the challenge to critical paradigms in children's literature criticism in a re-evaluation of theories of 'identification'. I place existing formulations of 'identification' (Chambers 1985; Stephens 1992; Nikolajeva 2010) in dialogue with Darren Shan's pulp horror series, *Zom-B*. My reading reveals the paradoxical pedagogy at the heart of these formulations of identification in children's literature criticism, which consistently fail to theorise reader agency in their reliance on the image of a passive, teachable child reader. I contend that *Zom-B* presents a grotesque subject in response to the child usually constructed in pedagogical readings. The grotesque identification offered by the zombie returns to the text aspects of identity that children's literature typically disavows. Shan's zombie manifests those aspects of identity repressed in readings of children's literature erected on binaries such as the reading / non-reading child, the middle-class / working-class child, and the teachable / unteachable child. Tracing a 'line of flight' akin to that made by Deleuze and Guattari's 'war machine', Shan's zombie embodies a grotesque nomadism that rejects 'Classical' being and a dominant construction of the child as middle class and teachable. Shan's use of the zombie further prompts a rereading of accounts of the zombie that dominate Gothic Studies. It is a critical commonplace to read the zombie as symbolic of cultural and social anxieties. However, I argue that in children's literature, the zombie becomes an affirmative and attractive figure of identification.

Chapter 3 focuses on the long-maligned form of Gothic Romance and its female readers. I explore the dismissive attitude towards 'feminine' forms of Gothic present in Gothic criticism from Samuel Richardson's savage critique in the eighteenth century, to Fred Botting's rejection of feminine romance novels in his 2008 study, *Gothic Romanced*. Further developing my critique of the dismissive tendency in Gothic studies towards popular, mainstream works, I also interrogate the recent critical backlash against 'Paranormal Romance', looking at the complexity of the interrelation between Romance and Gothic. I challenge the way that audiences for works labelled as 'feminine' have been constructed as passive dupes, even in critical accounts dedicated to exploring the experience of female readers. In twenty-first-century children's Gothic Romance *both* heroes and heroines are exiled from the domestic space and must reconfigure their identities as nomadic. The Romance mode (in its much maligned popular manifestation as romantic fiction) also plays an important part in this reconfiguration of identity since it suggests that romantic love and desire are affirmative processes for the becoming subject. Rejecting a negative formulation of desire as lack that comes from psychoanalysis, a formulation common in critical accounts of romance, children's Gothic Romance locates the exile within a Spinozan model of subjectivity as an active agent whose passions reveal a persistent and affirmative 'will' to be.

Chapter 4 counters the elitism of Gothic Studies through a reading of two animated children's films. As I have suggested in this introduction, twenty-first-century children's Gothic includes numerous film and television adaptations of novels, as well as multimedia series narratives and franchises. Of course, it is not just children's culture. As Linda Hutcheon asserts, adaptation is everywhere and increasingly self-conscious (2006: 2). The films I examine in Chapter 4 are explicitly self-conscious in their adaptation of literary and filmic Gothic tropes, illustrating some of the ways that the Gothic has developed as a mode through film production throughout the twentieth and twenty-first centuries. Examining these films also allows me to consider the way nomadic subjectivity can be constructed not only in a verbal medium, but through the visual and aural production techniques of Gothic cinema. These techniques produce a particular aesthetic that feeds back into children's Gothic more generally and films are as much an influence on print culture as they are influenced by print culture.

As I have outlined in this introduction, some critics suggest that twenty-first-century popular forms of Gothic (particularly works for children) represent a diffusion and degradation of the form, which more properly belongs on the margins of culture. The parodic strategies of the films *Frankenweenie* and *Paranorman* (both released in 2012) work to dismantle the notion of 'authenticity' often invoked in these arguments. The double-voicedness of parody reveals the impossibility of 'authenticity', but does not empty the works of their potential affective power. The films' parodic repetition of Gothic cliché does not result in a reduced power to affect audiences. Rather, they imagine a 'sophisticated-naïve' reader who is able to decode the parody while also feeling the spine-tingling effects of Gothic horror. Furthermore, these films reconfigure the image of the home as a site of belonging for the child protagonists, who are represented as outsiders and misfits. Spaces that are experienced as uncomfortable or repressive in the opening of the films are reconfigured as welcoming when the actions of the outsider protagonists transform their homes and communities. In these works, the nomadic subject brings together the 'margins' and the 'mainstream'.

Chapter 5 returns to literature to explore the way that children's Gothic appropriates elements of the Weird tradition inaugurated by the early twentieth-century writings of H. P. Lovecraft. A deeply contradictory mode of writing, Weird fiction has inspired radical challenges to Western philosophy *and* a proliferation of pop-cultural manifestations. Both of these forms of the Weird (philosophical and popular) appear in Derek Landy's *Skulduggery Pleasant* and Anthony Horowitz's *Power of Five*, which deploy the Weird to destabilise narratives of maturation typical in 'Young Adult' fiction. Not only are the protagonists un-homed in these fantasy adventures, their entire ontology is swept away by an encounter with a Weird universe. Thus, rather than creating safe, bounded spaces for the exploration of maturation, Weird children's fiction opens out into a horrifying encounter with what Lovecraft calls 'cosmicism'. At the same time, the child continues to be constructed as an agent capable of pleasure and empowerment; the protagonists of the stories battle successfully with indescribable and monstrous creatures. These texts do not simply re-create the 'haute' Weird of the early twentieth century: they remake it, countering traditional narratives of maturation and mastery popular elsewhere in children's fiction. Drawing on recent developments in speculative materialist philosophy, I suggest that the Weird offers an encounter with the strange objects of material reality, propelling the nomadic subject beyond the confines of the humanist conception of the 'I'.

The conclusion draws the various readings of the different works together in a final articulation of nomadic subjectivity. It asserts the importance of critical attention to children's fiction, which represents both a space of innovation and imaginative adaptation of the Gothic, as well as being the forum in which young readers develop their subjectivity as readers and actors in the social realm. Surveying a range of twenty-first-century children's Gothic fictions, this book follows the nomadic subject through very different landscapes and spaces. This journey will trace a productive, transformative figuration of subjectivity that counters both the pedagogical interpretation of the 'psychoanalytic child', which dominates children's literature criticism, and the image of a tragic, or riven, subject offered by deconstructive psychoanalysis. Nomadic subjectivity instead offers an affirmative image of being as becoming. Inspired by the agility of the nomadic subject, I suggest that critics of children's Gothic must occupy a number of different theoretical positions to account for the myriad ways that writing for children can reconfigure the Gothic and make use of its transformative potential.

Notes

1. In *A Series of Unfortunate Events: The End*, page numbering begins again at the end of the book in a section titled, 'Book the Last: Chapter Fourteen'. Here 'pp. 1–2' refers to this last section of the book. That the work begins again after having seemingly ended signals its playfulness regarding narrative structure. The second ending is also a beginning, and acts as an exhortation to readers to keep the reading process open rather than seeking closure and restitution in the final pages of a novel, another manifestation of a nomadic project.

2. Key texts founding this 'constructivist' method include Philippe Ariès's *Centuries of Childhood* (1973); Jacqueline Rose's *The case of Peter Pan: or, the impossibility of children's fiction* (1984); Karín Lesnik-Oberstein's *Children's Literature: Criticism and the Fictional Child* (1994) and James Kincaid's *Child-Loving: The Erotic Child and Victorian Literature* (1994). The phrase, 'the child does not exist' is articulated by Karín Lesnik-Oberstein in *Children's Literature: Criticism and the Fictional Child* (1994: 9).

Chapter 1

Un-homing Psychoanalysis through Neil Gaiman's *Coraline*

From Gothic *Alice* to the Canonisation of *Coraline*

Coraline, published in 2002, was one of the first novels to be warmly praised in an academic discourse championing children's Gothic in the twenty-first century. In an essay titled 'Between Horror, Humour, and Hope: Neil Gaiman and the Psychic Work of the Gothic', Karen Coats suggests that children's Gothic fiction is a 'cultural symptom' indicative of an underlying trauma at the heart of childhood (2008: 77). For Coats, Gaiman's work exemplifies the way that new children's Gothic fiction responds ethically to the 'demands' of child readers and meets their fundamental psychic 'needs' (2008: 78). Coats's essay demonstrates how critics have seized upon *Coraline* as a particularly apposite text for the modern child reader. Counter to this dominant reading of the novel as exemplary of the 'uncanny' nature of childhood, I suggest that *Coraline* instead offers an explicit exploration of the intertextual and mutually constitutive relationship between Gothic, psychoanalysis and children's fiction. In place of the psychoanalytic child, *Coraline* suggests a nomadic alternative, prompting its reader to explore relations and connections beyond a limiting psychoanalytic framework. A nomadic text, rather than an 'uncanny' one, *Coraline* adds its voice to those seeking to debunk what Deleuze and Guattari see as the great ruse of psychoanalysis. That is, 'its claim to enable individuals to finally speak in their own name, when it was actually only getting them to reproduce the statements of a specific assemblage – the psychoanalytic oedipal complex' (Holland 2013: 96). Psychoanalysis, and the critical tradition it inaugurates, constructs identity as singular, while Deleuze and Guattari suggest that subjectivity is always a multiplicity, always incorporating self and others. That is, subjectivity is 'several Wolves' not just one (2013: 25–44). Gaiman plays on such theories of identity, a playfulness that is signified by the confusion of the book's title. Here, the unusual name of 'Coraline' echoes the more common name, 'Caroline'. Throughout, *Coraline* presents singular identity as something of a tricky game. I find it suggestive that Gaiman (also author of the *Sandman* comic series), followed *Coraline* with the 2003 picture book, *Wolves in the Walls*. This is a writer, then, whose overt intertextual strategies suggests theoretical awareness. Certainly, in *Coraline*, Gaiman's rather irreverent deployment of the 'uncanny' suggests not psychoanalytic therapy, as Coats would have it, but nomadic playfulness.

To understand why *Coraline* has come to be so valued, I need to go back to Lewis Carroll's *Alice's Adventures in Wonderland* (1865). In this book, the Cheshire Cat accuses Alice of madness, grinning 'we're all mad here. I'm mad. You're mad' (Carroll [1865] 1982: 58). The cat's diagnosis foreshadows a long tradition of psychoanalytic interpretations of this most famous of Victorian children's books. Kenneth Kidd argues that a history of psychoanalytic case writing on *Alice* exerts a significant influence on children's literature criticism and has also shaped popular attitudes about childhood (2011: xxiv). Associations between *Alice* and madness, explicitly psychoanalysed through the twentieth century, forms the basis for an explicitly gothicised *Alice* in the early twenty-first century. Numerous examples of Gothic *Alice* abound in print and visual culture, epitomised by the computer game, *American McGee's Alice* (2000) and Alan Moore and Melinda Gebbie's graphic novel, *Lost Girls* (published between 1991 and 2006). The former is set in an asylum, its spooky sanatorium aesthetic indebted both to Jan Svankmajer's surrealist film *Alice* (1988) and a late twentieth-century penchant for the neo-Victorian Gothic. Moore and Gebbie's graphic novel draws on the popular interpretation of *Alice* (influenced by psychoanalytic case writing on the novel) as containing evidence of a sexualised relationship between Dodgson and his child muse. As well as supporting a popular theory that implicates Dodgson in paedophilic desire, Moore and Gebbie depict Alice herself as perverse. She admits, 'I did spend a number of years in a sanatorium' (Moore and Gebbie 2006: 1:8). This declaration chimes with American McGee's *Alice*, the trailer for which features a haunting voiceover: 'Something's broken . . . I am.' Though these two texts are adult fictions, they represent a shift in representations of *Alice* from innocent golden-age heroine to morbid Gothic captive. This shift paves the way for the twenty-first-century proliferation of children's Gothic fictions.

Following these adult versions of *Alice*, children's literature critics have been keen to rebrand the original text as 'one of the great
uncanny classics' of children's literature (Rollins and West 1999: 36).
The twenty-first-century proliferation of Gothic fiction for children,
as well as an attendant critical discourse championing this fiction,
are built on the foundation of a psychoanalysed, gothicised *Alice*.
Jackson, Coats and McGillis read Carroll's Wonderland as a 'world
which seems to invite exactly the same kind of psychoanalytic reading that the gothic genre as a whole insistently calls for' and claim
that *Alice* is the starting point for the overturning of a didactic tradition of children's fiction, paving the way for the re-emergence of
Gothic for children in the twenty-first century (2008: 3, 2). Likewise,
David Rudd traces a line from *Alice* to *Coraline* by identifying a long
'tradition of exploring the darker side of life' in children's fiction
(2008: 160). These assessments of *Alice* as Gothic, uncanny and
'dark' are seemingly confirmed in *Coraline*, which rewrites Carroll's
Through the Looking Glass and What Alice Found There (1871)
alongside Freud's essay on 'The uncanny' (1919). For Coats, Rudd,
and others, *Coraline* confirms an *essential* sympathy between Gothic
and children's literature, and *proves* a psychoanalytic narrative of
the child's subjectivity. However, as Kidd notes, *Alice* has long been
'used for psychoanalytic explorations of identity and agency, often
in "looking-glass" worlds in which identity is suspect and unstable'
(2011: 76–7). Bearing in mind this intertwined history of *Alice* with
psychoanalysis, *Coraline* is perhaps best understood not as a *confirmation* of psychoanalytic ideas about childhood, but as an exploration of an intertextual network that spans *Alice*, psychoanalysis and
the Gothic.

Coraline tells the story of Coraline Jones, a girl aged around nine
years old, who moves to a new apartment in a crumbling Gothic
house. Left to her own devices, Coraline explores the corridors of the
new apartment. She finds a small, locked door in the corner of the din-
ing room, which, initially, when unlocked, reveals only the bare bricks
of the partition wall of the neighbouring apartment. However, when
Coraline returns to the doorway one night, she discovers a portal that
takes her into another world. The other apartment beyond turns out
to be an uncanny mirror image of her own, home to alternative parents who have buttons instead of eyes. The attentions of Coraline's
'other' mother and father soon become disturbing when Coraline's
other mother captures her real parents and threatens to trap Coraline
in the other apartment forever, replacing her eyes with buttons too. In
the course of her explorations, Coraline finds the remnants of children

previously trapped by the 'other mother'. They are nothing more than ghostly wisps who cannot remember their names. To escape this fate, which is read by critics as the 'uncanny' resurgence of an infantile desire to return to a pre-Oedipal and pre-linguistic dyadic state, Coraline must outwit the 'other mother'. With the help of a neighbourhood cat, who interlocutes for Coraline as the Cheshire Cat does for Alice, Coraline successfully tricks the 'other mother', and is able to return home. She locks the door to the other apartment and throws the key down a well. Aside from *Alice*, *Coraline* overtly references Freud's essays on 'The uncanny' and 'Beyond the Pleasure Principle', as well as E. T. A. Hoffman's *Sandman*, some snippets of Lacanian theory, and a little-known Victorian fairy tale by Lucy Clifford, 'The New Mother' (1882), a disturbing moral tale in which two young girls are punished for disobedience when their mother disappears and a new mother, with glass eyes and a wooden tail, appears to take her place. *Coraline* is overtly Gothic, invoking the claustrophobia of the Victorian Gothic house; it is overtly psychoanalytic, depicting an animistic realm, populated by symbols readily interpreted as repressed psychological material; and it also signals itself as a fairy tale, referring to a tradition in which fairy tales have long been used for the moral and social instruction of children.

Since *Coraline* so neatly incorporates 'the uncanny' into its Gothic aesthetic and, moreover, invokes a particularly gothicised version of *Alice*, critics are keen to champion the text as a paradigm of twenty-first-century children's Gothic. Partly, this is because *Coraline* confirms the psychoanalytic narratives that underpin much children's literature criticism. For example, it has become a critical commonplace to declare 'the uncanny' as one of the most apt tools for understanding children's fiction, and, by extension, the child. A 2001 special issue on 'the uncanny in children's literature' of *Children's Literature Association Quarterly* attests to this tendency. In the introduction to the issue, Roberta Seelinger Trites urges readers to recognise 'the primacy of the *unheimlich*, the uncanny, in determining the form and content of much children's literature' (2001: 162). Rollins and West go further in their assertion that childhood in itself is uncanny, claiming that children's classics like *Alice* depict 'direct links to our uncivilised selves – to the uncanny that represents true childhood' (1999: 36). *Coraline* explicitly mirrors such critical ideas, holding up a looking glass, as it were, to critical discourse and cultural ideas about childhood. It is not surprising, then, that initial critical analysis of the novel echoes such ideas. Karen Coats gives Gaiman's novel a prime position in twenty-first-century children's fiction, arguing that his 'well-made' Gothic nourishes children, 'giving concrete expression to abstract psychic processes' (Coats 2008: 91). David Rudd claims *Coraline* is a 'rich and powerful work', a modern Gothic fairy tale (2008: 160–1). Likewise, Nick Midgely urges adults to *thank* Gaiman for providing the child with exactly the kind of scary fiction they need on their journey through life (2008: 140). In addition to this praise, *Coraline* has won a plethora of mainstream awards and accolades, indicating an accord between the academy and other gatekeepers of children's fiction. Critics seem to be in agreement: *Coraline* is so worthy because it is an explicitly psychological Gothic fiction.

Though critics have made an investment in *Coraline*, the novel is hardly representative of twenty-first-century children's Gothic. Gaiman is well known as a writer of adult fiction but has written relatively few works for children. Revealing how much children's works have to appeal to adult gatekeepers, the canonisation of *Coraline* demonstrates that it is Gaiman's credentials as a writer of adult fiction that recommend him. Richard Gooding's 2008 essay on *Coraline* heralds Gaiman as 'a major writer for children', and yet Gooding admits that when *Coraline* was published, Gaiman had only written one other children's book, *The Day I Swapped my Dad for Two Goldfish* (1997). To prove Gaiman's competency as 'a major writer' of children's Gothic, Gooding offers the writer's adult graphic novel series, *Sandman,* as evidence of previous form (Gooding 2008: 391). Gaiman has since published a number of picture books, and three other children's novels in various genres, but his output in terms of children's Gothic is minor compared to more prolific writers in the field, particularly given the position he continues to be afforded by critics. The mass-market fiction of Derek Landy, Joseph Delaney, Darren Shan, Cassandra Clare, Anthony Horowitz, Philip Reeve and Charlie Higson, to name a few, is arguably more representative of the wider field of children's Gothic than *Coraline*. *Coraline*, a stand-alone novel, contrasts with the mass-market serial fiction that elsewhere dominates children's Gothic. *Coraline* is now also over fifteen years old and so the position it has been accorded as a monumental and paradigmatic Gothic text for children belies the fact that the field of children's Gothic fiction is dynamic and continues to grow.

Critical readings of *Coraline* in part seek to remove the novel from the commercial context of children's literature publishing. In contrast to Neil Gaiman, writers such as Derek Landy, Darren Shan, and others that will discussed later in this book, are not afforded much academic attention because children's literature critics tend to be wary of mass-market fiction. Revealing this prejudice, Jack

Zipes regards series fiction as one of the main forms of cultural violence done to children, turning their reading habits into 'nothing more than acts of consumerism' (2002: 59). The selection of *Coraline* as an exemplary children's Gothic text is, in part at least, motivated by this lingering suspicion toward mass-market series fiction. Implicitly eschewing more commercial fictions, the various essays on *Coraline* by Karen Coats, David Rudd, Richard Gooding and Nick Midgely argue for the novel's importance in a literary canon of psychologically important children's *literature*. These readings reproduce the novel as what Bakhtin describes as a 'monumental' work, that is, self-evident and self-enclosed (Vološinov and Bakhtin 1986: 72). Furthermore, these readings of *Coraline* are part of a monologising discourse at work in the criticism of children's Gothic more generally, one that privileges a psychoanalytic narrative of childhood and so shuts down the play of meaning at work in the form.[1] I begin my own exploration of children's Gothic with *Coraline* not to confirm this discourse, but to scrutinise it and suggest that Gaiman's novel is just one possible manifestation of twenty-first-century children's Gothic, rather than exemplary of it. *Coraline* is the point of departure for my nomadic critical journey through children's fiction. I want to show that its use of Freudian Gothic tropes is self-conscious and playful, suggesting that the novel's 'uncanny' representation of the child anticipates the critical readings performed of it. *Coraline* situates itself in dialogue with Freud and the Gothic, asking to be read as a 'text' in the terms suggested by theories of intertextuality. *Coraline* produces 'a multidimensional space in which a variety of writings, none of them original, blend and clash' (Barthes 1977: 146). Through its intertextual connections, *Coraline* recontextualises Freud's essay via a Gothic concern with surfaces to counter psychoanalytic depth readings of both the Gothic and the child, offering a nomadic figuration of subjectivity in its place. This nomadic subject will emerge in the aftermath of this chapter, in which I undertake the necessary work of dismantling of the claimed authority of psychoanalytic criticism, and the child it constructs. As Deleuze and Guattari insist, such *dismantlings* (of discourse, of authority, of the self) do not mean 'killing yourself, but rather opening the body to connections that presuppose an entire assemblage, circuits, conjunctions, levels and thresholds, passages and distributions of intensity, and territories and deterritorializations' (2013: 185–6). *Coraline* is not a self-enclosed, monumental work, but a textual assemblage, a threshold to other narratives, to other ideas and other selves.

In order to dismantle some of the critical commonplaces I feel are holding back engagement with children's Gothic fiction, I ask *Coraline* to speak back to the readings performed of it, a methodology I derive in part from Shoshana Felman's work on psychoanalysis and literature, and from Virginia Blum's study, *Hide and Seek: The Child Between Psychoanalysis and Fiction* (1995). Felman argues that 'literature is a subject, not an object; it is therefore not simply a body of language to interpret, nor is psychoanalysis simply a body of knowledge with which to interpret' (Felman 1982: 6). Felman thus suggests that the literary critic should 'initiate a real exchange . . . a real dialogue between literature and psychoanalysis' (1982: 6). Despite Felman's persuasive call 'to consider the relationship between psychoanalysis and literature from the literary point of view', similar frustrations about psychoanalytic criticism continue to be articulated (1982: 6). Virginia Blum argues that the truth claims of psychoanalysis dominate literary criticism, particularly in relation to readings of the child. Blum follows Felman by employing a methodology that 'invite[s] the imaginative text to "read" psychoanalytic theory in much the same way that to date psychoanalysis has erected a truth claim against which imaginative literature plays out its frail symptoms' (1995: 12). Literature has, in its irony and imaginative space, the capability for addressing the absences and gaps psychoanalysis does not (Blum 1995: 12, 8). *Coraline's* 'other' apartment is one such imaginative space.

In Felman's terms, *Coraline* might, 'by virtue of its ironic force', be used to 'fundamentally deconstruct the fantasy of authority' wielded by psychoanalysis (1982: 8). In its disruption of psychoanalytic mastery, *Coraline* returns its reader to the encounter between Alice and the Cheshire cat and to Alice's indignant question, 'How do you know I am mad?' Though the cat reasons that Wonderland is full of mad people, ergo Alice must be mad to have come, Alice remains unconvinced: He has not 'proved it at all' and she has no desire to 'go among mad people' (Carroll [1865] 1982: 58). Alice is one of the few people to remain unconvinced by her diagnosis in a tradition of psychoanalysing children's literature that has largely ignored her resistance. This resistance returns in the character of Coraline, who proves an equally unwilling analysand. *Coraline* reveals that the child is an intertextual construction, produced through the interconnections between psychoanalytic writing and Gothic literature. Through its representation of a doubled, Gothic house and an uncanny childhood encounter, *Coraline* works to un-home staid psychoanalytical critical narratives, offering routes beyond them to other readings of the child. Finally, the novel does not submit to narrative of childhood development that resolves with mastery of the self. In so doing, *Coraline* offers one of the first figurations of the nomadic child in twenty-first-century children's Gothic. Coraline is a nomad located in an intertextual network that challenges dominant conceptions of subjectivity and instead offers a figuration of identity as an open-ended process.

'How do you know I am mad?': The Psychoanalytic Child

As I suggest in the introduction, current criticism of children's Gothic rests upon the idea of a real child found by the critic through analysis of the text. At the same time, the critic claims to *know* the child a priori, drawing on a narrative of maturation and development adapted from psychoanalysis. As Lesnik-Oberstein argues, the task children's literature criticism has set itself – 'to find the good book for the child' – ascribes a developmental function to the book and takes the 'extra-textual child as ultimate goal and reference point' (1994: 3, 131). Emerging criticism of twenty-first-century children's Gothic values *Coraline* because its themes, tropes and trappings accord with a psychoanalytic narrative of the child, a child they already know and can find in the book. At least, on the surface, this seems to be the case. In the various analyses of the book I have found, the novel provides both a pedagogical and therapeutic function in the eyes of the critic. However, the psychoanalytic child, whose existence is confirmed (tautologically) by a psychoanalytic reading of children's Gothic, is not 'real' at all. It is the product of a complex textual interrelation between children's literature and psychoanalysis, a relationship that requires more interrogation than it has hitherto been given in discussions of children's Gothic.

Though the relationship between psychoanalysis and children's literature is mutually constitutive, critics often construct a master-slave dialectic in which the truth claims of psychoanalysis are applied to children's books. The particular dominance of psychoanalysis within children's literature criticism is not surprising given that, as Blum explains, 'psychoanalysis is the preeminent twentieth-century discourse about childhood' and so inevitably informs discourses of childhood and children (1995: 8). In her exploration of the child in psychoanalytic theory, Michelle Massé adds 'we are all Freudians now: the "psychoanalytic" in "psychoanalytic child" almost seems a redundancy, so thoroughly have its concepts been naturalized'

(2003: 162). Current criticism of children's Gothic echoes a tendency extant elsewhere in children's literature criticism, which claims psychic insight into the lives of children even when critics do not necessarily see themselves as adopting a psychoanalytic, or even overtly psychological outlook.

The influence of psychoanalysis on children's literature tends to produce monologising accounts of the child reader and the function of texts. This is because critics

> assume that child psychoanalysis is a body of expert knowledge that has discovered the truth about children and that therefore psychoanalysis can help both to locate truthful depictions of children in fiction (which book gets the child right?) and to predict with some degree of accuracy the way children will read a book (how they will understand it or experience it, and therefore what it will do to them). (Lesnik-Oberstein 2000: 225)

Psychoanalysis seemingly provides a route to a knowable child beyond unstable textuality. However, when critics uphold the psychoanalytic view they often do so 'in contradistinction to all other evidences of false consciousness' (Blum 1995: 6). Upholding the psychoanalytic child as universal, critics ignore the constructedness of the child and, so, other possible constructions. Kidd explains that 'the teleology of psychoanalysis seems especially totalising in the case of children's literature', so that even where critics begin to acknowledge the dialogue between literature and psychoanalysis, they seem only to repeat what Felman criticises as a 'unilateral monologue of psychoanalysis about literature' (Kidd 2011: ix; Felman 1982: 6).

Psychoanalysis and children's literature share an intertwined history that undercuts the master-slave relationship constructed in children's literature criticism. Kidd notes that 'while Freud and the first analysts did not think of themselves as engaging with "children's literature," their work helped advance and reshape that literature' in such a way that children's literature has since firmly 'appropriated psychoanalysis' (Kidd 2011: vii). Kidd charts a dialogue between psychoanalysis and children's literature, showing how the forms have been mutually constitutive across the twentieth century (Kidd 2011: 204). *Alice* is an important text in this dialogue. Along with other classic children's books, such as *Peter Pan* (1911), *Alice* coexists with psychoanalysis, sharing its themes and concerns, influencing its theories. One of the most important texts in this relationship between psychoanalysis and children's fiction is Bruno Bettelheim's *The Uses of Enchantment* (1976), which argues that fairy tales help the child to master the problems of their unconscious. A number of the readings of *Coraline* I have mentioned draw explicitly on Bettelheim's ideas. For example, Rudd appeals to Bettelheim's argument that children 'need' to explore dark, psychological themes in his evaluation of *Coraline* as a 'rich and powerful work' (2008: 160). Rudd's appeal to Bettelheim demonstrates Lesnik-Oberstein's argument that *The Uses of Enchantment* proves key in cementing the psychoanalytical assumptions of children's literature criticism (Lesnik-Oberstein 2000: 225). Exploring Bettelheim's influence, Kidd explains that 'the psychoanalytic literature on the fairy tale gradually began to intersect with the widespread belief that the fairy tale is "for" children, so that by mid-century, the fairy tale was broadly received both as a psychological genre and as a cornerstone for children's literature' (Kidd 2011: xxiii). Readings of *Coraline* by Rudd and others, however, do not take this complex history into account. Rather, they assume an essential sympathy between fairy tales and children, reading *Coraline* as a modern fairy tale.

The Uses of Enchantment sets out a pedagogical paradigm for psychoanalytic accounts of children's literature. To an extent, *Coraline* deliberately leads critics down the garden path as it were, by locating itself in this psychoanalytic fairy tale tradition. The opening epigraph suggests a link between the text's psychoanalytic imagery and the fairy tale form by paraphrasing G. K. Chesterton's assertion: 'Fairy tales are more than true: not because they tell us that dragons exist, but because they tell us that dragons can be beaten' (Gaiman 2002: 1). Gaiman's version of Chesterton invokes a particular concept of the fairy tale as part of a child's emotional and psychological education. Specifically, that monsters are symbolic of the difficulties that must be overcome on the route to maturity. In framing the novel in this way, *Coraline* draws on a wider discourse about why children's books, fairy tales and fantasy are *valuable*. As Kidd explains, 'fairy tales were made authoritative in our own time through a rhetoric of children's psychological, emotional, imaginative needs' (2011: 24). Kidd argues that, through Bettelheim's influence, fairy tales have become synonymous with childhood development and even regarded as a form of therapy (2011: 118). Despite Kidd's work, a number of critics who previously rejected a psychological reading of fairy tales have recently returned to the psychoanalytic fold. Maria Tatar's *Off With Their Heads!: Fairy Tales and the Culture of Childhood* offers a cultural materialist reading of fairy tales, but her more recent study *Enchanted Hunters: The Power of Stories in Childhood* returns to a psychological reading.

At its root, the idea that fairy tales perform a psychological function is pedagogical. Gooding articulates this pedagogy when he argues that *Coraline* 'provides the kind of preparation for adult life that Bruno Bettelheim once imagined for the fairy tale genre' (2008: 405). Likewise, Rudd concludes that *Coraline* is a fairy tale about finding one's place in the world (2008: 167). Reading *Coraline* as a psychological fairy tale, Gooding and Rudd reveal that their use of the text is aimed at educating children emotionally but also, by implication, socially. The claim for the universal appeal of fairy tales inevitably positions the adult critic as knowing what is good for the child, who needs the fairy tale in order to become mature. As Zipes has argued:

> the fairy tales we have come to revere . . . are not ageless, universal, and beautiful . . . and they are not the best therapy in the world for children. They are historical prescriptions internalized, potent explosive, and we acknowledge the power they hold over our lives by mystifying them. (1983: 11)

Though analyses of the fairy tale in children's literature criticism might employ terms such as amusement, play and fantasy, they make recourse to the 'language of child development, not displacing didacticism or rationality, but giving them a makeover' (Kidd 2011: 24).

The pedagogical framework offered by Bettelheim's analysis of fairy tales originates in ego-relational psychology and a sequential narrative of psychological development that pervades children's literature criticism. Kidd shows that throughout Bettelheim's analysis 'a traditionally Freudian outlook meets the utopian perspective of ego psychology' and that '*The Uses of Enchantment* is not only a book of interpretation but also a child-rearing primer, its readings designed for practical use' (2011: 19). Following Bettelheim, children's literature and its criticism typically favours stories structured around a teleological narrative of progressive development and eventual mastery. In other words, the 'good' book is 'frequently described in terms of resolution (or mastery) of emotional problems or conflict' (Lesnik-Oberstein 2000: 227). Moreover, children's literature criticism puts psychoanalytic criticism in service to its ideological ends, using Lacan and Freud to produce a psychoanalysis of 'resolution and stages – not multiplicity and inherent division' (Lesnik-Oberstein 2000: 227). Children's literature and its criticism has

> been reading the wrong Freud to children . . . The unconscious is not an object, something to be laid hold of and retrieved. It is the term

> Freud used to describe the complex ways in which our very idea of ourselves as children is produced ... Childhood persists as something which we endlessly rework in our attempt to build an image of our own history. (Rose 1984: 12)

In an interpretive model of psychoanalysis, childhood and the unconscious are not real, stable objects, but texts produced through the narrative of psychoanalytic interpretation. Drawing on psychoanalysis to produce a uniform and stable meaning thus misappropriates the fundamentally interpretive methods of Freudian psychoanalysis. Influenced by Bettelheim, children's literature reworks Freudian interpretive methods to construct a child through a 'myth of developmental progress' (Blum 1995: 147). Rose asserts that 'in most discussions of children's fiction which make their appeal to Freud, childhood is part of a strict developmental sequence at the end of which stands the cohered and rational consciousness of the adult mind' (Rose 1984: 13). Despite the challenges brought to children's literature criticism by Rose, Lesnik-Oberstein and others mentioned here, narratives of development ending in mastery continue to be expressed in children's literature criticism, particularly in relation to the Gothic.

A narrative of maturation as mastery is evident in analysis of *Coraline*. Nick Midgely's analysis of *Coraline* argues that experiencing fear helps children grow, stating that 'Freud's work makes clear the way in which confronting the terrifying and the horrible is an important aspect of emotional development' (2008: 131). Likewise, Coats describes *Coraline* as 'psychically effective' because it 'facilitates psychic integration' and thus aids maturation (Coats 2008: 79, 78, 77). Both Coats and Midgely read *Coraline* as offering a representation of a regressive desire to return to a sense of unity imagined in pre-linguistic infancy. The novel's animistic realm, presided over by a predatory other mother, reveals the way childhood subjectivity passes through stages that threaten to return the child to the chaotic mire of undifferentiated subjectivity. For Midgely, the novel provides a confrontation with this fearful desire; for Coats it offers a scheme whereby the child can negotiate the desire, passing through to a stage of integration and stability. This psycho-symbolic function for Gothic fiction insists that it offers a true depiction of a universalised psychic reality and plays a vital function in the child's development. These critics reframe psychoanalytic theories within a staged, developmental narrative of childhood, charting the child's growth out of infantile neurosis and dependence on its parents into a healthy acceptance of its own desires as an independent and mature subject.

Yet, something strange is happening to the 'child' constructed in these critical accounts. An insistence on the psychological/ pedagogical function of *Coraline* as a Gothic fairy tale is based on a binary between dependence and independence that ultimately disavows the child. The privileged term, independence, is associated with the adult and a secure sense of selfhood; the subjugated term, dependence, relates to the child's dangerous existence in a realm of regressive desires. Nick Midgely explains that at the beginning of the novel Coraline does not have a 'clearly defined' identity: 'she is dependent and emotionally attached to her . . . parents' (2008: 136). Gooding also concludes that *Coraline* narrates the successful negotiation of the dangers inherent in childhood subjectivity: 'Traces of infection by the fantasy world retreat into the background. Coraline seems a little older, a little more mature . . . she is not "nervous and apprehensive" before starting a new school year, and she seems to have *definitively emerged* from the world of animism' (2008: 405, my emphasis). The inclusion of the detail that Coraline is starting a new school year further connects Gooding's analysis to a pedagogy invested in progressive maturation within a social and educational framework. In this framework, the 'child' is constructed as that which must be erased, done away with.

In these readings, Coraline the character is offered up as a universal subject. These critical accounts of her journey naturalise a narrative of maturation as mastery. However, this is problematic in terms of gender since psychoanalytic developmental theories tend to assume a masculine bias. Rachel Blau DuPlessis argues that Freud's account of the oedipal conflict and its phases 'has a linear and cumulative movement' (1985: 36). Anne Cranny-Francis adds that 'this linear and cumulative movement is sometimes read as the psychoanalytic narrative of "human" growth and development, a narrative which characteristically encodes a male gender bias and linear causal fallacy' (1990: 16). DuPlessis and Cranny-Francis draw on a body of critique, developed by Cixous, Irigaray and others, that reveals how psychoanalytic theories disavow the feminine, constructing it as passive, or even monstrous. This disavowal of the feminine is notable in Rudd's assertion that *Coraline* highlights the necessity of leaving the mother behind in the world of animism. Rudd argues that Coraline's defeat of the other mother demonstrates the importance of setting aside the maternal 'in order for a person to take up their place in the world' (2008: 166). Midgely also characterises the other mother as 'an anti-developmental object, who offers gratification at the expense of individual identity' (2008: 136). For Rudd, Coraline only gains the confidence necessary to defeat the other mother when she identifies with her father. Rudd states that Coraline acknowledges 'the significance of her father in her' when she draws on a memory from her childhood in which her father demonstrated bravery after being stung by wasps (2008: 165).

Rudd's insistence on the disavowal of the mother shores up a social patriarchal figuration of the family and contributes to a discourse that makes motherhood monstrous. He insists that 'henceforth [Coraline's] mother must always stand slightly apart' (2008: 165). Here, Rudd echoes a 'patriarchal fantasy devised in the service of solidifying and perpetuating a gender system in which the woman is marked as lacking the very thing she has most clearly – the child' (Blum 1995: 9). Rudd's exposition of *Coraline* reveals a discourse in which 'while the woman's relationship to the child is metonymic, a relation of proximity and physical connection, the man's metaphoric relationship is forged out of a combination of social law (legitimacy) and psychological necessity' (Blum 1995: 9). Rudd explains that 'the other mother's offer to reinstate this earlier state of oneness, to remove any gap between word and thing, is alluring but it is also repulsive', concluding with the assertion that 'Coraline has internalised the voice of her father, of the Symbolic' (2008: 165). Rudd does not interrogate the gendered positions implied here and misappropriates Barbara Creed's notion of the 'monstrous feminine' in support of his reading. In Rudd's analysis the maternal body must by necessity be represented as monstrous because it 'incarnates all that we need to set aside in order to live' (2008: 166). This does not account for how the 'monstrous feminine' 'speaks to us about male fears', nor how the term might encourage a critical interrogation of key aspects of Freudian theory' (Creed 1993: 7).

As well as constructing the feminine as monstrous, this developmental narrative pathologises the child, even as it constructs childhood as a privileged space outside of language and textuality. The child becomes a repository of negation: 'it functions as an exponent of the "non-adult" and "non-reason"' (Lesnik-Oberstein 1994: 26). In conflict with the developmental teleology underpinning the pedagogical logic of children's literature criticism, there lies a 'primitivization of infancy', a portrayal of the child as 'imperfect in relation to the accomplishment of adult' (Blum 1995: 30). Here, children's Gothic fiction intersects with an adult Gothic also influenced by psychoanalytic ideas. Particularly in horror films of the twentieth century, the child appears as abject and horrifying, representing a repellent image of regression and dependency (Paul 1994: 297, 311). In these adult horror narratives, notably *The Exorcist* (1973), the child is demonised and punished for its helplessness, which figures as an alien intrusion into the existence of the family (Paul 1994: 328, 324). Influenced by this image, criticism of children's Gothic filtered through a popular appropriation of psychoanalysis invested in maturation and independence, constructs the child itself as uncanny and abject. Moreover, childhood is made uncanny or abject because the anxieties of adulthood are 'thrown off' onto it. James Kincaid argues that

> Freud exposes the ways in which we take the variety of children's play, open to any interpretation, and construct a single restrictive story: the child plays at one thing and for one reason; and that is how you must see it. Why should we see it that way? Freud says it will 'help in the child's upbringing.' Telling the story in this way allows us to use the child's own activities to get what we want, namely for the child not to be an adult, merely an adult in training. (1994: 278)

Current analysis of *Coraline* follows Kincaid's assessment of Freud's reasoning since it accords with the pedagogical aim attributed to children's literature. Coats, Rudd, Gooding and Midgely read *Coraline* as a therapeutic intervention, a form of psychoanalytic treatment for the child who is really an aberrant (or, not-yet) adult. Coats suggests that *Coraline* 'may help children cope' with the traumas of maturation, positing Gothic both as a symptom of and cure for a pathologised childhood (2008: 77). This assessment implies that childhood is that which one survives, rather than enjoys, and characterises the child at best as a work in progress, or, at worst, as a symptom of psychological ill health. Accordingly, Midgely describes Coraline's escape from the other apartment as 'overcoming the persecutory split between idealisation and denigration' (2008: 136). Similarly, Gooding notes that 'traces of infection' of the fantasy world retreat at the close of the novel, echoing the pathologising language of psychoanalytic accounts of the child (2008: 405).

Psychoanalytic readings of children's Gothic through *Coraline* call into being a child who can be inculcated into a staged journey of maturation, ending in mastery and a stable sense of self. At the same time, the child as an image of dependence and regression is abjected in favour of a coherent adult subjectivity. The totalising tendency of psychoanalytic narratives of the child produces a blind spot in literary criticism, in which the heterogeneity of children is not accounted for, and the novel's intertextual playfulness is glossed over. The assumption that psychoanalysis tells the truth about the child does not allow space for exploring the complexity of children's literature, nor of exploring difficult issues 'such as the relationship between fiction and truth, the status of the author with regard to the meaning of the text, the multiple and various interpretations of texts, or the manifest unpredictability of any (adult or child) reader's emotional responses to a text' (Lesnik-Oberstein 2000: 226). Children's Gothic fiction read exclusively through psychoanalysis is thus replete with textual aporia. Rather than confirming these totalising psychoanalytic readings of the child, I contend that *Coraline* opens up these aporia and reveals a Gothic concern with surfaces that subverts depth readings of the text.

A Flow of Fictions: Psychoanalysing Gothic Surfaces

Gothic is popular with children's literature critics because, like children's literature, it has often been read through psychoanalysis. Also, like children's literature and psychoanalysis, Gothic and psychoanalysis are to an extent mutually constitutive. Gothic literature informed the development of Freud's theories and, in turn, psychoanalytic theories shaped Gothic literature after the late nineteenth century. William Patrick Day argues that Freud's ideas remain persuasive in readings of the Gothic because they offer a way of reading the text as a literally true depiction of psychic reality (1985: 188). The assumption that Gothic is also inherently psychological informs current criticism of children's Gothic, and of *Coraline* in particular. In their overview of the field, Jackson, Coats and McGillis allegorise Gothic as the child's unconscious:

> As a child grows, more and more experiences good and bad, displace into memory, forming the intricate passages where bits of his or her past gets lost, only to re-emerge at unexpected times. The child's mind thus becomes a crowded, sometimes frustratingly inaccessible place at the same time as his or her body morphs in uncomfortable ways. (2008: 4)

Gothic is posited as the best expression of infantile cathexes and the means by which these can be worked through. Jackson, Coats and McGillis assert that 'Gothic landscapes and conventions remain familiar to us because they are, to some extent, inside us' (2008: 4). Here, they essentialise the Gothic as the child's unconscious rather than acknowledge the mutually constitutive intertextual relationship between psychoanalysis and the Gothic, which developed from the late nineteenth century into the twenty-first.

A psychological depth reading fails to recognise the dialogic nature of Gothic. Jackson, Coats and McGillis totalise Gothic in their assertion that 'part of the reason for the persistence of the Gothic across centuries of children's literature must be due to the ease with which the typical Gothic chronotope can be allegorized as the mind . . . a place, very often a house, haunted by the past that remains present' (2008: 4). Here, they imply a straightforward relationship between psychoanalysis and Gothic: the concepts of the former are used to explain and evaluate the symbols of the latter. Jackson, Coats and McGillis argue that Gothic depicts universal unconscious depths, invoking the idea of a 'Gothic chronotope' without engaging with the dialogic implications of the term. For Bakhtin, chronotopes are mutually inclusive and are able to coexist within a text; 'they may be interwoven with, replace or oppose one another, contradict one another or find themselves in ever more complex interrelationships' (1981: 252). Current criticism of *Coraline* fixes upon one chronotope: the unconscious as Gothic house. Karen Coats's analysis of *Coraline*, for example, argues that the Gothic gives expression to 'cultural symptom' of the trauma of childhood and maturation (2008: 77). David Rudd argues that Coraline's house, 'with its cellar and attic, its dark corridors', is the perfect topography of the child's unconscious (2008: 161). Richard Gooding argues that Gaiman's uncanny Gothic landscape is the perfect space for children to play out the fantasies of their id (2008: 393). Counter to these readings, I suggest that *Coraline* engages in a dialogic interplay of multiple chronotopes, even parodying the idea of the Gothic house as a symbol for the unconscious through a 'double-voiced' reference to Freudian theory.

Like psychoanalysis and children's literature, psychoanalysis and Gothic are mutually constitutive: Gothic narratives informed psychoanalytic theories in the late nineteenth and early twentieth centuries. This relationship leads Day to suggest that Gothic and psychoanalysis are 'cousins', responses to the same problems of selfhood and identity (1985: 178–9). Conceiving of the two forms as a set of responses to a specific socio-historic moment problematises a psychoanalytic reading of Gothic. For Day, Gothic fiction was revised and redirected into Freudianism, and he questions the way in which Freudian readings of Gothic turn what had been a 'culturally produced anxiety' into a description of 'reality outside time . . . nature and civilisation' (1985: 184). Robert J. C. Young is less tentative in his assessment of the relationship, reading *The Interpretation of Dreams* as a work of fiction (1999). Elsewhere, Young argues that 'Freud is as much literary as psychoanalytic, which makes a psychoanalysis of literature somewhat tautological' (2013). Steven Marcus likewise concurs that 'Freud is as much a novelist as he is an analyst' (1984: 67). The danger of a psychoanalytical reading of Gothic, then, is that it may become what David Punter calls 'a flow of fictions' (1989: 6). This is particularly true of contemporary texts which are themselves shaped by, or may even reference, as *Coraline* so evidently does, specific psychoanalytic ideas.

Psychoanalytic readings also ignore theorising within Gothic Studies that suggests critics should not so readily dismiss the 'trappings' of Gothic fiction in order to plunge into its psychic depths. Drawing on the work of Eve Kosofsky Sedgwick, Catherine Spooner argues that Gothic denies depths and insists upon its surfaces, 'on the mask rather than the face, the veil rather than what lies beneath, the disguise rather than what is disguised' (Spooner 2006: 27). However, a psychoanalytically informed critical tradition in Gothic Studies has tended to dismiss these surfaces. Sedgwick argues that critics

> intent on grasping the essence of the Gothic novel whole have also been . . . impatient with its surfaces . . . but their plunge to the thematics of depth has left unexplored the most characteristic and daring areas of Gothic convention, those that point the reader's attention back to surfaces. (1981: 255)

Sedgwick's arguments are pertinent for children's literature criticism, which is keen to posit the uncanny as the depth and truth of children's Gothic. Her insistence on surfaces accords with Day's assessment of Gothic, which, he claims, refuses answers where Freud seeks them (1985: 187). If the uncanny is not the 'depths' of a text, but a part of its textual surface, it cannot provide the final meaning for the text, only a set of tropes that tantalisingly hint at depths but that return the reader back to a surface of textual connections. The 'inside' depths of Coraline's Gothic house are not the locus of the child's subjectivity; *Coraline* transforms psychic depths into surface trappings. One example of Sedgwick's redirection to surface and convention is her analysis of the doubling of dreams. In her analysis, the psychological import of the dreams is less important than the fact of its doubling. The content of the dream is a side issue in comparison to the fact of its doubled nature, and the dreams she analyses are experienced with the same terror by the characters regardless of whether they are innocuous or disturbing in content (1986: 30–4).

The same might be said of the use of 'the uncanny' in *Coraline,* an essay that it knowingly reproduces. It is in this doubling and repetition of Freud's essay that significance lies.

The depth readings of *Coraline* performed by Coats, Gooding and Rudd reproduce the motifs recounted in Freud's 'The uncanny' already reproduced in the novel. In this way, they are caught in the very gesture of repetition that *Coraline* parodies. Coats explains that the novel's 'multiple womb images' communicate 'the dubious pleasure of regressing into an infantile state of undifferentiation . . . marking it as a death drive' (2008: 88). Coats's psychoanalytic reading makes a series of unacknowledged references to Freud, catching in *Coraline*'s playful mobilisation of the uncanny 'compulsion to repeat' (Freud [1919] 1955: 238). Coats's reading of the other mother's severed hand, described by Gaiman as akin to a spider, makes no mention of Freud's inclusion of 'dismembered limbs . . . a hand cut off at the wrist' in his list of uncanny images (Freud [1919] 1955: 244). Instead, Coats notes that hands and spiders are 'traditionally' linked to mothers in the 'child's psycho-symbolic world': 'it is no small leap to think that a breastfed child, especially, might bear a residual image of her mother as a breast with arms, i.e., a spider' (2008: 89). With a startling assumption of obviousness, Coats's reading of the uncanny nature of the other mother's body repeats Freud without acknowledgment. Not only does Coats not interrogate *Coraline*'s reference to Freud *as a reference*, she offers her own repetition of the motif as evidence of the novel's psychic depths.

Though Gooding suspects Gaiman 'has been reading Freud', he too fails to explore the intertextual connection this suggests and posits the uncanny as a critical tool best able to 'offer clues to the psychological cost of Coraline's renegotiation of her relationship with her parents' (2008: 391, 392). Like Coats, Gooding (re)repeats motifs *Coraline* repeats from Freud, calling Coraline's house 'a near-literal manifestation of the *unheimlich* . . . an instance of what "ought to have remained hidden and secret, and yet comes to light"' (2008: 393). Gooding lists the motifs, echoing the patterning of Freud's essay: 'There are doubles, the dead, talking animals, toys coming to life, the constant threat of blindness and mutilation . . . the apparent reading of Coraline's mind, immediate wish fulfilment, and so on' (2008: 393). Gooding reiterates Freud's list of uncanny images without reflecting on the process of its doubling. Instead, he insists that the narrative is 'a test of Coraline's capacity to surmount an infantile desire for permanent (re)union with the mother' (2008: 398). If Gaiman's imagery is perhaps 'heavy-handed', Gooding muses, it is because he has to express 'the too forceful return of repressed drives' (2008: 402).

Of the three critics, Rudd articulates the most awareness of *Coraline*'s intertextual relationship with 'The uncanny', though his reading continues to posit the essay as the source of the novel's meaning. Rudd argues that *Coraline* produces 'an overt fictional representation of the Freudian uncanny – not by merely invoking the motifs that Freud enumerates in his essay, but by animating the very etymology of the German term *das unheimlich*' (2008: 161). For Rudd it is 'noteworthy that Gaiman first became famous as a writer of graphic novels featuring a sandman character' (2008: 162). He suggests that Gaiman's previous engagement with Freudian themes authenticates an exposition of the novel as performing a psychological function. For example, Rudd notes how the spool of cotton the other mother brandishes when threatening to sew buttons onto Coraline's eyes 'brings to mind' the *fort-da* game described in *Beyond the Pleasure Principle*. In Freud's analysis of the game, the boy uses the spool to come to terms with becoming an independent being; for Coraline, the spool represents the temptation to reintegrate with the mother (Rudd 2008: 163). Following Coats and Gooding, Rudd does not explore the intertextual connection any further than reading the references to Freud as confirmation of his depth reading.

In contrast to these depth readings of *Coraline*, I read the novel as an intertext in a network that includes Freud, but also other works, and which recontextualises these works through a double-voiced parody. Following Barthes, I suggest that the anterior texts to *Coraline*, namely Freud's essay, should not be 'confused with some origin' (Barthes 1977: 160). Had Rudd explored the connection to *Sandman* further, he would note that this intertext undermines Freud as an authenticator of symbolic meaning. In *Sandman #15*, 'Into the Night', one character tells the protagonist, Dream, what Freud theorises about dreams of flying: 'it means you're really dreaming about sex'. Dream responds, sardonically, 'Indeed? Tell me, then, what does it mean when you dream about having sex?' (Gaiman: 1990). The exchange between Rose and Dream in *Sandman* recontextualises psychoanalysis in 'an arena of battle between two voices', and through Dream's scorn, Freud is subject to ridicule (Bakhtin 1984b: 193). Continuing this open dialogue with Freud, *Coraline* appropriates motifs from 'The uncanny' in a 'doubly-voiced discourse' at odds with Freud's 'original' (Bakhtin 1984b: 19).

The novel more than echoes the thematic material of 'The uncanny'; its references to Freud are so numerous as to be parodic. On meeting the other mother, Coraline emphasises her bird-like appearance, noting the 'too long' fingers, with nails that are 'curved and sharp' (Gaiman 2002: 38). Later, the other mother crunches on a bag of insects, smiling at Coraline with 'a mouth full of black beetles' (Gaiman 2002: 93). These references to the other mother as bird-like evoke Freud's recollection of the Sandman's children, whose 'hooked' beak-like mouths 'peck-up' the eyes of naughty children (Freud [1919] 1955: 228). The text's tendency to paraphrase Freud becomes more marked as the story progresses. Freud relates the uncanny experience of wandering 'about in a dark, strange room', colliding time after time with the same piece of furniture ([1919] 1955: 237). Similarly, Coraline finds herself lost in a darkened, but ultimately familiar, room when she emerges from the portal between houses: 'She closed her eyes against the dark. Eventually she bumped into something . . . an armchair in her drawing room' (Gaiman 2002: 59). Though the situation evoked in *Coraline* is not quite the one Freud describes, it is familiar. Like Freud, Coraline finds herself back where she started: the drawing room of the apartment she has just left.

This repetition of another of Freud's examples, finding oneself back at the same spot, appears again in *Coraline*, this time recalling the passage in which Freud imagines himself 'caught in a mist perhaps . . . every attempt to find the marked or familiar path may bring one back again and again to one and the same spot' ([1919] 1955: 237). Coraline is also caught in a mist when she attempts to escape the other house by walking away from it:

> And then it took shape in the mist: a dark house which loomed at
> them out of the formless whiteness. 'But that's – ' said Coraline.
>   'The house you just left.' (Gaiman 2002: 89)

The 'milky whiteness' of the mist forms a series of images that links the other apartment to the maternal body. Freud famously asserts that when one states that 'this place is familiar to me, I've been here before, we may interpret this place as being his mother's genitals or her body' ([1919]1955: 245). Images of the mother's body are overtly appropriated in the climactic scene of *Coraline* which dramatises the heroine's escape from the other mother's clutches through a narrow passage between the worlds: 'The wall she was touching seemed warm and yielding now . . . It moved, as if it were taking a breath . . . This time what she touched felt hot and wet, as if she had put her hand in somebody's mouth' (Gaiman 2002: 156). Parsons, Sawer and McInally criticise the way in which *Coraline* uses bodily imagery such as this to represent the mother, noting that the 'repulsive' sexualised imagery of the maternal body and the phallus evoked throughout the novel is either 'a psychoanalytic tour de force, or, indeed, a smutty farce of comic proportions' (2008: 381). I agree that *Coraline*'s representation of the child's relationship with the mother reproduces the gender biases of Freudian psychoanalysis, but I think the element of 'farce' Parsons et al. detect goes some way to undermining this sexist discourse. The references to Freud that recur throughout the novel draw attention to their status as repetition. As in Sedgwick's reading of the dream, it is the repetition that is significant, rather than what is repeated. Producing a double-voicedness through repetition, *Coraline* casts a 'shadow of objectification' over psychoanalytic discourse (Bakhtin 1984b: 19). Stylising and parodying Freud in this way, the novel suggests it is alert to well-rehearsed psychoanalytic readings of Gothic tropes.

By including so many of the signifiers of 'the uncanny' from Freud's long list, *Coraline* points to the fact that Freud's text is simply that: a list of signifiers. Freud's list of signifiers only constitute a definition, a meaning for 'the uncanny', by pointing to texts outside the essay, which, in turn, provide only more examples and signifiers. As Cixous argues, Freud's investigations are circular: the dictionary is called upon to corroborate his definitions, but the one has no more reality than the other, because Freud merely confirms his interpretations by another interpretation. He remains within a hermeneutic circle, unable to distinguish between the literal and the metaphorical (Cixous 1976: 528). Repeating signifiers from Freud's 'definition', *Coraline* becomes another instance in a chain of deferral. Thus the novel itself points to the fact that Freud's essay cannot provide its meaning, or an answer, for 'all such answers to the initial question merely provide other signifieds which themselves become signifiers' (Allen 2002: 32). *Coraline* points not to one meaning, then, but to its plurality as 'text' by allowing for 'the infinite deferment of the signified' (Barthes 1977: 158). Rudd, Coats and Gooding cannot progress through the signifiers in *Coraline* to the depths of the text, or the child's unconscious. This is not 'a hermeneutic course of deepening investigation, but . . . a serial movement of disconnections, overlappings, variations' (Barthes 1977: 158). For example, the word 'mist', repeated many times in *Coraline*, not only recalls Freud's essay, but also the 'formless mist' of Heinlein's science-fiction story, *The Unpleasant Profession of Jonathan Hoag*, which itself is quoted by Slavoj Žižek as an apt signifier of the Lacanian Real, Lacan's (re)theorisation of Freud's ideas of pre-Oedipal subjectivity (1992:

14). 'Mist' also signifies the Sandman volume, *Season of Mist*, itself a quotation from Keats. Thus, the signifier 'mist' points outside of the text, not to some original or authentic meaning, but to a plethora of texts, which themselves continue the process of deferral.

From Dora to Coraline: The Elusive Analysand

Signalling its intertextuality, *Coraline* reveals that psychoanalysis constructs a myth about the child from various fictions. The story psychoanalysis tells about the child is particularly persuasive for children's literature criticism, which purports to speak for the child in the child's demonstrable absence. Rose accuses children's literature criticism of hypocrisy since it 'sets up the child as an outsider to its own process, and then aims, unashamedly, to take the child in' (1984: 2). A children's book is one of the forms through which the child is discursively constructed and yet critics write 'as if the "child" were in the book' (Lesnik-Oberstein 1999: 16). Coats and Rudd claim that *Coraline* successfully reveals the child's psyche. Coats argues that the novel is a response to a 'demand' originating in the child; it feeds their 'appetite' for images of childhood as they actually experience it (2008: 78). For Coats, the opening of the novel in particular allows the child to recognise and express her own desire in an adult world that largely overlooks her (2008: 87). On a shopping trip with her mother, Coraline asks for Day-glo green gloves, but is instead bought 'an embarrassingly large pullover' she will grow into (Gaiman 2002: 11). Coraline's mother carries on a conversation with her daughter oblivious to the girl's sullen silence, later not realising that Coraline has wandered off when she discusses the pullover with a shop assistant. Coats and Rudd read this scene as staging the child's need to be recognised in her own right (Coats 2008: 87; Rudd 2008: 160). However, by speaking on behalf of the silent Coraline, the critics repeat the behaviour of Coraline's mother. They insist that the book, like the pullover, is good because it imagines the child's growth. Opening with a scene in which the child, ignored by the adults speaking on her behalf, wanders off, *Coraline* does not so much reveal the interior psyche of the child as the process of psychoanalytic children's literature criticism.

Coraline foregrounds the problematic nature of its own authority as a text about a real child, and so undermines any reading that speaks on behalf of that child. *Coraline*'s critics conflate character with child in their psychological depth readings of the novel, which quickly become psychoanalytic case studies. However, the title of the novel undermines this methodological leap by drawing attention to the titular character as a narrative: Coraline is *Coraline*, and so not representative of a child outside the book. The novel also repeatedly shows adults misidentifying Coraline by getting her name wrong. Coraline corrects them: '"It's Coraline. Not Caroline. Coraline," said Coraline' (Gaiman 2002: 12). The repetition of two similar names is deliberately confusing. Whereas Rudd cites the mispronunciation of Coraline's name as evidence for her 'frustration of feeling neglected' and need to assert her identity, I contend that the confusion reveals that 'Coraline', the 'child' in the book, is a particularly elusive construct (Rudd 2008: 164). The name Coraline is deliberately wrong-sounding, off-kilter, slightly unreal, the name of a character, the title of a book. Read in this light, 'Coraline' is a reminder that 'character' is no more than a collection of 'semes' (elements of the semantic code), lent the illusion of real existence by a proper name. As Barthes indicates: 'As soon as a name exists . . . to flow toward and fasten onto, the semes become predicates, inductors of truth, and the Name becomes a subject' (1974: 191). The quirkiness of 'Coraline' undermines the illusion that a name indicates a fixed subjectivity.

While Coats, Gooding and Rudd offer their readings of the novel on behalf of the misunderstood Coraline, their treatment of her as an analysand repeats the gesture of misidentification carried out by Coraline's neighbours who continue to call her Caroline. Gooding misidentifies Coraline when he argues that the neighbourhood cat is a 'physical manifestation of the emotions Coraline now recognizes' but was previously unable to accept (2008: 399). A reference to Carroll's Cheshire Cat, *Coraline*'s cat recalls the moment where Alice refuses diagnosis. Rather than Coraline's interlocutor, then, the cat is the voice of the insistent therapist. Gooding insists he knows Coraline despite her unresponsiveness. Noting that the narrative of *Coraline* is consistently opaque when it comes to revealing Coraline's feelings, Gooding states that 'Coraline's muted responses . . . delicately identify the limits of Coraline's self-awareness' (2008: 395). He claims the lack of emotional content in the narrative as evidence of the 'unuttered feelings' of the child (Gooding 2008: 395). Gooding's knowledge of Coraline is based on the absence of her response. He notes that the text makes Coraline's emotions difficult to establish. Most usually they are articulated by the narrator in a very general way, through the non-specific word, 'feel' (Gooding 2008: 395–6). Developing his interpretation, Gooding takes Coraline's 'opacity' as evidence that she is undergoing repression. He suggests that Coraline's decision to enter the uncanny 'other' apartment is triggered by her father leaving town and by a quarrel with her mother, which he characterises as a 'defeat by a rival' in specifically oedipal terms (2008: 401). Accepting the oedipal complex as explanatory principle, Gooding identifies the 'primal scene' of *Coraline* as the moment Coraline passes her parents' bedroom door: the closed door presents Coraline with 'evidence of her parents' sexuality' that proves 'challenging' for her to accept (2008: 401). For Gooding, Coraline's refusal to consider a sexual act taking place beyond the door reveals her repression. Displaying no emotion, Coraline wonders what the other mother and father may be doing behind the door, concluding that 'it was an empty room and it would remain empty until she opened the door' (Gaiman 2002: 80). Gooding reads this as Coraline's retreat from confronting her understanding of her parents' sexual activity: Coraline has 'entered the territory of repression that Freud marks as the second source of uncanniness' (Gooding 2008: 401). Coraline's opacity legitimises Gooding's assertion of the uncanny as explanatory principle.

Positioning himself as analyst, Gooding initially claims to follow the child's lead. However, credit for discovering what the child does not know about herself is given ultimately to the analyst. Throughout Gooding's analysis the emphasis is that the child's anxieties are 'constructed upon a foundation she is unwilling to recognize' (2008: 402). Gooding's insistence on Coraline's ignorance of her emotions reveals how child's 'nonknowing' is a key to the construction of the 'psychoanalytic child'. Massé argues that 'the injunction to the child is "Thou Shalt Not Be Aware"', and that 'his state of nonknowing means that the analyst can . . . speak for the child's awareness in a way that they can't for any other (nonpsychotic) group' (2003: 153). Coraline's silence seems to allow the critic to take the privileged position of the analyst, and speak directly to the child for its own good. 'She has to accept', says Rudd, 'that she cannot be all to her parents, who have each other' (2008: 164). Going beyond evaluating whether the book is 'good' for the child, Rudd imagines that the adult can (and should) intervene directly in the psychic life of the child.

As she is constructed by the critics, Coraline has much in common with Dora, Freud's famously difficult patient. Coraline's name seems to partially echo Dora's. Freud's case study, 'Fragments of a Case of Hysteria', charts the analyst's desire to get to a truth about Dora – her repression – in the face of her obvious resistance to his analysis. Freud's frustration with Dora leads to a hubristic tone similar to that in Rudd and Gooding's diagnoses of Coraline. Gooding's 'treatment' of Coraline recalls Freud's of Dora insofar as both analysts admit that the 'material' making up their diagnosis 'required supplementing' in the face of the analysand's refusal to cooperate (Freud, quoted in Marcus 1984: 55). Freud's case study also presents us with a narrative in which the analyst is increasingly unaware of his own role in the story he is telling. Steven Marcus argues that 'Fragments of a Case of Hysteria' constitutes the least self-aware narration found in any of Freud's writing: 'It becomes increasingly clear that Freud and not Dora has become the central character in the action' (Marcus 1984: 69, 76). Similarly, when Coats asserts that 'hands and spiders are traditionally linked to mothers in a child's psycho-symbolic world', she produces 'a personal anecdote by way of example' (2008: 89). Coats discusses her youngest daughter's recurring dream of being chased by a spider, asserting 'I most certainly was in that dream' (2008: 89). This passage reads as though it were a case study of the critic, rather than an analysis of the novel.

Coraline's analysts are mirrored in the novel by the figure of the 'other mother', who wants to confine the girl to her uncanny realm forever. The button eyes that the other mother wishes to sew onto Coraline are interpreted by the analysts according to Freud's oedipal narrative and as the loss of individuation threatened by the regression to a dyadic union with the mother (Rudd 2008: 162–3; Gooding 2008: 394; Coats 2008: 90). I contend that the image of the buttons is overdetermined by critics repeating the uncanny reading offered within the novel, and in fact serves better as a sign of the blankness Coraline must enact when critics speak on her behalf. Like Dora's grudging silence in the face of Freud's analysis, Coraline does not dignify her mother within the text, nor the critic external to the text, with a response. Thus, they are able to make their observations without her participation. Therefore, the novel reveals the child as a hollow category filled with the desires of the adult writing. As James Kincaid argues, 'a child is not, in itself, anything. Any image, body, or being we can hollow out, purify, exalt, abuse, and locate sneakily in a field of desire will do for us as a "child"' (1994: 5). Coraline's plan to defeat the other mother reveals and relies on this desire when she puts on the 'protective coloration' of behaving as an innocent girl at play, having a tea party with her dolls (Gaiman 2002: 180). Convinced she is seeing an innocent child at play, the other mother sends her severed hand to steal the key to the other apartment back from Coraline, but she is tricked and tumbles into a deep well where she remains buried, unable to prey on any more children. The trap works because Coraline plays an artificial role that the other mother fills with her desire.

Coraline echoes the image of the child offered by *Alice*, who is, for Kincaid, the quintessential fantasy child. For Kincaid, *Alice* fantasises that inside the magical world perhaps the child 'can be *held*, kept as a child' (1994: 279). However, Alice always eludes the writer's grasp, never more than the adult's dream of a child, 'always on the edge of disappearing' (Kincaid 1994: 296). *Coraline* recalls this disappearing act both through Coraline's opacity, and in the children the other mother has previously captured in her web. These children are wisps, bearing only traces of once having been a child. Trapped behind a mirror, these are 'shapes of children . . . nothing more than afterimages, like the glow left by a bright light in your eyes after the lights go out' (Gaiman 2002: 102). The psychoanalytic depth reading attempting to fix Coraline as a real child insists that these children are warnings as to what will happen to Coraline if she is tempted by the offer made by the other mother (Rudd 2008: 163; Gooding 2008: 398). Yet, these 'hollow, hollow, hollow' children stand in for the child constructed by this psychoanalytic discourse (Gaiman 2002: 102). Like Alice, Coraline and the ghost children are only as real as 'a photograph we can set in the past and tell stories about . . . a child who never was' (Kincaid 1994: 289). Elusive, revealing the hollowness of the child constructed by psychoanalysis, Coraline becomes a mobile, nomadic figure located in the intertextual relations of a long-standing dialogue about the (psychoanalytic) child. Encompassing Freud's writings, the *Alice* texts and its subsequent psychoanalytic criticism, as well as numerous rewritings, Coraline is a playfully resistant analysand. She sits within a trend of rewriting Alice as an analysand who speaks back to psychoanalysis: Moore and Gebbie's Alice gently mocks that 'notable professor of the mind practising . . . in Vienna' while Bruce Bauman's short story, 'Lilith in Wunderland', imagines Alice's older sister, Lorina, rejecting the process of psychoanalysis – just as Dora does – when Freud attempts to speak for her (Moore and Gebbie 2006: 1:8; Bauman 2006).

Beyond the 'I'

Towards the opening of *Coraline*, a short passage occurs that has become the crux of psychoanalytic readings of the novel:

> Coraline tried drawing the mist. After ten minutes of drawing she still had a white sheet of paper with
> M   ST
>   I
> Written on it in one corner, in slightly wiggly letters. (Gaiman 2002: 26–7)

In the psychoanalytic readings I have explored here, the 'I' in 'mist' is particularly significant. Coats, Gooding and Rudd retell *Coraline* as a story about attaining secure subjectivity: The 'I' seems unstable at the beginning of the novel, floating away from the other letters in 'mist', but the child claims it back at the end, where it becomes a fixed point of meaning anchoring identity. However, in my intertextual reading, the subject position indicated by 'I' is always floating, never fixed. This is because I follow Deleuze and Guattari in privileging becoming over being, and 'a line of becoming has neither beginning nor end, departure nor arrival, origin nor destination' (Deleuze and Guattari 2013: 341).

The critics I have examined in this chapter insist that Coraline is finally given her proper name at the close of the novel, attaining a secure position in the Symbolic order. By insisting on the 'I' as confirmation of a psychoanalytical depth reading of children's Gothic, critics value the text under the terms of a strictly pedagogical discourse: Gothic is good because it helps the child to grow up. This reading glosses over the fact that Coraline continues to correct adults addressing her as 'Caroline' right up to the closing pages, and that the child continues to be an elusive figure. For Barthes, 'I is nothing more than the instance saying I . . . a "subject", not a "person" . . . empty outside the very enunciation which defines it' (Barthes 1977: 145). While a psychoanalytic reading wishes to fix the 'I', *Coraline* constructs a subject that eludes the totalising grasp of monologising criticism. In my intertextual reading, then, the 'I' is a red herring. It is the word 'mist' that attests to the continued instability of meaning in *Coraline*, meaning beyond the grasp of one single interpretation. Mist indicates that – in Bakhtin's terms – 'the word in language is half someone else's', referring as it does to many texts outside of *Coraline* and so resisting appropriation by one discourse (Bakhtin 1981: 293). Mist offers what Kristeva calls an 'intersection of textual surfaces rather than a fixed point of meaning' (1980: 65). Insisting on its intertextual surfaces, *Coraline* keeps meaning open and mobile.

Although *Coraline* and children's Gothic have been appropriated for therapeutic ends, neither has to be understood in these terms. It is possible to move beyond a therapeutic, humanist application of psychoanalysis in children's literature criticism, and *Coraline* offers itself as a model for this shift. As in Braidotti's theorisation of nomadic subjectivity, the 'fictional unity of a grammatical I' offered in the image of Coraline as character indicates not a fixed self, nor an absence, but a subject in the process assembling a 'fictional choreography of many levels into one socially operational self' (Braidotti 2011a: 18). An intertextual construction, Coraline is a nomadic subject located across textual and temporal locations. Elusive, often opaque to adult analysis, Coraline 'sustains a critique of dominant visions of the subject' (Braidotti 2011a: 7). That is to say, her 'uncanny' adventures in the Gothic house estrange the critic from monologising psychoanalytic explanations of the Gothic, and of the 'child'. The text's insistence on Gothic surfaces, however, does not lead to an emptying out of meaning, but rather mobilises a reading of the text that offers a multiplicity of contingent and relational meanings.

The psychoanalytic child is paradoxical: it is imagined to contain depths, but turns out to be hollow; it is determined but abjected by adult discourse, contained and limited by a developmental narrative of maturation that aims at its expulsion. In contrast, the nomadic child is 'self-organised and relational' offering the opportunities for an 'opening out toward an empowering connection with others' (Braidotti 2011b: 3). In his praise of the novel, writer Philip Pullman asks readers to applaud *Coraline* as 'the real thing', invoking a discourse in which there is such a thing as the good book for the real child and suggesting that critics need look no further (2002). Academic criticism has followed Pullman, valuing *Coraline* as exemplary in the field of children's Gothic and thus limiting their conception of the form to a narrow psychoanalytic pedagogy. *Coraline* is the real thing, perhaps, but only because its intertextuality opens out to a plethora of texts and possible subject positions available to children's Gothic. Leaving the reader, in Barthes's words, 'at a loose end' (1977: 159), *Coraline* reconfigures the home as an uncanny Gothic mansion that is not the unconscious, but a nexus point for the meeting of many threads and *fibers* of becoming. It is from this nexus point that I want to journey outward to other locations constructed by twenty-first-century children's Gothic. *Coraline* is, then, only the beginning.

Note

1. I take the word 'monologise' from Bakhtin's *Problems of Dostoevsky's Poetics*, in which Bakhtin criticises early commentators on Dostoevsky who try to 'monologise' his work (1984b: 8).

Chapter 2

Fleeing Identification in Darren Shan's *Zom-B*

The Zombie Apocalypse – a 'Line of Flight'

From Coraline's 'uncanny' house, I want to follow the nomadic subject of children's Gothic into very different territory: the urban cityscape of the zombie apocalypse. In this location, Gothic challenges the pedagogical assumptions of children's literature criticism by destabilising the process of identification that critics imagine exists between the child reader and the protagonist in the book. This process has been theorised differently by various critics, but, at root, it suggests that through identification with (or against) the protagonist, the child reader learns the valuable lessons the book has to teach. Darren Shan's *Zom-B* presents a number of problems for this critical model. At the same time, the migration of the zombie from adult into children's fiction reconfigures this particular Gothic monster, suggesting a different reading of its function to those currently circulating in Gothic Studies. Gothic critics tend to read zombies as negative cultural metaphors or symbols of social or political anxieties. In many readings, the zombie is a lesson for late capitalist, neo-liberal society. Darren Shan's *Zom-B* reconfigures the zombie as a hero protagonist who refuses to be co-opted by these dominant discourses in both children's literature criticism and Gothic Studies.

Drawing on the imagery and language of the grotesque, *Zom-B* constructs a child zombie protagonist as an image of nomadic subjectivity. This zombie nomad positively embodies gendered and classed identities that have been disavowed in pedagogical accounts of children's fiction. My reading of this grotesque nomadic subjectivity employs the spatial metaphors of Deleuze and Guattari. The continually mobile zombie in Darren Shan's series is a nomad and a 'war machine', mobilising a line of flight from repressive power relations. Shan tells a story in which being a zombie offers a possible mode of becoming and positive embodiment beyond the restrictive pedagogy of developmental models of maturation. This is Deleuze and Guattari's 'war machine of metamorphosis' composed from rotting flesh, a grotesque body able to carve a 'creative line of flight' from within striated, restrictive spaces (Deleuze and Guattari 2013: 420, 492). Matt Fournier argues that a 'line of flight' designates the possibility of escape in a moment of change, 'when a threshold between two paradigms is crossed' (2014: 121). Shan's child zombie marks one such line of flight, produced at the intersection between zombie horror and children's fiction.

The mass-market, high-action series *Zom-B* (2012–16) is very different to *Coraline* and so demonstrates the multiplicity of twenty-first-century children's Gothic. *Zom-B* also reveals how children's Gothic draws on and, in turn, influences Gothic in adult culture. Consisting of thirteen novels in total, published at three-monthly intervals, *Zom-B* follows Shan's previously successful horror series, *The Saga of Darren Shan* (2000–4) and *The Demonata* (2005–9), which were released in thirty different languages worldwide. Shan's novels are inspired by splatter horror and gross-out cinema aesthetics and their content and style is shaped by the demands of a rapid publication schedule. Their success indicates a pattern: as elements of Gothic become popular in adult culture, they migrate into children's works. The success of *Zom-B* is due in part to the resurgence that the zombie has enjoyed in print, film and television over the past decade in adult culture. This resurgence is evident across narrative forms and media, from the success of the US television series, *The Walking Dead* (2010–current), based on the graphic novel series of the same name, the BBC series, *In the Flesh* (2013–14), and the organisation of zombie walks and flash mobs involving participants across the globe since 2001 (Flint 2009: 224). More recently, the format of the live-action zombie survival game has also been televised by BBC3 as the game show, *I Survived a Zombie Apocalypse* (2015). An increase in the variety of zombie fictions, as well as the zombie's increasing mainstream visibility, has opened up a space within children's literature for the zombie to occupy. Children's literature is the next space within popular culture into which zombie can migrate. Shan's work is in dialogue with these adult texts, but it is also a *re*configuration of now familiar zombie tropes, suggesting a new way of reading the genre.

Zom-B has been very successful in critical as well as popular terms, further demonstrating the value accorded twenty-first-century children's Gothic by adult gatekeepers. In fact, critics have lavished praise on the series even though it draws on the aesthetics of pulp horror, a form not usually associated with 'good' children's literature. *Zom-B* has received favourable reviews in broadsheet literary supplements and a number of accolades, including being shortlisted for the Children's Book of the Year competition in Ireland. Though the awards it has gained are minor compared to the acclaim garnered by *Coraline*, *Zom-B* indicates that pulp horror (as well as literary Gothic) is beginning to be valued in critical discourse. However, these positive evaluations continue to be made according to pedagogical criteria. *The Telegraph*'s Martin Chilton describes *Zom-B* as 'a clever mix of horror, fantasy and realism about the damaging "virus" of racial hatred and social paranoia' (2012). For Chilton, *Zom-B*'s characters function as moral compasses, but also prompt children to think for themselves; the text is not simply didactic. For Chilton, the pulp horror elements perform a vital pedagogical function: they teach without seeming to.

Chilton's review echoes a paradox that lies at the heart of *Zom-B*: the idea that 'good' children's literature teaches important moral, social or maturational lessons, but that it ought not to impose or dictate these lessons. In commentary on the novels, Shan argues that the series provides an important pedagogical function, but is keen to avoid accusations of didacticism: 'I never set out to preach . . . but I do feel like I have to wear something akin to a teacher's hat' (Shan 2012b). His anxiety recurs throughout this essay as he insists that writers do not need to 'hold the reader's hands, but . . . should provide some sort of guiding light' (Shan 2012b). His equivocations attempt to cover over a paradox at the heart of his pedagogical project. This paradox is summed up in debates about an earlier children's series, Philip Pullman's *His Dark Materials* (1995–2000), which famously decries what it sees as dogmatic Christian ideology. Pullman's stated aim to teach child readers to be wary of ideological control (such as religious 'propaganda') is itself an attempt to assert ideological control. David Gooderham argues that Pullman's attack on the 'traditional complex of Christian beliefs, values and practices and the construction of an alternative system' actually inhibits an imaginative reading and that Pullman thus lays himself open to the charges of 'indoctrination which [he] so disapproves of in other writers' (2003: 166). Stephen Thomson also states that 'the reader's imagined relationship to the text that is said to coax her into freedom sounds dangerously passive' (2004: 145). Thomson uses Pullman's series to argue that any appeal to 'readerly freedom' from authorial didacticism 'leaves even the putatively unrestrictive text firmly in control' (2004: 145). In Shan's case, the desire not to be didactic is overridden by his belief that book (and author) must guide the reader to the right reading. Shan inherits this paradoxical pedagogy from a liberal humanist formulation of children's literature evident elsewhere in twenty-first-century children's Gothic. Charlie Higson, author of another children's zombie series, uses horror tropes to make his writing 'grimmer and more violent and nastier' (Higson quoted in Flood 2014). Higson implies that horror is an affective form and that zombies function foremost as violent spectacle. However, as I suggested earlier, for Higson this spectacle actually serves the therapeutic and maturational function of children's literature, which ought to teach children how to 'cope' and 'deal' with their fears (Higson quoted in Flood 2014).

Zom-B negotiates this paradox by offering two competing functions for horror. On the one hand, a gross-out horror aesthetic is deployed as pure spectacle; on the other hand, horror is employed in service of pedagogy and education:

> I wanted to write about racism and xenophobia in 21st century England and Ireland, but I wanted to do it in an exciting way, so that I could reach more readers. Zombies seemed like a good way to do that. (Shan 2014c)

The pedagogical function of the zombie is not something particular to children's fiction, as Shan notes when he acknowledges the influence of George A. Romero, whose zombie films 'held a mirror up to society' (Shan 2012b). Taking his cue from Romero's *Night of the Living Dead* (1968), Shan reveals how the zombie has come to be ascribed a pedagogical function more generally, not just since its migration into children's literature.

However, Shan's contradictory use of horror actually undermines his posited 'zombie pedagogy'. Principally, a pedagogical function for horror is undermined by Shan's recourse to a splatter horror aesthetic, seen in low budget horror comedies of the 1970s, 1980s and 1990s. These films, designated 'gross-out' cinema by William Paul, refuse a role of social utility in favour of pleasurable indulgence in a spectacle of gross-out violence (Paul 1994: 420–1). Shan also borrows from more recent 'inversion' texts that transform the zombie from negative cultural symbol into empathetic protagonists, including *Warm Bodies* (2010, 2013) and *Breathers* (2009). *Zom-B*'s competing images of the zombie form the book into an 'assemblage' in the terms suggested by Deleuze and Guattari. As an assemblage, the book is 'unattributable', a 'multiplicity' that cannot serve one function or one politics (Deleuze and Guattari 2013: 34). Like the zombie itself, Shan's series fiction is a 'body without organs' whose multiplicities and contradictions dismantle any organising principle or master schemata (Deleuze and Guattari 2013: 25).

Pedagogy is a central theme of *Zom-B*; it relocates the zombie apocalypse to a school. In the first novel of the series a hoard of zombies and mutants sweep through a high school, drawing the protagonist B Smith into a seemingly typical zombie apocalypse survival scenario. Yet, the zombie attack on B's classroom precipitates a line of flight away from the avowed pedagogical intentions of the text and of pedagogical readings of the zombie more generally. B Smith is an aggressive working-class teenager who, at the start of the series, holds overtly racist views expressed through truculent first-person narration. The novel initially offers B as a point of counter-identification for the imagined reader, who is meant to find fault with B's morally reprehensible actions and beliefs, thus learning a lesson about racism. Nonetheless, the attack on the school offers B the opportunity to occupy a heroic position within the narrative, bravely leading a group of teenagers through the zombie-infested chaos. In a twist at the climax of the novel, B is killed by a former classmate, Tyler, a boy who has previously been the target of B's racist bullying. However, at this point in the novel, the 'lesson' constructed around B becomes confused, a result of the contradictory locations B occupies as the narrative progresses. The second novel in the series, *Zom-B Underground* (2012) sees B return as a 'revitalized' zombie. Shan offers a very different function for the zombie in the figure of this 'revitalized' zombie, who retains their memories and personality. The subsequent novels follow B as a zombie, the titular 'Zom-B', and chart a transformation from rebellious, reprehensible human to undead hero.

Though seeming to offer a straightforward moral lesson about the ways racism damages both object and subject, B's transformation initiates a nomadic trajectory of continual motion. Throughout the series B never remains in one location or in one role for very long. Typically, she occupies one or two key locations and positions in each novel before moving on somewhere else. She is variously a prisoner, an itinerant, a mother, a fugitive, a bride, a soldier, a gladiator. In this way, B eludes the pedagogical structures of the text that would offer the zombie as a moral and social lesson. Though B's flight from the zombie-infested school is initially presented as an 'escape', the series charts journeys through post-apocalyptic London that illustrate the other meanings of the word flight (*fuite*), 'not only the act of fleeing or eluding but also flowing, leaking, and disappearing into the distance' (Deleuze and Guattari 2013: xv). This trajectory disappears into the distance, into a place not in the here and now, but also not the determined future: this is the fantastic elsewhere of the post-apocalypse. I also find it significant that the zombie attack on B's school involves 'mutants' as well as the undead. Mutants, circus freaks and grotesquerie abound in Shan's post-apocalyptic London suggesting that this line of flight is also a moment of mutation. In Deleuze and Guattari's account of power relations, a 'mutation' in code, in language, or in biological life, prompts variations and transfers within and between cells, species and languages, offering the chance to challenge hegemonic structures (2013: 261). Furthermore, Shan's mutants and zombies, B included, are leaky bodies, manifesting the 'leakage', or 'runoff' of the line of flight from restrictive bodily identities. Thus, as the inclusion of carnival and circus imagery suggests, Shan's Zom-B is also a grotesque body, offering an embodied, nomadic subjectivity beyond the constraint of a classical mode of being.

B's transformation further undermines the avowed pedagogical intentions of the text by offering the zombie as a grotesque, undecidable point of identification in place of an ideal child reader. B's grotesque zombie body returns identities that are disavowed by the text's identification with an ideal reading child. The ideal child traditionally imagined by children's literature is male and middle class. Children's literature emerges when the growth of the middle class creates a lucrative market in publishing for children. Consequently, a paradigm of bourgeois childhood dominates that literature and its criticism. As John Morgenstern argues, the bourgeois child is both the imagined consumer of children's literature and the object of its representation (2002: 136). Moreover, it is the middle-class school-*boy* who becomes the reading child as schooling in literacy comes to dominate conceptions of children's literature (Morgenstern 2002: 141). However, as Shan's horror fiction exemplifies, this image of a middle-class reading child is complicated by the presence of another child: the reluctant reader. Resistant to the text's pedagogy, the reluctant reader is courted through gory, action-packed content. Shan draws on an explicitly 'masculine' horror tradition in this process of identification. Characterised by violence and monstrosity, this masculine horror tradition has dominated Gothic in literature and film in the latter half of the twentieth century. The valorisation of masculine horror works 'in tandem with youth culture's male rebels and the rejection of the cosy domestic world fetishized in the books, radio and television programmes of the post-war period' (Reynolds 2001: 5). Shan's mobilisation of the horror aesthetic, then, paradoxically imagines its reader as both a rebel and a schoolboy. These ambivalences emerge in B who offers an alternative point of identification to the ideal middle-class reading child. Though the text initially disavows B's violent, working-class masculinity, B's transformation into a zombie returns a working-class masculinity *and* a female identity that have been disavowed or written out of the pedagogical project. Zombie B is a girl and her wounded but savage body both satirises and rehabilitates the appendages of violent masculinity within a body firmly designated female. Thus, Shan's zombie disavows neither the masculine nor the feminine, embodying a grotesque *un*decidability that is both repulsive and attractive.

The grotesque imagines a line of flight from binaristic gender and classed identifications through its representation of an undecidable body. Here I designate the grotesque as an aesthetic and structure of undecidable ambivalence, drawing on formulations of the term by Philip Thomson (1972) and Mary Russo (1994). Philip Thomson defines the grotesque as 'the unresolved clash of incompatibles in work and response . . . paralleled by the ambivalent nature of the abnormal' (1972: 27). For Thomson, this unresolved clash centres on an incompatibility between the comic and the terrifying, but is also a wider structural component of the grotesque, resulting in a form that is anti-rational and disorientating (1972: 21, 42). On the one hand, this positions the grotesque as the perfect literary aesthetic for a pedagogy that aims at producing an actively questioning subject, the particular pedagogy at work in *Zom-B*. On the other hand, the grotesque also works to undermine the assertive maturity that this pedagogy aims at since the tension within the grotesque remains unsolvable and continually discomfiting.

Russo's notion of the female grotesque is also useful in my reading of *Zom-B* since it considers the gendered aspects of the grotesque aesthetic. Russo's reconfiguration of the grotesque critiques the tendency to essentialise gender often found in critical uses of the grotesque, while maintaining that the grotesque remains both a potentially positive and dangerous force. On the one hand, the grotesque is potentially positive for feminist politics, since it posits a body that is open, dynamic, boundless, and can thus counter a static and contained model of femininity (Russo 1994: 8, 61, 63). On the other hand, the grotesque also powerfully re-inscribes the status quo and negatively abjects the transgressive female body (Russo 1994: 56, 60). In the end, the grotesque remains a 'painfully conflictual configuration' that is useful for examining the transformation that B undergoes from macho tomboy to female zombie (Russo 1994: 159). Zombie B produces an image of the female grotesque that disrupts a male-gendered hero paradigm favouring aggressive activity and, at the same time, counters a 'feminised' image of the reading child, that is, the image of the bourgeois schoolchild passively subject to pedagogy. The grotesque zombie thus offers an alternative figuration of identity to the ideals constructed by pedagogical formulations of children's literature. Refusing the position of object in a lesson directed at a middle-class reading child, the grotesque zombie becomes a nomad, a mobilising agent within the multitudinous assemblage of Shan's text.

Identification as Pedagogy

Zom-B first foregrounds and then disrupts the process of identification theorised in pedagogical formulation of children's literature. Identification is crucial to the pedagogical project of children's literature because critics want to establish which characters the reading child will identify with, and how active or critical their identification will be, to know what the child will *learn* from the book. However, as the reading child is a construction (of the critic, the book, the writer), these questions of identification are oriented in the wrong direction. Rather than ask with whom the reading child will identify, it is more pertinent to ask which particular child the book identifies as its reader. What kind(s) of reading child(ren) does it construct and why? *Zom-B* foregrounds identification in distinct ways that draw attention to this problematic. Initially, *Zom-B* offers an antagonistic first-person narration that aims to locate its reading child in opposition to the narrator. However, this aimed at identification is undermined because the addressee constructed by B's narration occupies an undecidable position, oscillating uncomfortably between empathy and disagreement. Once B becomes a zombie, this fraught process resolves. The grotesque figure of the zombie eventually replaces that of the ideal reader. B's transformation into a zombie produces an identifiable hero-protagonist, reconciling B with the book's imagined reading child. However, this child is not the one initially imagined by the author. To unpack these complex textual manoeuvres, I need to place Shan's stated authorial intentions in dialogue with the book.

Shan's authorial commentary on the novel reveals what Lesnik-Oberstein calls 'the classical paradox of liberal humanism' that offers children's literature 'as the supposed ideal medium of non-intrusive, non-authoritarian teaching of children' (Lesnik-Oberstein 1998: 19). Shan's ideal reader is constructed for this medium: they are ideally active and critical of hegemonic ideology, but also passively subject to the tutelage of the book; a reluctant reader who needs to be seduced by the pleasures of the horror, but eminently teachable; they seek pure indulgence, but receive sound instruction. Shan explains:

> I felt I had to do what I could to get young readers questioning the ways of their elders, to decide for themselves what is right or wrong, to look for the truth behind the cloud of lies. The main message I wanted to impart was – QUESTION EVERYTHING! (Shan 2012b)

Shan's capitals anxiously assert that the novels seek to teach, without being didactic, how the central character has internalised the pernicious views about people of other races and religions espoused by 'certain sections of our media and society' (Shan 2012b). That is, he needs to teach his reader why B has become racist and why this is bad. The realisation of 'how B ended up in that situation' allows the imagined reader to critique these incorrect ideologies, thus accepting the right ones (Shan 2012b). While overt didacticism is rejected, the reading child is nonetheless constructed as a subject who must be the willing recipient of a lesson. Put simply, the paradox is that Shan's exhortation to 'QUESTION EVERYTHING' requires a child reader that is passive.

Moreover, Shan's exhortation to 'question everything' imagines that his novel is able to place the child outside of ideology. However, as Stephen Thomson explains, 'the claim to ideological neutrality is profoundly ideological' (2004: 146). Even as Shan dismisses the 'cloud of lies' offered by pernicious media representations, he asserts a 'truth' in its place. This truth implicitly constructs certain identities, the young and the economically disadvantaged, as less able to make ethical and moral judgments: 'Many people believe the lies, especially people who (like me when I was younger) don't travel much or get to mingle with people from other cultures' (Shan 2012b). Limited life experience and limited opportunities for travel are barriers to the openness and active engagement Shan seeks in his ideal reader. This openness is yet another paradox in the liberal humanist formulation

Shan inherits from children's literature. Writers and critics that insist upon the openness of a text still have a message to transmit. Shan asserts that there are 'correct' ways of reading and positions the child as passively subject to tutelage of the book.

The paradoxes plaguing Shan's formulation of his pedagogy for *Zom-B* originate in children's literature criticism, which has not satisfactorily theorised reader agency. One of the founding texts of children's literature criticism, Aidan Chambers's *The Reader in the Book* (1985), attempts to establish the reading child as an active participant in the process of making meaning. However, in Chambers's theory the child's activity is prompted by and reliant on the book (or, its adult author). As Neil Cocks points out, Chambers's dualism between author and reader ends up with the author 'in total control of the text and the response to it' (2004: 95). Attempts to revise Chambers's ideas question this dualistic power relationship so as to rescue the child reader from didacticism. John Stephens's *Language and Ideology in Children's Fiction* points out that the reader is not separable from the text since it too is constituted by language (1992: 55). However, Stephens's linguistically constructed child reader is still forced to 'conform' to the discourses that constitute it and so Stephens replicates the problems he seeks to overcome (Cocks 2004: 111). Though Stephens theorises a reader constituted by language, his formulations of agency still rely on a child outside the text. He prefers texts that 'situate the reader as a separately constructed subject firmly outside the text', but he struggles to conceive of a pedagogy outside didacticism (Stephens 1992: 252). Even here the adult-authored text is in control, constituting a child reader that can – through the machinations of the book itself – learn to be an independent and mature subject, not a passive recipient of the book's ideas.

Maria Nikolajeva's essay, 'The Identification Fallacy' (2010) represents a more recent intervention in this debate, but like Stephens and Chambers, it fails to theorise reader agency within the pedagogical formulation of children's literature. Nikolajeva criticises literacy and educational professionals who advocate identification with fictional characters as beneficial to the child reader. For Nikolajeva, identification with a character will not encourage the reader to develop good critical faculties (2010: 188). Instead she insists that writers must 'subvert the identification compulsion' if they wish to help their readers develop empathy and critical engagement with the world (2010: 189). Nikolajeva imagines a naïve child reader who wishes to identify with characters in the book, but must not be allowed to do so for its own good. For this purpose, Nikolajeva prefers first-person narration since it is inherently dialogical and creates a dissonance between the narrative voice and the implied reader that will produce a critical response in the reading child (2010: 201). However, her theorisation of the dialogic nature of first-person narration is one directional and points to a single way to interpret the text, against the narrator's voice. Nikolajeva concludes by stating that instead of identifying with characters, child readers must identify with the implied reader, or 'narratee', who will aid it in interpreting the text (2010: 190). She implies that if children learn to read in the right way they will then become more mature and better able to detect ideological manipulation. Thus, Nikolajeva offers her counter to the identification fallacy as the 'correct' way to read and also imagines a child located outside of ideology.

Zom-B reveals and negotiates these failures to theorise reader agency through its narrator B, who is initially offered as a counter-point to the imagined reader, but whose narration eludes the pedagogical function it is ascribed. Shan expresses anxiety about B in his commentary, noting that *Zom-B* was 'the most daunting task I've yet to face as a writer' (Shan 2012b). His main concern is that his reader will incorrectly identify with the 'wrong' character, a worry that prompts a number of redrafts (Shan 2012b). B presents a problem for Shan from the outset. According to Nikolajeva's argument, Shan's choice to use first-person narration would seem exemplary: the ideal child reader will judge everything B says and does to be wrong, and thus learn to think for themselves. However, aspects of the first-person narration complicate this, not least because many of B's actions and attitudes prove successful in the context of the zombie survival narrative. B becomes increasingly undecidable since it is unclear whether she is a point of counter-identification, or an exemplary hero. Furthermore, the narration is candid and self-aware, positioning B's perspective as ultimately dominant since it explicitly invites and anticipates judgment. The narration oscillates between distance from and proximity to an imagined reader, whose position likewise becomes increasingly undecidable.

B is distanced from an ideal reading child through an expressed distaste for school, scribbling 'crude drawings' on exercise books and deliberately disrupting classes, but the narration is also shot through with self-reflective pathos. After provoking a fight with a classmate, B offers an uncomfortable interpretation:

> I know I should feel ashamed of myself, and to a degree I do. But to my surprise and dismay, I also feel smug because I know Dad would be proud if he could see me now, bringing an interfering black girl down a peg or two. (Shan 2012a: 66)

B is racist and misogynist, obviously reprehensible. Yet, the reference to her bullying father offers a partial justification: B is seeking approbation where she finds only rejection. The uncomfortable oscillation between empathy and judgment is articulated by B, who expresses 'dismay', even as the word 'smug' undercuts this expression of remorse. Here, B's narration does not address itself to an oppositional child reader, but it does offer a narrating subject unable to comfortably occupy one position.

As the novel shifts from a domestic school drama to zombie survival horror, B morphs again. In the context of a zombie survival scenario, which is also informed by the tropes of the classic 'hero' narrative, B's violent and aggressive behaviour is justified. Attacking fellow humans (former classmates) infected by a zombie bite and abandoning fallen comrades to make good an escape are common tropes of zombie survival horror. B's single-minded, utilitarian approach to survival is necessary in her ascension to the position of group leader and hero. 'They're finished. No time to feel sorry for them', she declares as she leaves friends who have been cornered by zombies (Shan 2012a: 156). From this narrative position, B displays aggressive masculine qualities with impunity. When the group of boys she leads takes down their first zombie, B knocks knuckles with Cassius, aptly named after Muhammed Ali, approvingly exclaiming, 'Sweet!' (Shan 2012a: 139). This part of the story does not begrudge B any pleasure in her performance of violent masculinity, even though earlier this very same performance has been held up for judgment and criticism.

An 'Honorary Man'? Performing Female Masculinity

B's uncomfortable position as a point of identification is also a result of the way gender is constructed in the story as part of its pedagogical project. *Zom-B* offers a pedagogical lesson about gender, but ends up expressing contradictory ideas about the feminine and the masculine through its ambivalently gendered protagonist. *Zom-B* initially marks its protagonist, B, as masculine. The name B Smith is a gender-neutral designation, but B's behaviour is marked as masculine through vulgar speech, rebellious behaviour at school, boyish clothing, short hair and sexist comments about the 'hot and easy' girls at school (Shan 2012a: 19). Only in its closing pages does the novel reveal that B is a girl, just before she is killed. The aim of the text seems in line with Shan's stated exhortation to 'question everything'. The marking of B as a boy produces a trap for the imagined reader, who is led to a mistaken assumption so that they can be corrected. The text imagines its reader naïvely asking, 'do I think only boys can be heroes in these kinds of action stories?' A paradoxical pedagogy is again evident here since this twist imagines a reader in need of, but also receptive to, critical literacy strategies that will aid it in rejecting received notions of gender.

Yet, the withholding of this crucial information about B disrupts the aimed-at process of identification because it again shifts B's function within the narrative. From a villainous point of counter-identification, B moves to a victim position, not only because she gets brutally attacked by a zombie, but because her masculine behaviour is reframed as a pathological performance, a response to the trauma she suffers at the hands of her violent father. The revelation also sees B shift from the position of anti-hero to hero. The text suggests that B's behaviour as a boy is typical, but as a girl it is marked as extraordinary. Qualities marked as aberrant in the text's construction of its ideal reader (B's violence, her lack of sympathy) are the very qualities the reader is asked to accept once B's gender is revealed: girls can be heroic too, the text suggests, reframing those suspect masculine qualities as heroic when enacted by a female subject. Thus, B occupies an uncomfortable, undecidable position between these shifting constructions of the masculine and the feminine.

The text's 'twist' presents another problem for identification and pedagogy since it only reverses the hero paradigm it seeks to interrogate. As Margaret Hourihan notes, female heroes transposed into adventure stories are, with some exceptions, 'little more than honorary men' (1997: 68). Cranny-Francis also points out that the problem with role reversal is that 'it does not challenge the nature of the role itself . . . the role is preserved at the cost of the individual character [and] its masculine gender coding is barely threatened' (1990: 84). Certainly, masculine coding remains in place for the last third of *Zom-B* when displays of callous machismo are demanded by the genre. Moreover, B's attitude is directly contrasted within the text with the more obviously feminine-coded emotional responses of the girls in the group. For example, B's female friend Suze collapses in fear and guilt when the group kills an infected classmate (Shan 2012a: 139). Femininity is coded as oppositional to heroic masculinity, suggesting that B is only a viable hero because she eschews her femininity. This does nothing to disrupt a history of genre fiction in which women have had no presence other than 'an idealist construct composed from the negatives of masculinity' (Cranny-Francis 1990: 24). The notion that female functions as negative to male is coded into the structure of the twist itself: we learn that B is a girl only when she turns out not to be a boy.

Despite the evident problems with the novel's 'twist', I read B's gender identity as a performance that resists binaristic representations of masculinity and femininity. I want to read B through Jack Halberstam's theorisation of female masculinity, which offers an alternative to dominant masculinity because it is produced by both male and female bodies (1998: 1, 2). Within the novel's domestic setting, femininity is revealed as exactly that which B cannot afford to identify with, since it offers only victimhood and oppression. This is emphasised through B's mum, Daisy, who is bullied and belittled by her violent husband. The passive position allotted femininity is a result of a performance of violent masculinity, epitomised by B's father. B's performance of female masculinity, as the only role available in a cultural location that provides little in the way of agency for female characters, destabilises this power relationship by revealing the conditions in which it is produced. B's refusal to adopt the feminine position shows how femininity is abjected by association with 'passivity and inactivity' (Halberstam 1998: 269). Furthermore, as a performance of female masculinity, B demonstrates that masculinity is not the sole province of male sexed bodies and so disrupts the process whereby masculinity comes to be associated with power and privilege. B's behaviour demonstrates that the 'immense social power that accumulates around masculinity' does not have to be 'reserved for people with male bodies' (Halberstam 1998: 269). In terms of genre conventions, masculinity is exactly what B needs to embody in order to survive the zombie apocalypse, a fact that in itself does not necessarily deconstruct the hero trope, but nor does it wholeheartedly endorse it, since B's masculinity is designated as a contingent and context-dependent performance. In fact, B's performance of masculinity is the first stage of her 'flight'. In Deleuze and Guattari's terms, she is lodged on a particular 'stratum' and 'experiments with the opportunities it offers, find[s] an advantageous place on it, find[s] potential movements of deterritorialization, possible lines of flight' (2013: 187). B's experimentations with masculinity in the first book of the *Zom-B* series prefigure the more radical line of flight taken when she becomes a fully fledged zombie.

Initially the novel shows B mimicking her father in her performance of masculinity, but the flow of power is more complex than simple mimicry. For Halberstam, 'the question . . . might be not what do female masculinities borrow from male masculinities, but rather what do men borrow from Butches?' (1998, 276). Following this, B's performance of masculinity becomes the example which others imitate. Her friends follow her lead: *she* makes the jokes, *she* confers the nicknames and *she* leads the fight against the zombies. Her exaggerated performance of masculinity prompts the boys around her to perform too, a situation that suggests female masculinity is not simply the aping of masculinity by an oppressed subject. B's performance mobilises a 'shift' in the 'flow of power and influence' imagined by Halberstam's model of female masculinity. Thus, when B turns out to be a girl at the end of the novel, the revelation of her gender does not function as the correction of a misidentification, nor as a disavowal of heroic masculinity in favour of femininity. Rather, the fact that B is a female offers additional information through which to read her masculinity, rendering it an explicit performance of female masculinity. She continues to be referred to by the ambiguous designation, B, despite her father briefly identifying her as 'Becky'. B remains an ambivalently gendered nomination that marks the character as female *and* masculine as the series progresses. B is not a disempowered female 'longing to be and have a power that is always out of reach' (Halberstam 1998: 9). Rather, B's performance constitutes a productive reversion of the structures – generic and social – that produce masculinity as dominant.

Though B's female masculinity suggests a critique of essential and binary notions of gender, it is not wholly liberating. Nor does B's awareness that her behaviour is a performance posit performativity as radical freedom from gender norms. Instead, B's female masculinity critiques a particular idea about performativity through its reference to Iain Banks's *The Wasp Factory* (1984). *The Wasp Factory* has become a canonical text in Gothic Studies, often read alongside Shelley's *Frankenstein* as a study in Gothic masculinity. *Zom-B* invites comparison with Banks's novel because its 'twist' is similarly conceived. *The Wasp Factory*'s narrator, Frank, who also suffers abuse at the hands of a violent father, is revealed at the close of the novel to be a girl. Berthold Schoene-Harwood asserts that this revelation 'ironically unwraps patriarchal masculinity' and constitutes a deconstruction of traditional gender formations in line with Judith Butler's theorising of gender as performative, fluid and open to re-signification (1999: 132). Schoene-Harwood's reading values performativity as a radically transgressive act, but does not fully explore the dangerous and conflictual nature of performativity.

Mary Russo argues that simply recognising the performative nature of gender does not constitute freedom from gender norms. Performativity is – in Judith Butler's seminal *Gender Trouble* – a 'compulsory practice' (Russo 1994: 48). While the agency of the subject is not entirely foreclosed in Butler's model of gender, performativity does not automatically grant her control over identity. Performativity is not the result of deliberate and wilful choices (Russo 1994: 48). Schoene-Harwood's claim that Banks's 'coup' is to 'dismantle' masculinity by 'presenting his readers with a typical boy's tale whose hero is really a girl' does not fully confront the limiting and compulsory nature of gender performativity. B's performance of female masculinity, however, makes it clear that performativity is contingent on cultural location, rather than being a wilful choice or an act of radical subversion. B's performance of female masculinity is a critique of the fate of femininity in a gender structure dominated by masculinity, but it is also a survival strategy. B's self-aware narration notes that her behaviour is a social act, a necessary camouflage, which extends to a pretence of racism (when she is with her father) and sharing in derogatory sexist commentary (when she is with the boys).

Class Politics: The 'Laff Riot'

B's performance of masculinity also disrupts the text's attempt to identify with a middle-class reader. The novel's 'lesson' about B's gender relies upon its reader interpreting B as a negative image of working-class masculinity. This negative conception of working-class masculinity is constructed in opposition to an imagined middle-class reader and also draws on a wider context of specifically 'disgusting' representations of the working class in British culture. Imogen Tyler argues that contemporary culture vilifies the 'chav', a designation of the working class that is symptomatic of 'middle-class desire to re-demarcate class boundaries' (2008: 21). Tyler identifies 'the emergence of the grotesque and comic figure of the chav within a range of contemporary British media', arguing that it is a sign of 'heightened class antagonism that marks a new episode in the dirty ontology of class struggle in Britain' (2008: 18). Elsewhere, Tyler traces this class antagonism and abject representations of social others, including the working class, to efforts by New Labour in the 1990s to make class a revolting subject. This was a time when 'questions of class-based inequalities were repressed, reconfigured and reformulated within sociological and political discourses and, latterly, within wider popular and public culture' resulting in the 'popular reconfiguration of the underclass discourse in the figure of "the chav"' (Tyler 2013: 16). Tyler's work gives a wider context for the representation of B in *Zom-B* and prompts me to suggest that Shan's representation of class is influenced by a wider social and political discourse, by the figure of the 'chav'.

Often B's working-class masculinity is figured as revolting: crude language, swearing, violence and racism echo negative media representations of the working class, positioning B in direct opposition to the imagined middle-class reader. The school setting cements this opposition. The middle-class child is a learning child, whereas B expresses her hatred for school and pays 'little or no attention to the teachers' (Shan 2012a: 85). Moreover, B's school is identified as a poor school. There isn't money for trips, she states, 'plus we're buggers to control when we're let loose' (Shan 2012a: 64). Tyler further notes that class disgust is also tied to racial difference and chav disgust is racialising (Tyler 2008: 25). The 'chav foregrounds a dirty whiteness – a whiteness contaminated by poverty' and, importantly for this discussion of B, represented complexly by the chav's 'filthy white racism' (Tyler 2008: 25). This language of racialised abjection appears frequently in descriptions of B's father, who attends National Front meetings. B recalls 'rooms full of angry white men muttering bloody murder' (Shan 2012a, 21). B's 'filthy white racism' is most emphatically represented in the fight with a black girl, Nancy, whom she goads by saying 'I know your kind aren't the most civilized in the world', defending herself with the retort, 'at least I'm white scum' (Shan 2012a: 49). The novel thus faces a problem in its formulation of an anti-racist message since it relies on a counter-identification that racialises B as a member of the 'filthy white' working class. Racism is abhorred, but B's repellent racism marks her as a member of the revolting working class, whose abjection in popular culture manifests through racial disgust.

However, as was the case with gender, B's narration subverts the identification strategies that would position her as an object of disgust. She offers astute reflective commentary about her performance of working-class masculinity, anticipating the listener's disgust. In her encounter with Nancy, for example, she describes 'slipping into hateful character with alarming ease' (Shan 2012a: 49). B narrates in the present tense, but simultaneously offers reflective retrospective commentary. In part, this is a result of Shan's need to provide a space for his imagined reader from which to judge B's behaviour rather than simply go along with it. However, the result is an increasingly admirable B, whose reflective first-person narration is the source of the 'good' analysis as well as of the 'bad' ideology. B's performance of white, working-class racism and aggressive masculinity are refigured as neither wholly elective, nor entirely essential. B explains that 'the trouble with putting on an act is that sometimes it's hard to tell where the actor stops and the real you begins. It's rubbed off on me to an extent, the years of pretending to hate' (Shan 2012a: 21). Through reflection, B's narration combines the seemingly rejected first-person character and the backgrounded authorial voice. The authority of B's reflections increases as the novel shifts mode into the survival scenario in which B excels. The result is that statements made early in the novel revealing B's seemingly 'bad' macho swagger are retroactively endorsed. Thus aspects of B's performance of working-class masculinity, elsewhere critiqued, gain authoritative status. This includes the early pronouncement: 'I'm B Smith. This is my turf. Any zombies on the loose should be worried about *me*' (Shan 2012a: 43). This confidence and swagger fit well when framed by the tropes of the zombie survival scenario. As B later jokes, she may receive 'straight F's in most courses . . . but A plus in zombie survival!' (Shan 2012a: 187) In the fast-paced action of zombie survival horror B becomes a clear point of identification. The oppositionally constructed idealised child reader disappears as B's voice becomes increasingly assertive and *Zom-B* mobilises its zombies. The character initially located as an objectified point of counter-identification becomes the hero, a nomadic subject who escapes the pedagogical structure of the text.

The dialogic nature of B's narration, and various shifts in position, work alongside the push and pull of a 'gross-out' aesthetic, which revels in a spectacle of gory violence for its own sake. The gross-out aesthetic clashes with the backgrounded moral pedagogy outlined by the author. B revels in this violence, describing how classmates turn on each other: 'Drives the knife deep into her head, panting like a dog. Again. Blood flows. Bone splinters. He doesn't stop. Moments later he's gouging out chunks of brain' (Shan 2012a: 152). Here, fragmented sentences give an impression of the breathless gratification of the viewer of the gory spectacle. Shan's vocabulary also evokes excessive gore and violent action: blades 'sink' into chests, 'guts ooze' and the school is plastered with 'trails of blood' and plenty of vomit (2012a: 150, 127, 170). In this way, *Zom-B* invokes the gross-out aesthetic exemplified by low-budget horror films such as *The Evil Dead* (1981). Paul argues that such films celebrate bad taste and aggression and 'transform revulsion into a sought-after goal' (1994: 4, 10). For Paul, gross-out is the 'art of inversion', offering an undecidable oscillation between attraction and repulsion: 'In the confusing process of the push-pull aesthetic we are forced to consider what we mean by both *repellent* and *attractive*' (Paul 1994: 420). Gross-out is thus structurally grotesque, remaining undecidable in terms of pleasure and disgust.

Undecidable gross-out aesthetics represent a stumbling block for any pedagogical project and the material conditions of the gross-out cinema Paul examines are relevant to Shan's work. Both are rapidly produced cultural products, seeking high sales and a good return: gross-out offers 'a radical challenge to taste and value . . . simply to make a buck' (Paul 1994: 20). Though gross-out aesthetics are subversive, they cannot be appropriated by a left-wing critical discourse that gives subversion a pedagogical function. As Paul points out, the central problem with valuing subversion is that works that are not sufficiently 'subversive' are designated symptoms of what is wrong with culture and pop-cultural products are returned to a role of social utility (1994: 420–1). In other words, even subversive cultural products must teach the audience something. Gross-out, in contrast, is pure spectacle seeking only '*indulgence*' and 'all spectacle must be suspect for both the right and the left because it bypasses rationality to appeal directly to the desire for pleasure' (Paul 1994: 421, 16; emphasis in original). Tracing the debates surrounding bad-taste cinema and its supposed effect on vulnerable 'young people', Paul concludes that a film's moral content cannot be equated with an educational experience, since the film is spectacle rather than instructional: 'No matter what kind of attitudinizing one may try to encase in them, there always remains something of an appeal in the *shows* of violence' (1994: 12). This spectacle of violence increasingly characterises the tone of *Zom-B* as it reaches its climax. Furthermore, like the films Paul explores, its concluding scene is merely a prelude to the next instalment, not a summation of its moral and educational content. The sacrifice of B to the zombie hoard is framed as punishment for B's racism, but really it is a necessary plot turn enabling the next instalment in the series in which B is resurrected, and the whole carnival of gross-out horror can be repeated.

Paul suggests that there is something of the carnivalesque in the public, mass enjoyment of films denoted as 'bad taste'. This is the 'laff riot', a public 'circus of bad taste' (Paul 1994: 13). While gross-out aesthetics revel in spectacle that undercuts any educational intent, the 'laff riot' tag line attached to many gross-out films politicises the act of spectating. The deliberately incorrect spelling offers an 'aggressive assertion that the phonetic attempt of an uneducated writer, the "wrong" way, is in fact the right way. After all, we don't go to '"laff riots" for schooling' (Paul 1994: 13). The title of the *Zom-B* echoes 'laff riot', explicitly rejecting proper spelling in its hybridisation of zombie and B. 'Laff Riot' politics are also evident in Shan's eighth novel, *Zom-B Circus* (2014). Set in a circus run by mutants who prey upon the survivors of post-zombie apocalypse London, the book follows one of B's former teachers, whose family is being held as collateral so that she will perform humiliating and dangerous acts for the assembled crowd of mindless zombies and mutants. The teacher is ostensibly being taught a lesson: she has treated many people badly in her bid to survive the apocalypse, and must now sacrifice herself to save her family. In the end, she makes the 'right' choice, but the ringmaster, a grotesque mutant clown, kills her family anyway, jettisoning her infant nephew from a cannon over the stadium walls. Throughout these events, the reader is positioned as a spectator. Originally, the teacher is set up in opposition to the reader because of her selfish behaviour (echoing *Zom-B*), but becomes a more sympathetic character when she is captured. However, the circus setting ultimately positions the reader as a spectator of gleeful violence as the supposed 'lesson' comes to nothing, subsumed in a gory carnivalesque spectacle played at the expense of a figure of authority, the teacher.

The laff riot of *Zom-B* complicates the class demarcations the novel seeks to emphasise. A gross-out aesthetic is embraced by working-class B from the beginning. She is first introduced viewing a YouTube video of a supposed zombie outbreak in Ireland. B and her father 'crack up laughing' as B jokes about what they would do if zombies really attacked: 'Put my head between my legs and kiss my arse good-bye!' (Shan 2012a: 16) B watches the clip over and over, fascinated by the scream of the woman when a zombie 'chews off a chunk of her skull' and the sound of the cameraman vomiting. Despite these gruesome details, B describes the footage as a 'bit of fun' (Shan 2012a: 19). Unlike the ideal reading child, B rejects education for the spectacle of gross-out, participating in the 'gleeful uninhibitedness' of the laff riot, watching the news footage as though it were a 'video nasty' (Paul 1994: 20). B narrates in the language of the 'laff riot', rambunctious, rowdy and profane. She is callous about the slaughter onscreen, laughing along with her dad's racist and sexist comments. However, B's assertive response in the face of the zombie crisis reframes her as active and engaged, not a mindless spectator.

B's narration and her role as active spectator offer a direct contrast to the novel's prologue, which describes the fate of a young boy in Ireland, Brian Barry, who passively watches the zombie attack. 'Crying, moaning, shivering', Brian watches helplessly as his mother devours his father (Shan 2012a: 6). He aimlessly wanders the streets looking for 'a police officer, a teacher, a priest . . . anyone' before falling prey to a zombie who 'feasts' upon his brain (Shan 2012a: 6, 11). Brian is a nice child, but his demise is retroactively made into a spectacle when B views the news footage. He becomes the object of the spectacle, while she is its viewing subject. Though B seems callous, she also conveys an admirable self-sufficiency: 'I head home alone through the dark. And do I worry about zombies? Do I bugger' (Shan 2012a: 29). The shift in narration style also suggests this move from passivity to activity, for while Brian is narrated B narrates. A member of the 'laff riot' mob, B is positioned as active and empowered in contrast to the passive child.

Skipping School: The Zombie Eludes Objectification

At first, *Zom-B* seems to echo a critical discourse that reads the zombie as an object lesson. Shan's commentary resonates with the central tenets of 'Zombie Studies', a body of criticism that tends to position the zombie as a negative cultural metaphor and a symbolic indicator of social anxiety or crisis. Recent adult zombie texts are informed by this idea, too. Fred Botting notes that in the novel *Breathers: A Zombie's Lament* (2009), which portrays zombies sympathetically, the zombies are 'crassly' analogous to African Americans in pre-civil rights era United States (Botting 2012a: 30). Another recent 'inversion' text, *In the Flesh*, which aired a year after the publication of *Zom-B*, makes a similar move and uses the plight of its sentient zombie protagonist to work through issues of othering, scapegoating and civil rights in contemporary Britain, against a real-world political backdrop of anti-immigration rhetoric and increasing racism. *In the Flesh* and *Breathers* thus turn monstrosity 'to a good and moral purpose – a warning about the fate of the world in crisis' (Botting 2012a: 28–9). When Shan announces his intent to use the zombie to teach his readers about racism, he echoes this use of the zombie, common in adult zombie texts and criticism.

This use of the zombie belongs to a 'social anxiety' or 'socio-symbolic' reading model in which the zombie serves a broadly left-wing politics as a lesson about the degraded conditions of humanity in late-capitalist society. In an overview of 'Zombie Studies', Todd Platts claims that critics tend to read zombies as 'a monstrous tabula rasa whose construction registers extant social anxieties', citing Kyle Bishop (2009), Peter Dendle (2007) and Shawn McIntosh (2008), among others (2013: 547). Peter Dendle notes that 'the zombie holocausts vividly painted in movies and video games have tapped into a deep-seated anxiety about society, government, individual protection, and our increasing disconnectedness', adding that in recent fiction the zombie has become 'increasingly nihilistic' (2007: 54). This critical narrative is echoed in commentary from popular culture too, in feature articles such as 'Night of the Living Metaphor' from the *Independent* in 2013 (Haynes 2011), *The Guardian*'s 2009 article 'March of the Zombie' (Billson 2009), and the comparison in *The New York Times* of modern life to a 'zombie onslaught' (Klosterman 2010). I find this dominant critical reading of zombies persuasive in relation to specific texts, specifically those that, like *In the Flesh*, draw on and thus confirm the critical discourse. However, this discourse has become something of a master narrative used by critics to homogenise a broad and varied body of work. Reading zombies in *Dawn of the Dead* as symbolic of the 'mindless consumer' caught up in a 'capitalist economy fuelled by a pathological need for growth' is convincing in relation to the specific (Dendle 2007: 51). The film asks to be read in these terms. However, to argue that 'the zombie holocausts vividly painted in movies and video games have tapped into a deep-seated anxiety about society, government, individual protection and our increasing disconnectedness from subsistence skills' makes a conceptual leap from the particular to the general that I find less persuasive (Dendle 2007: 54).

Recently, the idea of the zombie as object lesson has developed further recently through the emergent discourse of 'zombie pedagogy', which puts forward the idea that zombies are 'good to think with' (Gonzalez-Tennant 2013). Higher education classrooms, in particular, have embraced the zombie. In the US, Monmouth University offers a course titled 'Zombies: Social Anxiety and Pop Culture'; in the UK, the 2013 Higher Education Academy conference featured a keynote on 'Zombie Pedagogies' by American academic Jesse Stommel. Gonzalez-Tennant notes that zombies reveal 'cultural reactions to social anxiety' and that 'analysing zombie cinema supports a critical engagement with the unrecognized ways media can influence our understanding of cultural difference' (2013). In this zombie pedagogy, the zombie is located as an object of social and cultural utility, and does not provide a positive formulation of identity and subjectivity.

These zombie pedagogies meet resistance in the body of the zombie, who is located both as antagonist and protagonist in *Zom-B*. In *Zom-B*, the zombie is the antagonist against whom B pits herself in order to escape the slaughter of the school. At the climax, B shoves a classmate into the zombies at the behest of her racist father, but immediately regrets the action. Acknowledging that she must pay for her behaviour, she decides to:

> take my chances among the zombies [rather] than go along with the racist beast who made me kill Tyler Bayor . . . That's the last thing I see in this life, Tyler chewing on my heart, grinning viciously – revenge is obviously as sweet as people always said it was. (Shan 2012a: 141)

B's first-person commentary makes the moral lesson overt as she tells her father, 'you're a bigger monster than any bloody monster' (Shan 2012a: 197). The snarling, mindless zombie is equated with racism, aggression and small-mindedness, with all the 'bad' ideologies the book aims to critique. At the same time, however, the zombie is also the victim (Tyler Bayor), a figure scapegoated by racist ideology, made monstrous by hate. When Tyler kills B, the zombie becomes the avenger, meting out a gory punishment to the wrongdoer. The lesson of the zombie thus becomes difficult to read, not least since B's death is also an act of sacrifice that cements her position in the narrative as hero. The zombie's grin further muddies the moral lessons as the scene presents its pleasurable spectacle of gory violence and gleeful revenge. Thus, *Zom-B* locates the zombie in multiple and competing functions. It becomes increasingly unclear what the zombie *means*.

Rather than figuring as heroic sacrifice or deserved punishment, B's transformation into a zombie offers a release from a fraught identity constructed around problematic binaries of class and gender. Through this transformation the zombie becomes a subject, not an object; active, rather than passive. In the second novel, *Zom-B Underground*, B adjusts to life as a zombie, incarcerated in an underground military base. She is asked to watch CCTV footage that shows her in a mindless state, attacking and eating a living person. The military organisation which has captured B offers the footage as a lesson *and* a threat. They want to convince B that she is a monster, and could easily degenerate if she does not cooperate. They threaten to withhold food (processed human brain), which would cause B to return to a savage state. The footage is also offered as a teaching moment for the imagined reader, and prompts an extended passage of reflection from B, who recalls the words of a former teacher, Mr Burke: 'always remember that you might be the most black-hearted and mean spirited [person] of the lot, so hold yourself the most accountable of all' (Shan 2013b: 56). B initially objectifies the monster onscreen as the part of her identity that is being punished, dutifully promising to 'never forget' her reprehensible behaviour. At the same time, however, B finds a place within herself to 'house the horror, somewhere close to the surface, but not too close that it would get in the way of everything else' (Shan 2013b: 57). Though B's narration moralises, it also recognises that the zombie cannot really be paralysed with guilt. This is a problem for Shan's pedagogy: neither the series format, nor the zombie narrative, have space for continual moralising and introspection, for accusations of guilt and accountability. The fast-paced zombie serial, and its zombie hero, must leave pedagogy behind.

The footage of B also offers an image of the zombie as active subject, able to refuse the controlling power structure of the pedagogical text, to elude its controlling gaze. At first, B is horrified as she watches herself: 'All I can do is keep my eyes pinned on the girl – the *monster* – on the screen and stare' (Shan 2013b: 52). In terms suggested by Foucault and Deleuze, the CCTV camera is a *dispositif* in service of State power, the military organisation. It acts as a go-between, positioning B in a negative relationship with the image of herself, producing a line of force that makes the zombie visible and gives it negative meaning (Deleuze 1992: 160). The controlling gaze behind the camera is emphatically a male gaze, and it is the male military scientist, Dr Cerveris, who first offers the word 'monster' to interpret the images onscreen. Becky's narration initially echoes his analysis:

> The zombie has cut the boy's head open and is digging out bits of his brain, spooning them into its mouth with bone-distorted fingers. It looks like a drug addict on a happy high. The boy's arms are still shaking – he must be alive, at least technically. The zombie doesn't care. It goes on munching, ignorant of the trembling arms, the soldiers, everything.
>   The zombie is a girl.
>   The zombie is *me*. (Shan 2013b: 52)

Objectifying herself as the lesson, B at first refuses to positively identify with her image. Yet, the zombie on-screen disrupts this objectifying gaze through its uninhibited action. She ignores the soldiers, the camera, 'everything'; she is focused only on the pleasure of feeding. This pleasure reconfigures the initially uncomfortable moment of identification, offering some distance for B from which she can reflect on her new condition. Later, she thinks about the footage and considers her newly formed body. Though she admits that she has done 'plenty to be ashamed of', she does not reject her strong limbs, sharpened senses, nor her new appetites (Shan 2013b: 56). B begins to enjoy her monstrous body, announcing she is ready to 'face the world again', reconfiguring the zombie as an active participant, not passive object (Shan 2013b: 57).

As a zombie, B is sometimes heroic, sometimes selfish, but her actions continue to be described in the gory language of gross-out, revealing uncontrollable appetites. Although reflections on morality and ethics continue to feature in B's narration, her zombie body is simply not subject to the same rules as a living body. Her evident delight in feeding recurs in many scenes, emphasising an appetite that resists objectification and passivity. As I have noted, the metaphor of nourishment recurs in children's literature criticism, in which feeding is an act ascribed to the book (and its adult author), while the reading child is passively positioned as the one who is fed. Nikolajeva attempts to negotiate this passivity when she asserts that the child must 'learn to be critical toward what [it is] fed' (2010: 189). However, the child she imagines is passive a priori since it is in the position of having to be taught its critical faculties by the text. Nikolajeva's paradoxical proposition draws upon a vocabulary of nourishment and feeding freighted with a number of assumptions about the power dynamic between adult writer and child reader, and the text's responsibility to nourish the child in the right way.

In *Zom-B*, however, feeding is a gleefully unsanctioned act, offering a rabid sensory pleasure. Though initially sickened by the image of herself feeding, B nonetheless notes that the zombie 'looks like a drug addict on a happy high' (Shan 2012a: 52). Later, as a zombie, B admits to the desire to 'tuck into fresh, warm brains' (Shan 2013a: 196). She describes her own ravenous feeding when she stumbles on a corpse in the street:

> Like a monstrous baby taking to the teat, I latch on to the shattered bones and suck tendrils of brain from them. I run my tongue the whole way round the rim, not caring about the fact that it's disgusting . . . In fact, I'm ecstatic, getting an unbelievable buzz from the grey scraps, feeling myself strengthen as I suck. (Shan 2013a: 17)

B's description of herself as a 'monstrous baby' recalls and subverts the feminised figure of the reading child of children's literature
criticism. Cogan Thacker and Webb argue for a long-standing and
lingering association between stories for children and 'mother's milk',
a metaphor that denotes the nurturing function of stories for children (2002: 21). B is 'strengthened' by her feeding, but the body that
feeds her lies grotesquely inert and passive, a decaying corpse. Thus
the scene offers not a rejection of the model of feeding imagined by
pedagogical formulations of children's literature, but a grotesque and
parodic re-figuration of this act of feeding, one that refuses to locate
'being fed' in the passive position.

In *Zom-B*, nourishment does not lead to growth and so undercuts the preferred pedagogy of children's literature. Though B needs
human brains to survive, her inert zombie digestive system rejects the
majority of what is consumed. Brains must be vomited back up, or
else left to rot inside the dry tubes that once processed nutrients. In
a very literal way, B has become a 'body without organs', an assemblage of exteriority that takes nothing into it, internalises none of the
habits, identities, or lessons of dominant 'State' powers, here represented by the military and medical officers of the base where B is held
captive (Deleuze and Guattari 2013: 412). Yet, 'the body without
organs is not a dead body, but a living body, all the more alive and
teeming once it has blown apart the organism and its organisation'
(Deleuze and Guattari 2013: 34). *Zom-B* associates the zombie body
(without organs) to the carnivalesque, through its use of grotesque
and gross-out. B tells the reader:

> I can no longer process food or drink the normal way . . . it would
> sit in my guts, turn putrid and decay, unaided by digestive juices. The
> bits that broke down into liquid would flow through me and dribble
> out, meaning I'd have to wear a nappy. The solids would stay inside
> me indefinitely. If I ate enough, they'd back up in my stomach and
> throat. (Shan 2013b: 29)

Zombie consumption produces no growth, takes nothing in, but
evacuates like the earthy body of the Bakhtinian grotesque carnivalesque. And yet, this is a dried-up zombie body, which in part
counters the fluidity and positivity of the Bakhtinian grotesque and
its bodies in tune with natural processes. In Bakhtin, vomiting, along
with 'urine and other eliminations' that the zombie body cannot
produce, connotes the interconnectedness of life and death, and is

related to the 'lower stratum of the body and with earth' (Bakhtin 1984a: 180). For Bakhtin, the bodily element of the grotesque is 'deeply positive' and politically subversive; it counters the 'private and egotistic' forms of high culture, with something 'universal, representing all the people' (1984a: 19). *Zom-B* invokes elements of Bakhtin's carnival in its gory spectacle of consumption and vomiting, but its zombie remains undecidable, rather than politically radical. This zombie body is a stumbling block, an inert receptacle, lacking the ability to process (language) and change (its mind). The image of the zombie eating is a gory spectacle, in which the pedagogical language of nourishment can find no purchase. This is a body that cannot be co-opted for a subversive politics any more than it can act as object lesson for pedagogical purposes.

'Zombies, They're Us', They're the Female Grotesque

'Zombies, they're us' is often repeated in Gothic Studies, but it is not a positive symbolic identification and it fails to account for the affirmative subjectivity figured by the zombie in children's fiction. First, 'zombies, they're us' treats the zombie as a unit of the mass; it is undifferentiated and only symbolic in generalised terms. As a symbol of the masses, the zombie is mindless and blank, a fact that Platts acknowledges when he calls the zombie a 'tabula rasa' (2013: 547). Replete with significance on the one hand, representative of all manner of social anxieties, the zombie is, on the other hand, empty. Dendle describes the zombie as a symbol of 'supplanted, stolen, or effaced consciousness' (2007: 47). David Flint's assessment of the zombie in contemporary culture offers further evidence of this negative formulation of the zombie:

> A truly 20th century horror figure, the zombie . . . spoke directly to audiences who felt that civilisation was collapsing around them. The apocalypse seemed close, and zombie movies, with their unstoppable, expanding army of monsters who couldn't be reasoned with and who acted without feeling or emotion, seemed to capture a feeling of mass helplessness. (2009: 7)

Flint's zombie lacks agency, becoming simply a passive receptacle for the 'modern fears' of the reader or audience (2009: 7). There is no possibility for pleasure in recognising the zombie as 'us' in this way, nor any reading available that might counter a gloomy perspective on popular culture as the mirror of social breakdown and cultural catastrophe.

As Fred Botting has argued, 'zombies, they're us' is not a positive symbolic identification in zombie studies because zombies 'never seem satisfied, nor achieve the fullness of consumption or completion of death . . . Zombies are aimless, useless, destructive' (Botting 2013: 196). Identification with the zombie may seem to contain an element of attraction, but this attraction functions only to bring about expulsion: 'They're us. The identification may be desirable in that they are free from death, self-consciousness, enjoyment. It is also unbearable and demands expulsion' (Botting 2013: 200). Moreover, this act of identification is also an attempt to distance the zombie even as it claims it. This is signalled by the third-person plural, 'they', and by the physical arrangement of the film scene in which the phrase is first uttered. In *Dawn of the Dead* (1978), Peter identifies the zombies as 'us' while standing upon a high rooftop, looking down at the zombie hoard gathered outside the mall. He is separated from 'them', distanced from the clamouring mass below. Similarly, critics who make the identification now are also not identifying with the helpless, exploited masses they see represented in the zombie hoard. Zombies might be 'us', but they are very rarely 'me'.

Recent inversion texts seem to counter this process of (non)identification by presenting the zombie as the protagonist and encouraging identification with the monster. While some of these texts may have influenced Shan to cast the zombie as hero in *Zom-B*, I contend that their strategy, articulated by Botting as the exhortation to 'love your zombie', necessarily works to counter the trend towards non-identification and negative symbolic reading. There continues to be limited pleasure available in the identification with the zombie since the lines that have been crossed during the inversion are usually redrawn by the close of the narrative (Botting 2012a: 31). The close of the film *Warm Bodies*, for example, sees the zombie protagonist transform back into a handsome, living human – his monstrous state revealed as only temporary. Thus, 'love your zombie' is not really an affirmation of otherness. Even in *Breathers*, the pleasures that are momentarily expressed in identifying with a zombie body end up co-opted in service of a modernist politics, which rejects the pleasures of the here and now. Botting argues that the central 'drive' of *Breathers* 'seeks something other than an exhausted rapacious condition of equivalently consumptive zombie-humanity' (Botting 2012a: 34). However, 'something other' is never achieved and identification with the zombie ultimately expresses a 'world-weary and worn out' attitude (Botting 2012a: 34). Thus, in these 'inversion' texts, Botting's observation stands: 'While humans can be zombiefied, zombies . . . rarely find themselves humanized' (2012a: 26).

I offer Shan's B as a counter to these 'sympathetic' zombies in adult Gothic. B's grotesque zombie body offers an affirmative identification that eludes expulsion. Moreover, B as a zombie not only reimagines this negative symbolic identification, but also returns class and gender identities that the pedagogical project of children's literature seeks to disavow. Certain class and gender identities not reconcilable with an idealised image of the 'reading child' return in a grotesque form, repellent *and* attractive. The appearance of zombie B undercuts the structure of the first novel, which offers B as a point of counter-identification, identifying the zombie as 'me', positioning the reader in identification with a grotesque body. This grotesque body also allows B to escape the uncomfortable gender identification offered to her as a human girl and occupy instead an identity configuration that Mary Russo designates the 'female grotesque'. This configuration allows elements of femininity that were covered over by the necessary performance of masculinity to reassert themselves. In the figure of the zombie, the identification strategies already problematised by B's earlier performance of female masculinity break down altogether. When B makes the important identification with the zombie on the CCTV footage, this identification is explicitly female: 'The zombie is a girl. The zombie is me' (Shan 2013b: 52). Only when reconfigured as a specifically female zombie can B become a grotesque: unclean, repulsive, beautiful, powerful, ambivalent.

This new configuration is, in Russo's terms, 'painfully conflictual' since it must negotiate the effects of power that seek to limit and contain it (Russo 1994: 159). In *Zom-B Underground* the lines of force against which the zombie resists are mobilised by the military organisation, who keep B locked in an underground facility, performing tests and training her to be a fighter. B rebels against their discipline just as she previously rebelled in school, but she also allows her body to be subject to their regimes. In one scene, a medic files B's teeth with a power tool: 'splinters from my teeth went flying back down my throat and up my nose and into my eyes. My teeth got hot from the friction and my gums felt like they were burning' (Shan 2013b: 21). Though this is a violently repressive act, the zombie body offers resistance. B notes the fear on the medic's face and afterwards she realises that her zombie teeth are still incredibly sharp and dangerous. The soldier admits, 'they'll always be sharper than they were'

(Shan 2013b: 22). In her time in the military facility B negotiates repressive force, masochistically enduring the regimes her new body is subject to. In Deleuze and Guattari's terms this is 'less a destruction than an exchange and circulation' (2013: 181). Her grotesque body converts the force applied to it and is able to apply force in return. The majority of B's experiences in this novel chart this circulation of power effects back and forth along lines of force and lines of resistance, but it is only her escape from the facility that realises a line of flight leading out of this power struggle.

B's embodiment of the female grotesque reconfigures markers of masculinity that previously denoted binaristic gender identities required by the hero narrative. Her hair, clothing and attitude remain masculine, though her (now grotesque) female body is made visible. B invokes a tradition of butch women from Western cinema, exemplified in the figure of Ripley from the *Alien* franchise. For Halberstam, Ripley is not simply a 'stone butch', that is a dysfunctional rejection of womanhood by a self-hating subject who cannot bear her embodiment' (1998: 112). Rather, she offers a model of how female subjects can embody strength and aggression (Halberstam 1998: 186). The aggressive masculinity inscribed on B's body in the excessively long bones that pierce her skin and her sharpened, long teeth echo the prosthetics of heroic masculinity often exhibited by the action hero. There is an element of parody in this grotesquerie. Though the slightest scrape of her extended nails will kill a human, her overgrown teeth make it difficult to talk. At first, she struggles to make herself understood and her attempts to insult a military officer are framed as amusing: '"Skroo you, arsh hohl," I spat' (Shan 2013b: 22). B's aggressive response remains crude and rebellious, but it also constitutes an amusing critique of the excesses of heroic masculinity. Later, when B gains control of her bodily excesses, this aggressive masculinity can coexist with her newly visible female identity. As a zombie, B is attractive, powerful, female.

Though she continues to act in ways determined by a model of aggressive, heroic masculinity, she also uses her powers in new ways, explicitly directing her body against the military and medical organisations that would use it for their own ends. In *Zom-B City*, for example, she walks miles across London to cut down a zombie who has been strung up in the sunlight by cruel zombie-hunters. This shift in behaviour denotes a shift in the self/other, hero/monster, masculine/feminine binaries demanded by the tropes of the hero narrative on which the zombie scenario draws. In her flight from her human identity, and from the military forces that intend to use her body as a weapon, B follows the line of flight of Deleuze's nomadic tribe, who 'swept away everything in their path and found new weapons' (Deleuze and Guattari 2013: 239). Zombie B is, then, a nomadic 'war machine' engaged against 'apparatuses of capture or domination' (Deleuze and Guattari 2013: 492). Her masculine appendages take shape in a female body to act against the apparatus of masculine State power (medical and military) that would use B as a weapon.

As a zombie, B is able to identify as feminine in ways her masculine performance previously denied. She examines her ruined body in the mirror of her cell in an act of identification that eludes an objectifying male gaze that fetishises the female body as passive object. John Berger notes that the mirror is a common trope in this Western visual tradition; the mirror positions the woman alongside 'the spectators of herself' (Berger 1972: 50). Previously, B has looked at herself, and other girls, through the male gaze, disavowing and objectifying the feminine. In the first book, she colludes with the boys who share demeaning stories about the girls in their class, commenting on their female bodies while hiding her own: 'I was never a girly girl' she admits (Shan 2013b: 15). Now, though, she admits to 'feeling slushy' and expresses sorrow to see her feminine features destroyed in the transformation (Shan 2013b: 15). This is a painful recognition that reveals a misogynistic fear of losing one's femininity that is the result of a visual economy that privileges the masculine as bearer of the look and the feminine as 'to-be-looked-at-ness' (Mulvey 2009: 809). This fear is realised in brutal fashion in B's bodily wounds:

> My right boob is the same as it was before. But my left is missing, torn from my chest . . . a fair bit of the flesh around it is missing too. And my heart's been ripped out, leaving an unnatural grisly hole in its place. Bits of bone poke through the flesh around the hole, and I can see all sorts of tubes inside, veins, arteries and what have you. (Shan 2013b: 27)

B literally has a hole for a heart. There is nothing where the bodily signifier of her 'soft' femininity once was. Moreover, she can poke inside of herself, in a grotesque break down of bodily borders. Simply put, B's missing breast is a symbol of her rejected femininity.

However, this grotesquerie does not equate to a rejection of the feminine. Rather, it signals its transfiguration. B proudly displays her wound, deliberately ripping a hole in her T-shirt to make it visible, to display her undead, ruined body. This visibility of her bodily surfaces and disrupted bodily borders suggests that the female grotesque offers power. B studies her body in the mirror a lot and enjoys performing the role of monster and freak for her attractive military handler, Josh: 'I snarl . . . grin ghoulishly. "So I've turned into a big bad wolf. All the better to see, hear and smell you with my dear,"' B teases Josh, the 'good looking guy' (Shan 2013b: 46). Josh becomes the object of desire, B the bearer of a desiring gaze. Thus, the female grotesque allows B to operate (to an extent) outside the logic of the male gaze, allows her to express her desire without being subject herself to an objectifying gaze.

As a female grotesque, B also retains markers of her working-class identity, previously made abject. As Tyler shows in a variety of examples, from reality television programmes to news media, 'depictions of the white working class have always pivoted on appearance and, in particular, on a perceived excess of bodily materiality' (2008: 22). However, excessive bodily materiality and improper bodily functions become routine when B is a zombie and must regurgitate her food: 'The grey stuff come surging back up and I vomit into the bucket, shuddering as I spit the last dregs from my lips. "Not very lady-like, is it?" I grunt' (Shan 2013b: 30). B's identity has already been contaminated by working-class behaviour – racism, school rebellion and foul-mouthed rambunctiousness – marked with the class disgust identified by Tyler through contemporary popular culture. Here, though, the physical excess of her zombie body, its gorging, regurgitation and grunts, is represented as a form of rebellion. After B's transformation into a zombie, there is no uncontaminated identity upon which the text can anchor its image of an ideal reading child. B's grotesquerie remains marked by class but previously revolting aspects of a disavowed working-class identity are co-opted into the image of B as a powerful heroine.

As Russo points out, the female grotesque is carnivalesque because it is contingent on spectacle and performance. As such it offers a chance to escape limiting structures of femininity, though not the 'boundless flight' often imagined in narratives of women's liberation or fantasies of artistic transcendence (Russo 1994: 11, 44). Russo understands the female grotesque as a performance 'in error', risky and contingent on probabilities and circumstance (1994: 13, 11). As in my reading of female masculinity, performativity does not, in itself, offer freedom. In Banks's *The Wasp Factory* femaleness is figured as 'an unfortunate disability', a disavowal only remedied, in Schoene-Harwood's reading, by the revelation of the performative nature of gender (Banks 1998: 17; Schoene-Harwood 1999: 133). In contrast, the female grotesque is performative, but it offers a performance that acknowledges the ways femaleness continues to be figured as a disability in relation to masculinity, a disability that performance can only partially rehabilitate. B's female grotesque zombie identity transforms her into a freak, a performance that remains full of error. Like Russo's female grotesques, B is one of the 'odd, frightening women . . . stashed somewhere in the sideshow' (Russo 1994: 51). Rather than consigning female subjectivity to the sidelines, however, or placing it under scrutiny of the gaze, the image of the sideshow freak provides a position from which to make trouble. B as the female grotesque offers a brief chance for transformation. B's experiences as a zombie will not lead to maturity or progress, since she will remain forever trapped within her ruined (adolescent) body. Nonetheless, this body offers opportunities to create trouble, displaying 'irony and courage in the face of danger, ridicule, disbelief, injury or even death' (Russo 1994: 13).

The female grotesque becomes a powerful spectacle offering a chance for aerial freedom in contrast to the earthy grotto of an essentialised grotesque. Considering the usefulness of Deleuze's line of flight for transgender identity, Fournier counters Deleuze's translator who insists that a line of flight 'has no relation to flying'. Fournier argues that its English translation 'suggests an Icarian figure, an escape too glorious to already have happened but still there, open, somewhere between "right now" and the closest future' (2014: 122). This flight is staged in *Zom-B Baby* (2014) when B is challenged to climb the London Eye by a male rival, Rage. The climb is agonising, but B beats Rage to the top and with a 'triumphant shout' finds something of the aerial freedom promised by the female grotesque as she hangs on the uppermost pod. Her freedom is brief. Rage promptly pushes B off the top of the Eye and she 'plummet[s] towards the river like a stone' (Shan 2014a: 89). B's strong zombie body survives the fall, but the shock of it prompts her to reassess her situation. Yet again, B decides to leave behind the group with whom she has been staying: 'I turn my back and head off into the wilderness, abandoning the promise of friendship and redemption, becoming just another of the city's many lost, lonely, godforsaken souls' (Shan 2014a: 101). The grotesque as 'female bodily performance' in this sequence celebrates B's agile body as it beats the macho Rage to the top of the Eye (Russo 1994: 22). There is a brief moment of exhilaration associated with aerial elevation before B comes crashing back down. The brief moment of aerial freedom allows B to remobilise her nomadic trajectory, and she moves on, seeking new territory. As a nomadic subject, then, the female grotesque does not follow the sustained forward movement of progress, but embodies a constant motion that opens up temporary spaces for freedom and affirmative embodiment.

Throughout this chapter I have shown how the zombie of children's Gothic begins its life in the classroom, but is able to chart a route to another territory, another mode of becoming. Just as the Baudelaire orphans in *A Series of Unfortunate Events* decide not to remain shipwrecked and isolated, B's journey is not a 'running away from the world' but a line of flight that flows away from the grasp of repressive power relations, symbolised by the school, teachers, doctors and military organisations who constantly attempt to bring her under their control (Deleuze and Guattari 2013: 239). The zombie body may be a ruined body, but it does not enact a disavowal of either the masculine or the feminine, allowing a grotesque interplay between the two that complicates a pedagogical structure seeking to identify a particular idealised reading child. This newly grotesque, ambivalent zombie is designated 'me' and does not operate as a point of counter-identification or object lesson on behalf of a pedagogical project. Instead, the zombie body offers a risky opportunity of flight and freedom from restrictive conceptions of gender and class. Darren Shan's zombies display their gross-out lineage in their gruesome bodies and shows of gory violence. As such, they prove a difficult figuration for a pedagogical project: they are neither suitable objects nor subjects. Moreover, unlike the reading child, the zombie is neither a maturing nor learning subject. Thus, in *Zom-B* the zombie becomes a figuration of identity that avoids the active/passive and subject/object binaries built into pedagogical formulations of children's literature. Finally, this zombie counters critical formulations extant in Gothic Studies, which also positions the zombie as an object lesson. In children's literature, the zombie is a nomad, neither a teachable nor teaching object.

Chapter 3

Exiled Lovers and Gothic Romance in Jamila Gavin's *Coram Boy* and Paula Morris's *Ruined*

Rethinking Romance, Reconfiguring Desire

In the previous chapter I suggested that it is the *schoolboy* that is the traditional, or founding, addressee of children's literature. In this chapter, I want to think about the *young female reader*, arguably the addressee of the earliest Gothic fictions. In *Zom-B* the imagined male reader, or schoolboy, is courted through gross-out aesthetics and the trappings of a 'masculine' horror tradition. In contrast, the works examined in this chapter – *Coram Boy* (2000) by Jamila Gavin and *Ruined* (2009) by Paula Morris – evoke the explicitly 'feminine' tradition of Gothic Romance. The 'feminine' Gothic is separated from its 'masculine' counterpart in both critical discourse and popular histories of the form, but these gendered histories of Gothic tend to disavow Romance and devalue female readers. Gavin and Morris's books counter such negative evaluations of the feminine, rewriting tropes from eighteenth-century Gothic Romance alongside the love stories now most associated with mass-market romantic fiction. Bringing romance to the fore, *Coram Boy* and *Ruined* partake in a twenty-first-century 'feminine' turn in Gothic fiction. They reveal the mutually constitutive relationship between Gothic and Romance, and, in so doing, refigure Gothic's denigrated female reader as an active, nomadic subject.

Ruined and *Coram Boy* mobilise the affective power of desire as theorised by Benedict Spinoza. In Spinoza's *Ethics* desire expresses a foundational human essence, or *conatus*, that propels the subject to active self-dependence and self-affirmation (Spinoza 1996: 104).

Spinoza's desiring subject is positively self-determined, a nomad propelled by an 'ontological force of becoming' (Braidotti 2011b: 21).
I draw on this nomadic formulation of desire to suggest that Romance
promotes agency rather than passivity in its indulgence of romantic
desire. Expounding Spinoza, Beth Lord argues that desire promotes
agency because pleasure increases the body and mind's ability to act:
'when we feel good, our being swells' (2010: 100). In relation to
romantic desire, Lord asserts that the subject feels joy when they are
esteemed by another, and draws power from imagining themselves
as the cause of another person's love and affection (2010: 95). Lord
draws on Spinoza's formulation of love as an affirmatory affective
experience for both self and other: 'the greater the affect with which
we imagine a thing we love to be affected towards us, the more we
shall exult at being esteemed' (Spinoza 1996: 88). In their recourse
to a romantic narrative that fulfils this desire to love, and be loved,
by another, *Coram Boy* and *Ruined* position the romantic heroine in
an active role. The stories they tell echo Deleuze and Guattari's insistence that passionate intersubjective interactions result in the com-
position of 'a more powerful body' (2013: 40). Evoking this positive
formulation of desire, these twenty-first-century children's Gothic
Romances reveal that Gothic has long been shaped by positive feminine desire, which provides 'a recipe for transformation, motion,
becoming' (Braidotti 2011a: 114). In *Coram Boy* and *Ruined*, desire
is thus compatible with a feminist literary project that interrogates
patriarchal narratives that confine or limit women. Accordingly,
the female reader is constructed not as a passive consumer or dupe,
repetitively rereading the same unsatisfying romance novels, but as
actively seeking positive transformation through openness towards
other subjectivities.

The desire mobilised in these works of Gothic Romance posits
itself in opposition to psychoanalytical theories of desire as lack.
Rather than 'the entropic and negative theory of desire [found] in
Hegel, Freud, and Lacan . . . [it is] a notion of desire that is not built
on lack but rather constitutes a powerful force in itself' (Braidotti
2011b: 21). Braidotti draws on Deleuze and Guattari who conceive
of desire not as lack, or governed by the prohibition of pleasure (as in
the courtly tradition), but as a process that 'fills itself and constructs
its own field of immanence' (2013: 181). Nomadic desire counters a
critical discourse that posits romance reading as a compensatory act.
In her foundational study, Janice Radway draws on a psychoanalytic
theory of desire as lack to argue that the nurturance demands placed
on women by a patriarchal family structure produce an 'emotional

drain' that is appeased by romance reading (1991: 57). Radway suggests that readers' 'lack of emotional nurturance combined with the high costs of lavishing constant attention on others is the primary motivation behind the desire to lose the self in a book' (1991: 94). For Radway, the Romance is 'first and foremost' the story of what it feels like to be 'the object of someone else's attention and solicitude' (1991: 64). In identifying with the heroine, women are 'telling themselves a story whose central vision is one of total surrender . . . she is required to do nothing more than exist as the centre of this paragon's attention' (Radway 1991: 97). Radway argues that Romance performs a compensatory function, but is ultimately unfulfilling, since the persistence of the lack and the failure of the narrative to address it fully, leads to repetitive reading (1991: 9). However, the romantic plots of *Coram Boy* and *Ruined* position the heroine not as a passive object, but active agent. The romantic plot is not compensatory, but acts as a prompt to discovery, action and transformation (of self and others). In this way, Gavin and Morris engage in a political project that identifies an active female reader, without disavowing the aesthetic and sensual pleasures licensed by romantic fantasy.

In its appeal to Romance, children's fiction counters binary maps and histories of the Gothic. It suggests that Gothic is not separate from Romance and it does not devalue 'feminine' concerns in favour of promoting a 'masculine' horror tradition. Gothic Romance constitutes an interface in which desire traverses categories and connects male and female subjects in mutually transformative relationships. As Braidotti contends, 'desire need not be conceptualized according to the murderous logic of dialectical oppositions', but can produce an in-between space, a flow of self into other (2011a: 131). Conceiving of desire as active, of the beloved as agent, and of the romantic plot as charting the interconnectedness of self and other, *Coram Boy* and *Ruined* imagine a nomadic subject that affirms itself through its desire to be with others. In this figuration of desire as relational, gendered categorisations, which separate and differently value 'masculine' and 'feminine' forms of Gothic, collapse.

The Disavowal (and Return) of Romance

Coram Boy and *Ruined* occupy very different publishing contexts and represent two distinct types of Romance. *Coram Boy* is a historical Romance, published just before the critical discourse championing Gothic for children began to gain dominance. The novel won the

Whitbread Children's Book Award before going on to adaptation as a popular stage play. *Coram Boy* also won acclaim in the educational establishment. It is taught in Key Stage 3 and Key Stage 4 classrooms throughout the UK as a historical novel. In contrast, Paula Morris's *Ruined* (2009) represents a form of pop-cultural Romance, following Stephanie Meyer's *Twilight* (2004) and the burgeoning popularity of 'Paranormal Romance' in Young Adult publishing. While *Coram Boy* deploys Romance in its earliest sense as a literary mode dealing with past times and other places, *Ruined* deploys Romance in the sense of its popular usage to describe mass-market romantic fiction of the twentieth century. The New Orleans setting of *Ruined* also suggests the works of Anne Rice. A direct influence on Morris, Rice is also a key writer in the intertwined histories of Gothic and Romantic fiction on which *Ruined* draws. As befitting this 'romantic' lineage, *Ruined* appears in Scholastic's *Point* series, which is home to category romance fiction explicitly targeting a 'teen' audience.[1] The series includes titles such as *The Lonely Hearts Club* (2010) by Elizabeth Eulbery and *Girls in Love* (2010) by Hayley Abbott.

Despite these different publishing contexts, *Ruined* and *Coram Boy* reveal the different ways Romance is integral to Gothic narratives. Both rewrite conventions from eighteenth-century Gothic Romance within narratives charting a romantic relationship between hero and heroine. *Coram Boy* contains many elements typical of eighteenth-century Gothic Romance: an aristocratic family feud, an illegitimate child, and a tyrannical patriarchal villain whose past sins haunt the present in ghostly form. However, rather than focusing on a single Gothic heroine, *Coram Boy* focuses on a group of children, and on one particular hero. Alexander Ashbrook is stifled by his domineering father, Lord Ashbrook, and the expectation he will take over the family estate in Gloucester. His passions are for music and for Melissa, a poor ward of the family. Unable to pursue either, Alex flees the family home to find employment as a musician in London, unaware Melissa has borne their illegitimate child. Melissa is persuaded to give the child to the 'Coram Man', an unscrupulous peddler who takes unwanted babies ostensibly to deliver them to the charitable 'Coram' hospital in London, though most end up in a shallow grave on the roadside. In its second part, the novel follows the fortunes of Aaron, Alex and Melissa's son, and his friend Toby, both orphans in care of the Coram Hospital. The boys fall foul of the 'Coram Man', now posing as a respectable merchant and patron to the orphanage. Like Walpole's Manfred, this Gothic villain is a fraud, but his crimes are those of the emergent capitalist bourgeoisie, not of a decaying aristocracy. The

Coram Man supplements his profits from the slave trade by trafficking children from the hospital to clients overseas. Following the trajectory of eighteenth-century Gothic, the narrative of *Coram Boy* culminates in the revelation of family secrets and of the corrupt deeds of the Coram Man, allowing the Ashbrook family to reunite, restoring Aaron to his rightful place as Alex's heir and allowing Melissa and Alex to marry.

Gavin recontextualises Gothic Romance in several ways. Though she offers a romantic plot in the relationship between Melissa and Alex, she refocuses her narrative on male friendship. The novel opens by describing the friendship between aristocratic Alex and his lower-class friend Thomas, as they study together at the Cathedral School. In the second part of the novel, this male friendship is repeated as Aaron and Toby work together to uncover the corruption of the Coram hospital's patron. Gavin also relocates what Hogle calls the 'falsified antiquity' of eighteenth-century Gothic Romance, typically figured as medieval Catholic Europe, to eighteenth-century London (Hogle 2012: 498). Gavin thus disrupts the 'progress of abjection' in which anxieties plaguing middle-class Western identities 'are cast off into antiquated and "othered" beings' (Hogle 2012: 499). Though the novel is set in a London of the past, this is not the London of antiquity, but of incipient modernity, the very moment Gothic crystallises as a literary genre. Deploying Romance as a critique of Britain's colonial history, specifically its involvement in the slave trade, Gavin further counters what Robert Miles sees as Gothic's presentation of medieval barbarity as 'abject material . . . that must be expelled from the national body' (Miles 2001: 61). Gavin's villains are British merchants and officials, not foreigners. Gavin thus deploys Romance, in its sense as a story of the past, to refigure early middle-class Britain not as enlightened and progressive, but corrupt and barbaric.

Eschewing the historical setting of literary Romance, *Ruined* is set in contemporary New Orleans and follows a teenage girl, Rebecca, who has been left with her Aunt Claudia in an unfamiliar town while her father is away on business. As well as finding romance with a mysterious and handsome boy from a rich family, the heroine finds herself bound up in a supernatural mystery when she meets the ghost of a black girl, Lisette, in Lafayette Cemetery. Lisette's tragic history leads Rebecca to investigate New Orleans's most respectable and wealthiest family, the Bowmans. Rebecca uncovers the infidelity of the family's patriarch and the murder of his illegitimate daughter, Lisette, revealing the origin of a supernatural curse that has caused the death of a Bowman girl every generation for 200 years. Though it is marketed as Paranormal Romance and recalls aspects of the works of Anne Rice, *Ruined* also draws on the same tropes of eighteenth-century Gothic as *Coram Boy*. It tells the story of an orphaned heroine (Rebecca's mother is dead and her father is absent) discovering her aristocratic birthright after being persecuted by a corrupt aristocratic family. Rebecca discovers she is a member of the Bowman family, and the revelation of her identity undoes the curse that has haunted the family since the murder of Lisette 200 years before. Joseph Crawford notes that Paranormal Romance novels typically focus on a romantic relationship between the heroine and a mysterious romantic hero (2014: 63). However, *Ruined* places the Gothic mystery centrally, with the romantic plot between Rebecca and Anton acting in support. The romance between Rebecca and Anton is paralleled by the strong interconnection between Rebecca and Lisette, suggesting the importance of female friendship and multiple relationality for the emergence of an active Gothic heroine. Furthermore, like *Coram Boy*, *Ruined* also deploys Romance in its sense as a story of the past to interrogate colonial histories, here revealing the racial inequalities produced by the slave trade, inequalities that Rebecca recognises as continuing to shape present-day New Orleans.

Ruined and *Coram Boy* weave the popular Romance (a love story) *and* the literary Romance (a story set in another time and place) into a Gothic narrative of violence, transgression and haunting, problematising existing critical formulations of Gothic that reject Romance as inimical to Gothic transgression. As Crawford argues, Gothic 'has overwhelmingly been interpreted as, to use Punter's influential formulation, a "literature of terror", and Gothic criticism has, accordingly, tended to focus on themes of horror, violence and fear' (2014: 5). Likewise, Eugenia DeLamotte argues that a 'masculinization' of the Gothic canon manifests as a critical tendency to see 'high' Gothic as written by men, and to see Gothic in its 'fullest development as centring on a male rather than female protagonist', citing Leslie Fiedler and William Patrick Day, whose studies of Gothic sideline female-centred writing (DeLamotte 1990: 12). The separation of Romance from Gothic into 'masculine' and 'feminine' histories tends to devalue the former, evident in the very earliest Gothic criticism. Montague Summers rejects 'Sentimental Gothic' in favour of 'terror-Gothic' and Robert Hume claims that 'horror-Gothic' is 'more serious and more profound' than 'sentimental' or 'historical' Gothic tales (Summers 1964: 28–31; Hume 1969: 282). Botting highlights

Gothic criticism's unease with Romance in his exploration of *Bram Stoker's Dracula* (1992), a film which he argues returns Romance to the Gothic, 'with a vengeance' (2008a: 1). Botting shows how reviews of *Dracula* formulate Romance in opposition to Gothic, decrying the film as reversing the affectivity of horror (Botting 2008a: 1, 4). Following these reviews, Botting argues that Romance cannot offer Gothic transgression, but works to 'recuperate gothic excesses' (2008a: 1).

The tendency in Gothic criticism to value transgressive works in contrast to romantic fantasy results in a disavowal of feminine forms of writing. Botting's book-length treatment tracing the relationship between Romance and Gothic quickly dismisses 'feminine' Romance in its opening pages, which it sees as occupying a separate literary history from transgressive Gothic. Botting summarises and dismisses this tradition from the 'embourgeoisified' Gothic romances of Ann Radcliffe, 'through the Brontës, Collins, Corelli, du Maurier and the host of popular romantic fictions packaged as "Harlequins", "Gothics", "Mills and Boon" . . . and on' (Botting 2008a: 11). *Gothic Romanced* instead recuperates Romance through texts such as *Neuromancer*, *Terminator* and rewritings of *Frankenstein*. Focusing on a 'masculine' horror tradition, Botting explores the 'female gothic' via science-fiction works like *Alien* and *Alien Resurrection*, not by considering romantic or domestic narratives.

The disavowal of Romance in Gothic criticism motivates much of the criticisms levelled at *Twilight*, and, by extension, the modern genre of Paranormal Romance. This disavowal is evident in Serena Trowbridge's assertion that '*Twilight* is a romance dressed up as Gothic: it has the trappings of the genre but not the substance' (2013). Trowbridge's formulation opposes Gothic and Romance, polarising the terms to assert literary value ('substance') for one at the expense of the other. As Eric Murphy Selinger argues, disdain for Romance 'remains a way to demonstrate one's intelligence, political bona fides, and demanding aesthetic sensibility, even in circles where resistance to such orthodoxies is the norm' (2007: 308). Crawford further reveals that even in Gothic criticism

> romances continued to be viewed not just as non-literature, but as a sort of anti-literature, and their readers continued to be pathologized and dismissed . . . The cultural legitimacy of Gothic fiction thus depended largely on its ability to maintain a proper distance from its despised daughter genre, the romance; and this was precisely what *Twilight* threatened. (2014: 223)

Crawford's central claim is that responses to Paranormal Romance have been so hostile because the genre represents a return to, rather than departure from, form for Gothic literature (2014: 5). In different ways, Gavin and Morris present a similar challenge to Gothic Studies in their multiple deployment of Romance. Their works offer a (re)turn to a 'feminine' romance tradition central to Gothic since its inception, but which has all too often been devalued in comparison with a 'masculine' horror tradition.

Romance also poses problems for feminist critics. As Kate Ferguson Ellis notes, 'feminist critics of the Gothic are divided on the issue of whether or not its heroines are submissive and thus models of patriarchally defined "goodness" for their readers' (2001: 458). This indecision comes from feminist critiques of Romance more generally. Critics express concern that Romance offers limited representations for women and so contributes to their oppression, even in studies that ostensibly recuperate the form. Lynne Pearce notes that Romance 'will, for many, continue to be regarded as a harmful "illusion" that is visited upon its unfortunate subjects as a kind of madness' (2006: 21). For example, Germaine Greer famously asserts that Romance represents women 'cherishing the chains of their bondage' (2006: 174). Greer's disdain colours the foundational studies of Romance, including those by Janice Radway and Tania Modleski that ostensibly aim to recuperate the form for a feminist project. Modleski argues that romantic novels 'perpetuate ideological confusion' for their readers, while Radway concludes that the formulaic structures recapitulate patriarchal ideology and that romance reading can potentially disarm the impulse for change that leads readers to seek out romance in the first place (Modleski 2007: 35; Radway 1991: 211, 213). Likewise, Cranny-Francis' celebration of genre fiction remains sceptical of Romance, which she describes as 'patriarchal fairy tales for grown-ups' (1990: 183). For Cranny-Francis, the Romance remains a 'bourgeois fairy tale'; for Radway, Romance perpetuates a fantasy that compensates women, but ultimately shies away from challenging the inequalities produced in patriarchal family structures (Cranny-Francis 1990: 192; Radway 1991: 148).

In their descriptions of Romance as fantasy and fairy tale, feminist critics inadvertently echo Enlightenment critiques of Gothic Romance from the eighteenth century, which derided the works of female Gothic writers as fanciful and irrational. Sue Chaplin notes that early Gothic Romance was derided for its lack of literary accomplishment and its moral impropriety. It was seen as a kind of literary 'madness', which would have particularly disastrous consequences for its legion of imagined female readers (Chaplin 2013: 199). The concerns of eighteenth-century critics such as Samuel Richardson were rooted in Enlightenment ideology, which valued reason, rationality and moral propriety. Their opposition of rational, moral literature with the irrational, immoral Romance constructs a gender binary, pitting the rational male critic against the irrational female romance writer and her readers.

Critics have attacked Paranormal Romance, particularly Stephanie Meyer's *Twilight*, in similar ways, questioning its moral, educational and political effects. Catherine Spooner argues that criticisms of *Twilight* 'are based on the assumption that literature should be "educational" for young women – teaching them something and providing moral guidance' (Spooner 2013). She cites criticisms of *Twilight* by UK government ministers, for example, who decry the books as unedifying. Their comments reveal 'plenty of prejudices about women's reading . . . not least the idea that young women can't make their own informed choices or be active critics of the texts they read' (Spooner 2013). Similarly, Crawford explores the criticisms of *Twilight*, concurring that they rehearse the old criticisms of Gothic Romance: that it is badly written, irrational and morally dubious, and, moreover, that its readers are unable to see the text's shortcomings (2014: 187–9). Both in the eighteenth century, then, and in the twenty first, criticisms of Gothic Romance undertaken on behalf of a female reader are concerned with the utility of Romance and insist upon its negative powers of influence. The choices of the female reader are deemed unworthy and unliterary, assumed to originate in her naïvety and lack of critical awareness.

Feminist critiques of Romance are grounded in a similar assumption that fiction ought to serve a pedagogical and political function. Moreover, concerns about the effects of Romance on its female reader uphold this construction of the female reader as a dupe. Murphy Selinger notes this when he criticises Radway's assertion that Romance fails to supply the reader with 'a comprehensive program for reorganizing her life in such a way that all needs might be met' (Radway 1991: 215; Murphy Selinger 2007: 310). For Murphy Selinger, this is 'the stuff of self-help books' and is not a demand we would make of other forms of fiction (2007: 310). Even Carol Thurston's more positive appraisal in *The Romance Revolution*, which sees romance reading as feminist influenced if not fully feminist, praises the form on the grounds that it offers readers empowering messages about sexuality that can have a positive impact on readers' lives (1987: 10). Like Radway, Thurston's concern with the personal uses of Romance reading leads to a concern with the texts' political function. Thus, Murphy Selinger argues that Romance criticism is too easily drawn into a restrictive debate: 'are these novels good or bad for their readers?' (2007: 319). This question insists on a broadly educational remit for literature for women, a remit which in turn constructs women as in need of education.

Children's Gothic Romance troubles existing criticism that casts Romance as a conservative and limiting force, constraining Gothic excesses and containing a feminist impulse towards freedom from patriarchal ideologies. *Ruined* and *Coram Boy* do not structure Gothic and Romance in opposition to one another, but reveal them as mutually constitutive. They offer a non-binary model of literary form and of subjectivity. In these novels, Romance acts as both an excessive and containing force, offering instruction in service of a rational pedagogy on the one hand and indulgence that exceeds social rules on the other. Both rational and irrational, Romance resolves a binaristic formulation of literature based on a text's political or pedagogical utility. Drawing on Spinoza's ethical schema, Romance suggests that 'we judge something to be good because we strive for it, will it, want it, and desire it' (Spinoza 1996: 76). In simple terms, the subject desires what is good for the preservation of its being, and since what preserves being is good and moral, desire is rational. *Ruined* and *Coram Boy* thus gesture towards a new ethics of Romance. One the one hand, Morris and Gavin deploy Romance to perform a pedagogical function, both for instruction about the past and to aim at an empowered and critical female reader. On the other hand, they offer indulgence in the sensuous and often politically ambivalent pleasures of nostalgia and fantasy, pleasures that are often constructed as naïve or disempowering by critics of Romance. These varying functions of Romance are not mutually exclusive, but integral to the figuration of a multifaceted nomadic subject.

Non-Binary Gothic Romance

Though the categories of 'masculine' and 'feminine' Gothic originate in feminist criticism, they are often invoked in support of a binaristic model of the form that disavows the 'feminine' Romance in favour of 'masculine' transgression. Ellen Moers's original formulation of 'Female Gothic' posits the Gothic as an important form through which female writers express their anxieties and dissatisfactions

(Moers 1985: 90–8). Kate Ferguson Ellis proposes the categories of 'masculine' and 'feminine' Gothic to establish the Gothic heroine as a proto-feminist figure, arguing that 'the Gothic novel expanded the female sphere to the point where women could challenge the basis of their own "elevation"' in a restrictive bourgeois ideology of separate spheres and domesticity (1989: xiii). Ellis locates the feminine Gothic as 'the center [*sic*] of [a] model for the development of the genre', arguing that the masculine Gothic is a reaction to the feminine (1989, xvi). However, the lowly status of feminine cultural production within literary criticism more generally often results in a disavowal of 'feminine' Romance in histories of the Gothic. Various critics have argued that mass or low culture is often gendered as 'woman' in contrast to modernism, or high culture (Huyssen 1986: 44; McGowan 1991: 20; Cranny-Francis 1990: 5). This feminised culture finds its most obvious expression in mass-market Romance fiction, of course, a form that originates in eighteenth-century Gothic Romance. In a move repeated elsewhere in Gothic Studies, Cyndy Hendershot marks this feminine form of mass culture as the repository of a 'mummified' form of Gothic (1998: 1). Hendershot dismisses 'Gothic romances in the Harlequin vein, replaying plots of simplified Radcliffean heroines threatened by enigmatic villains in foreign castles', preferring Gothic with 'disruptive potential' that she locates in the masculine genres of science fiction, horror film, adventure novels and detective fiction (1998: 1–2). Gothic criticism thus expresses contradictory impulses. On the one hand, it seeks to recuperate a once-vilified popular genre for academic study, including those works dismissed by eighteenth-century critics as unworthy 'women's poison' (Samuel Richardson cited in Chaplin 2013: 199). On the other hand, it continues to draw upon modernist-influenced notions of high art to defend the genre as radical, transgressive (hence valuable), disavowing feminine mass culture in the process.

Andrew Smith and Diana Wallace argue that gendered categorisations of the Gothic are increasingly questioned as essentialising (2004: 1). Nonetheless, such categorisations continue to be used. As Abby Coykendall argues, 'the supposition that gender predetermines genre is, in fact, so ubiquitous in Gothic scholarship that critics who would otherwise be little swayed by the formulaic encodings of gender and genre remain unwilling to abandon the paradigm altogether' (2005: 446–7). So – despite the feminist origins of categories such as 'female' and 'feminine' Gothic and later critiques of such categories – Gothic Studies continues to delineate the masculine from the feminine in a way that devalues the latter. As Hendershot's study demonstrates, the notion of a 'Radcliffean' versus a 'Lewisite' Gothic, for example, denigrates 'feminine' Romance as formulaic, but values 'masculine' Gothic for its transgressive potential. Botting echoes this evaluation in his swift dismissal of feminine Gothic from Radcliffe onwards, arguing that Radcliffe was 'very much the Barbara Cartland of her day' (2008a: 11). Botting favours 'male dark romance . . . licensing "masculine" tendencies towards power and violence' (2008a: 11). Though Botting expresses doubt about the categorisations 'masculine' and 'feminine', noting that 'dark-toned Romances in which love is more prominent than adventure' have been 'misperceived' as feminine, he nonetheless upholds a gendered binary by choosing to analyse texts from the 'masculine' tradition (2008a: 11, 12). Botting's comments illustrate the ways that even critics interested in popular or otherwise marginalised forms of literature continue to treat genres read and written by women with contempt.

Though gender categorisations inform Gothic criticism, there is no neat delineation between Gothic and Romance, nor between 'masculine' and 'feminine' histories of the form. Gothic's origins lie in the Romance, simply defined by Umberto Eco as 'a story of *elsewhere*' (Eco 1994: 574). For DeLamotte, the 'core' of Gothic Romance is a 'world set apart from normal quotidian experience and from the logical and moral laws of everyday reality' (1990: 18). Moreover, 'Gothic' and 'Romance', originally used in concert, were often interchangeable. Since they are mutually constitutive forms, Gothic and Romance should not be opposed in terms of their themes, narrative structure or effects. As Crawford's study of Paranormal Romance asserts, 'the histories of those genres which we now call "Gothic" and "romantic" fiction have always been heavily interlinked' (2014: 5). Crawford notes a shift in the twentieth century towards the male Gothic counter tradition, offering violence, horror and monstrosity, followed by a postmillennial (re)turn to Gothic narratives of love and romance (2014: 235). Crawford's history of Gothic and Romance is generous to a feminine tradition by demonstrating the Gothic history of popular Romance, but I would further add that Gothic texts often manifest both 'masculine' and 'feminine' impulses simultaneously. For example, *Wuthering Heights* (1847) has been read variously as a ghost story, a realist novel, a Gothic novel and a prototypical romantic novel. Cranny-Francis and Deborah Lutz both posit Brontë's novel as foundational for the development of mass-market Romance, with Lutz further arguing that 'all contemporary romance seems to grow out of the gothic . . . many of its dark and secret themes still resonate' (Cranny-Francis 1990: 178; Lutz 2006: 12).

Just as Gothic and Romance are interlinked, so are 'masculine' and 'feminine' Gothic. *Frankenstein* (1818), for example, a novel often placed in the 'masculine' Gothic tradition, draws together 'the "deep subversive impulse" of feminist protest . . . found in the Radcliffean tradition and the pervasive pessimism of the Lewisite tradition' (Ferguson Ellis 1989: 183). The novel separates a feminine sphere of domesticity from a masculine sphere of scientific discovery, but the relationship between its exiled anti-heroes is an exploration of the trauma of motherhood as much as it is of rebellion and monstrosity (Moers 1985: 93). Likewise, the male and female characters of *Wuthering Heights* (1847), a novel often cited as one of the proto-types of twentieth-century mass-market Romance fiction, are caught between masculine and feminine narratives and spaces (Ferguson Ellis 1989: 214). In *Wuthering Heights*, masculine and feminine positions shift between characters and the boundaries between the separate spheres blur. This is noted in Gilbert and Gubar's seminal reading, which argues that Heathcliff's character finds its origin in the many rebellious females of literature and myth and that he constitutes Cathy's 'almost identical double' (2000: 296, 298). A forerunner of the 'alpha male' hero of mass-market romance fiction, Heathcliff also embodies what Botting identifies, in a lineage of 'masculine' Gothic works, a 'darkly romanticised masculinity' that troubles social and sexual boundaries (Botting 2008a: 11–12). However, Heathcliff is also a feminised figure, initially lacking any social status or economic power. Heathcliff and Cathy exemplify DeLamotte's assertion that 'both the wanderer and the prisoner, shut into this alien world, are thereby shut out from ordinary life' (1990: 18). 'Masculine' and 'feminine' positions within Gothic Romance are thus interconnected, both embodying entrapment *and* exile simultaneously, often within the same texts.

Echoing these complex interrelationships between the 'masculine' and 'feminine' in Gothic, *Coram Boy* offers a masculine narrative of exile alongside a feminine narrative of entrapment, borrowing from eighteenth-century Gothic Romance, from *Wuthering Heights*, and *Frankenstein* in its romantic plot and exploration of maternal trauma. Romance and horror are mutually constitutive elements of this story in which a romantic attachment between an aristocratic male and a poor dependent female plays out against a back drop of infanticide and child abuse. The novel opens with a scene of child abuse as young Meshak, son to the 'Coram Man', is beaten as he helps his father collect abandoned children, stuffing them into sacks tied to their mule. Traumatised, Meshak sees 'trolls and witches; evil creatures crouching in shadows, lingering round trees, hanging in the sky; demons with hairless heads and glinting teeth' as he travels through the 'darkness of the forest' (Gavin 2000: 9). The novel evokes horror, describing revolting scenes in which Meshak buries live babies: 'Meshak let go the feebly moving bundle. He heard it splosh into the ditch. He backed away whimpering. He never did like burying the live ones' (Gavin 2000: 18). Misshapen and clumsy, with 'large watery, blue eyes', Meshak recalls Shelley's monster. Like the monster, he is an outcast and wanderer, watching the seemingly happy Ashbrook family in their home from the outside, unseen. At first, Alex and Melissa's romance is focalised through Meshak, a vantage point that feminises him as a desiring subject. Through Meshak, the novel vocalises a romantic desire normally associated with feminine romance plots: 'His heart tightened in his chest. He could hardly breathe with the emotion which swayed through him' (Gavin 2000: 104). Also like Brontë's Heathcliff, Meshak is feminised even as he occupies the position of the masculine exile because he possesses no social power or status. Later, he becomes 'mammy' to Melissa and Alex's abandoned child, saving it from death at his father's hands, playing a maternal role to Aaron in the second half of the novel (Gavin 2000: 162).

While Meshak is an exile, locked outside the home, Alex is trapped within it, occupying the enclosed position constructed and critiqued by 'feminine' Gothic (Ferguson Ellis 1989: x). Alex is confined and restricted by his tyrannical father, whom he is desperate to escape so he can pursue his dream of becoming a musician. Like Meshak, Alex is also figured as a desiring subject, and his love for Melissa is expressed in the sentimental language of Romance. He writes to her effusively, '*my dearest, sweetest and most treasured Melissa*' (Gavin 2000: 141; emphasis in original). Alex is also explicitly feminised by his father, who sneeringly calls Alex a 'songbird' and chides Lady Ashbrook for coddling him. Alex is uninterested in 'manly pursuits' and knows he is 'not the son his father hoped he would be' (Gavin 2000: 91). In her portrayal of Alex, Gavin explicitly draws on a feminine Gothic narrative of entrapment, noting that Alex is 'imprisoned by his wealth and class and forbidden the one thing he craved' (Gavin 2000: 92).

However, the gendered positions of *Coram Boy* shift when Alex decides to flee Ashbrook, running away to London in a self-imposed exile. The novel then brings Melissa to the fore; she takes up Alex's position of confinement. Gavin notes this shift when the lovers part after a final meeting. Melissa is 'swallowed up into the house' and Alex disappears into the night (Gavin 2000: 143). When Melissa realises she is carrying Alex's child, she confines herself to the nursey. The first part of the novel concludes with a traumatic birth scene that sees the child 'snatched' away as its cord is cut, given to the Coram Man. Here the romantic plot culminates in pain and trauma for the female protagonist, recalling the indictment of the separation of an enclosed female domestic sphere from a male worldly sphere offered in Ferguson Ellis's formulation of feminine and masculine Gothic (1989: x). Gavin presents Melissa's experience of romantic love ambivalently. Towards the end of the novel, before she is reunited with Alex and Aaron, she considers her reflection in a mirror at Ashbrook, where she has remained for the duration of the second part of the novel:

'Who am I? A mother without a child, a child without a mother.' She stared at her face, which was no longer a child's, but already bore the marls of anxiety, unhappiness and grief. Where was the joy? She asked herself. Would she ever again experience the joy of that childhood? (Gavin 2000: 287)

Through the shifting roles of Meshak, Alex and Melissa, *Coram Boy* presents a complex re-figuration of feminine Gothic Romance. Alternatively entrapped or exiled, desiring or desired, male and female characters occupy different positions within the narrative as a romantic plot interweaves with an exploration of female trauma and isolation. For Melissa, the affirmative powers of Romance are temporarily suspended while she is incarcerated at Ashbrook. However, *Coram Boy* does eventually reunite its characters in a resolution that fulfils her desire, redeems her lover's transgressions and heals their trauma.

Ruined likewise locates its characters within shifting 'feminine' and 'masculine' positions. The romantic plot is foregrounded when Rebecca meets the attractive Anton Grey. In this scene, Morris uses language typical of teen Romance: 'Rebecca couldn't help staring at the dark-haired boy. His face was angular, and though he was tall, he didn't seem gawky or clumsy. Even in the semidarkness, she could tell he was better looking than the other two boys ... She wondered if this was the famous Anton Grey' (Morris 2009: 51). Rebecca's desire for Anton echoes earlier teen Romance novels in which romantic desire

> brings heroines to womanhood, endowing their lives with meaning. Heroines' involvement in romance stimulates their interests in beautification which sexually objectifies them while simultaneously reproducing their positions in the sexual division of labor [*sic*] as consumers. (Christian-Smith 1987: 365)

According to Linda Christian-Smith's analysis of teen Romance, Rebecca's desiring look at Anton ought to propel her into a plot that will solidify patriarchal gender roles and normative notions of femininity. However, Rebecca's meeting with Anton in Lafayette Cemetery is incidental to a more important event. After spying on Anton, Rebecca meets the female ghost Lisette, whose presence signals the corruption festering at the heart of New Orleans. It is Rebecca's desire to see Lisette again that draws her back to the cemetery, where she sees Anton for a second time. Rebecca asserts, 'she wasn't here to ogle Anton, however good-looking he was' (Morris 2009: 68). Later, when Rebecca's romance with Anton progresses, Lisette intervenes to prompt Rebecca to turn her attention to the unsolved mystery. As the boy and girl kiss at a society ball, Lisette appears, 'just a foot away, staring straight at them ... looking as startled as Rebecca. ... The moment between them was broken, Rebecca knew' (Morris 2009: 169–70). Though Rebecca enjoys her desire for Anton, 'she hadn't wanted the kiss to stop', their romance is suspended. Rebecca is propelled into action by the mystery signalled by Lisette's haunting, not by her desire for the attractive boy.

Morris subtly reworks teen Romance in other ways too, drawing on Gothic narratives of entrapment and exile to demonstrate the fluidity of feminine and masculine positions. Though pensive, brooding, dark-haired and mysterious, Anton is not the typical alpha male hero of Gothic Romance. The novel flirts with this image of the dangerous, Byronic hero when Anton hounds Rebecca to discover what she knows about the curse, accosting her in the cemetery 'like some kind of sinister vampire, blocking her escape route' (Morris 2009: 262). Tall and physically domineering, Anton looks 'haunted' and Rebecca is momentarily frightened, though she refuses to give in to his demands to tell him what she knows. However, after the novel's climactic denouement, in which Rebecca is almost killed by the Bowman and Grey families,

Anton is revealed to be passive and weak. His investigations fail to uncover the information Rebecca finds, and he is unable to stop his family's plot to lure Rebecca to the cemetery where they intend to kill her. In the closing pages, he admits to Rebecca, 'I was real confused. I just didn't know what to do' (Morris 2009: 297). While Anton is self-pitying, Rebecca is assertive, chiding him: 'So you did nothing' (Morris 2009: 297). Anton's passivity reframes his earlier Byronic brooding, revealing that Rebecca has always occupied the more active position in their relationship.

Much like the aristocratic Alex of *Coram Boy*, Anton is a prisoner. In contrast, Rebecca, who is an outsider to New Orleans, is remarkably mobile. Not only does she navigate between social classes, gaining entry to high society functions despite her 'plebeian' standing, she also moves through different spatial and temporal zones of the city. Her connection with Lisette allows her to travel through districts of the city that Anton, and the other high society kids confined to the Garden District, never see. Lisette allows Rebecca to see images of the city's past, giving her privileged information denied to others. Rebecca's mobility is also contrasted with that of Helena Bowman, her romantic rival. In one scene Helena looks down on Rebecca from a window in her Garden District mansion. Helena is confined to her house, having supposedly taken ill, though this turns out to be a ruse to trick Rebecca into taking her place at the Mardi Gras parade where the Bowman family intend to kill her to appease the curse. Helena looks down at Rebecca, a predatory, 'tight smile' on her lips, and Anton comes to her side. Rebecca shudders at the humiliation, 'standing around in the street, gazing up at Helena and Anton like peasants gawping at members of the royal family' (Morris 2009: 223). Though Helena's smile is one of 'triumph', the position she and Anton occupy within the mansion is restricted, while Rebecca, on the street below, is free to explore the city and unravel a story that will bring the Bowman family to account. Morris draws on explicitly Gothic imagery to emphasise Anton's entrapment as Rebecca ponders his family's vault in the cemetery: 'It was weird to think of Anton getting buried in there one day. Or rather, getting *entombed* . . . so much of his life seemed circumscribed' (Morris 2009: 195; emphasis in original). The italicised word, *entombed*, emphasises Anton's restricted position within the novel in comparison to Rebecca's mobility.

Morris rewrites the feminine and masculine positions of Gothic Romance by reconfiguring Gothic space and remapping the heroine's claustrophobic location as a nomadic terrain. Morris draws on a discourse of the female Gothic to map New Orleans as a prison: 'New Orleans was a strange dream of a place, extreme and claustrophobic, where her universe was confined to a few blocks – school, the coffee shop, the cemetery. In New Orleans, she wasn't in exile: she was practically incarcerated' (Morris 2009: 182). Describing New Orleans as a 'strange dream', Morris offers the city as a romantic location, unreal and mysterious. Thus, New Orleans evokes a 'feminine' Gothic of confinement and incarceration. However, Rebecca's displacement to the city affords her the mobility experienced by many of Radcliffe's heroines despite their incarceration. These heroines 'scurry up to the top of pasteboard Alps, spy out exotic vistas, penetrate bandit-infested forests. And indoors . . . [they] scuttle miles along corridors, descend into dungeons, and explore secret chambers' (Moers 1985: 126).

Arriving in New Orleans in the aftermath of Hurricane Katrina, Rebecca views it as a city of refugees and so further identifies with the masculine exile 'sent hundreds of miles from home' (Morris 2009: 4). Gothic New Orleans is a 'city in ruins' and its decay represents displacement: 'Thousands of its citizens were still living in other parts of the country. Many of its houses were still waiting to be gutted and rebuilt; many had been demolished' (Morris 2009: 3–4). An exile, Rebecca sees the city as a location in transition, its past in danger of decaying, its homes, like Lisette's cottage in Storyville, 'about to fall down' (Morris 2009: 140):

> They pulled down all the old houses and the old trees so that the big road up there could go in. Lots of ghosts there are real unhappy still. All they got to haunt is a big pile of concrete. (Morris 2009: 141)

Rebecca's displacement allows her to navigate these different zones of the city and, eventually, through her investigations into Lisette's murder, reconcile them. Moreover, Rebecca's journeys through the city allow her to discover her origins within it. Discovering that she, like Lisette and Helena, is also a Bowman, affords Rebecca a double belonging. By the end of the novel she travels freely between New Orleans and New York, calling both cities home. Rebecca's nomadism allows her to escape the either/or binary of 'feminine' entrapment and 'masculine' exile, capitalising on opportunities afforded by both positions.

Remapping Gothic Romance, Morris imagines fluid gendered subjectivities as her characters occupy a variety of locations within the narrative. Anton shifts from occupying the role of romantic teen hero, to dangerous alpha male, to Gothic prisoner. Likewise, Rebecca plays the proto-feminist role of Gothic heroine, exploring the corridors of the Gothic castle refigured as the streets of New Orleans, and unravels the plot against her. Later she takes up the position of victim when she falls for the trap set by the Bowman family. Helena also shifts roles. Initially, she is located as the antagonist, the selfish and pushy 'other' woman of category Romance whose punishment restores the 'good' girl to the arms of the hero (Christian-Smith 1987: 385; Radway 1991: 131). However, Helena is increasingly drawn as a Gothic heroine too, incarcerated in her family's claustrophobic mansion. As Rebecca notes,

> however rude and stuck-up Helena had acted toward her, she didn't deserve so extreme a fate – either an illness too serious for her to attend school for an entire semester, or a fear so overpowering that her family wouldn't let her leave the house. Rebecca wouldn't be able to stand being locked inside all day, and she certainly wouldn't want to wake up each morning fearing for her life'. (Morris 2009: 191–2)

This contradictory representation of Helena suggests a further commentary on romance tropes. The oppositional patterning that pits the 'good' girl against the 'other' girl is complicated by the revelation that Rebecca and Helena are cousins, intimately connected by the Gothic plot. Though the Bowman family seek to sacrifice Rebecca to appease the curse, it is Helena who dies in the novel's climactic scene: a chunk of masonry from the Bowman family tomb is dislodged, falling onto Helena and killing her instantly. Helena's death is figured not as a triumph of the 'good' girl over the selfish antagonist, but as a tragic outcome of a situation that has forced two women to become enemies. Though the antagonism between Helena and Rebecca is intratextual, a result of the scheming of the Bowman family, it is also offered as a metatextual commentary on Romance conventions that construct women per a binaristic moral schema, only allowing the freedom of one at the expense of the other.

Rational Desire

From the outset, the 'feminine' Gothic Romance and its female reader were constructed as irrational and naïve. The earliest critiques of Gothic were rooted in Enlightenment ideology, which values reason, rationality and moral propriety. Eighteenth-century critics compared

Gothic Romance unfavourably with the new novel, which mirrored the real world and served a clear moral pedagogical function that aligned with an Enlightenment notion of 'reason'. Chaplin notes that 'the hostility to romance fiction was in part a consequence of its challenge . . . to Reason: its epistemological impropriety' (2013: 200). Critics argued that reading Gothic Romance was improper and that Gothic's young, female readers required rational and moral guidance lacking in the books they so voraciously consumed. For Enlightenment critics of Gothic Romance, the female reader should not be allowed to indulge in irrational desire, but instead inculcated into rational thinking.

These earliest denouncements of Gothic Romance are built on a binary that pits rational (i.e. good) against irrational (i.e. bad) forms of fiction, and it is a binary that continues to underlie discussions of romance fiction. In analysis of twentieth-century teen romance, for example, young female readers are imagined as needing guidance about their uneducational reading material. Berta Parrish describes how the release of 'Wildfire Romance' through Scholastic's Teen Book Club in the early 1980s found opposition from education groups in the US, who decried romance as detrimental for young girls (Parrish 1983: 612). Likewise, in the same period, children's literature critics debated the educational value of romance. Writing in *The English Journal*, Sharon Wigutoff argues that Romance has no literary quality and will not help educators produce critical readers. Even Parrish, who concedes that the books make young girls feel good, urges educators to 'guide' girls' reading with 'thought provoking questions' that will help them deconstruct the limiting patriarchal ideologies the books perpetuate (1983: 613). Christian-Smith's analysis of a range of romances from this period urges teachers to pass on the necessary 'tools for deconstructing' romance's limiting patriarchal narratives, insisting on the necessity of training naïve female readers to 'challenge' what they read (1987: 368, 393). These critical responses to romance assume that fiction written for young people ought to be educational and rational, and that it should challenge fanciful wish fulfilment, which is particularly dangerous to girls.

Recent commentary on Paranormal Romance fiction, which is the twenty-first-century successor to Gothic and teen Romance, inherits these attitudes about the rational, pedagogical function of literature for young female readers. In feminist critiques of *Twilight*, the reader, or 'fan' of Paranormal Romance is constructed as undiscriminating and irrational in their consumption of 'the impossible fantasy of Edward and Bella's relationship' (Crawford 2014: 201). Crawford argues that critics of *Twilight* assume that Romance is 'harmful to its readers, who – perhaps because of their presumed youth and femaleness – often seem to be assumed, a priori, to lack the critical faculties necessary to distinguish between fantasy and reality' (2014: 201). Crawford argues that critics of Paranormal Romance are concerned that the female reader will use fiction as a blueprint, reproducing damaging gender inequalities in her own life. Echoing the earliest critiques of Gothic Romance, these pronouncements construct the text as irrational and the reader as lacking in rational, critical faculties.

However, the idea that there exist separate categories of irrational and rational forms of literature is countered by the earliest Gothic writers. For example, Horace Walpole's blend of 'ancient' with 'modern' romance offers a deliberate mixture of romance and realism (Walpole [1764] 2014: 9). Developing Walpole's formulation of the Gothic, Clara Reeve draws on the categories of both Romance and novel to describe her work, *The Old English Baron* (1778). First she establishes a separation between the novel, which is 'a picture of real life and manners', and the Romance, which 'describes what never happened or is likely to happen' (1930: 111). Defending Romance against charges of irrationality and immorality in comparison to the respectable novel, Reeve points to works that 'partake of the nature of both, but . . . [are] a different species from either' (1930: 127). She asserts that her own work unites 'the most attractive and interesting circumstances of the ancient Romance and the modern Novel' (Reeve 2008: 3). Reeve writes passionately to argue that writing denoted as 'Romance' straddles and exceeds categories and evaluations projected upon it by the critics. Morris evokes Reeve by subtitling *Ruined* 'a novel'. She explicitly links Paranormal Romance to early Gothic's challenge to categorisations that would separate the Romance from the novel, and 'rational' from 'irrational' forms of literature. Partly, the label of 'novel' is a response to the scorn typically garnered by teen Romance. Like Reeve, Morris anticipates her critics by alluding to a literary category that has credibility. In so doing, Morris reveals that categorisations like 'novel' and 'Paranormal Romance' are overdetermined by suspect value judgments. Morris's use of the term 'novel' attempts to resolve an opposition between pedagogical, utilitarian literature (the novel) and irrational, disruptive fiction (Romance), following Reeve's argument that her works partake of both romantic imagination and novelistic rationality.

I want to resolve the binaristic opposition of 'rational' and 'irrational' fiction by drawing on the ethical schema proposed by Spinoza in which passion and desire are eminently compatible with reason and virtue, not their dark opposites. Desire is not irrational since it is a manifestation of the subject's *conatus*, that original, foundational desire to know (Braidotti 2011a: 18). The pursuit of rational knowledge, or adequate ideas, is part of a subject's desire to become self-affirming; likewise, desires and passion lead the subject to increase their rational knowledge. Lord explains that to pursue joy and indulge desire is the path to virtue since it 'involves increasing our understanding of ourselves and our world through empirical encounters' (Lord 2010: 114). The nomadic subject thus increases their agency and activity through indulging their desire, which works in concert with increasing their reason. *Ruined* is both an indulgent Romance, dealing in teenage love, desire and irrational supernatural events, *and* a rational novel, offering a pedagogical depiction of the troubled history of New Orleans in a hermeneutic narrative that positions its heroine as a rational investigator. *Ruined* thus reflects nomadic ethics and Braidotti's assertion that nomadic figurations refuse 'to separate reason from the imagination' (2011a: 18).

The prominence of the hermeneutic mystery plot in *Ruined* suggests that the Gothic heroine's indulgence in fancy and desire is linked to her acquisition of rational knowledge and agency. In this, Morris draws on Radcliffe's heroines, who were able to 'move beyond the restrictions of "the proprieties" set by critics' in their exploration of the Gothic castle and their investigation of the mysteries therein (Ferguson Ellis 1989: xiii). Ferguson Ellis's feminist reading of Radcliffe's Gothic heroine suggests that 'too much innocence is hazardous . . . she needs knowledge, not protection from the truth' (1989: xiii). However, unlike Radcliffe's heroines, who discover a rational explanation behind seemingly supernatural events, Rebecca must accept irrational and unreal events to acquire an adequate understanding of the mystery and danger that threatens her. At first, she cannot believe that Lisette is a ghost, protesting that it is 'just too weird', but as she holds Lisette's hand in the cemetery she becomes certain that she has passed over into a spectral world of ghosts (Morris 2009: 74). Rebecca's investigations force her to reassess her ideas of what is possible, of what is rational, as she works out the 'rules' for the new 'ghost-world' she has discovered (Morris 2009: 100).

This acquisition of knowledge through exposure to seemingly irrational events increases Rebecca's agency, following a Spinozan model of rational desire. As Lord explains, 'as the individual increases his activity of thinking (i.e. gains more adequate ideas) he becomes more active . . . increasing both his rational knowledge and his virtue' (2010: 113). Rebecca's discoveries about the 'surreal' town of New Orleans lead to self-affirmation and agency as she uncovers the circumstances of Lisette's death and her own origins. That is, Rebecca's investigations lead her to positive action based on the *rational understanding* she develops of the *seemingly irrational* events she experiences. Moreover, her desire to pursue a romantic relationship with Anton (despite his obvious unsuitability) and her willingness to believe in ghosts (in contradistinction to reason) is what preserves Rebecca in the climax of the novel. However illogical Rebecca's attraction to Anton or her belief in Lisette may be, these attachments are what preserve Rebecca's existence. Facing death in Lafayette Cemetery, Rebecca is saved first by Lisette, who makes Rebecca invisible and allows her to climb to safety, and then by Anton, who helps her flee. The climax of the story thus illustrates Spinoza's proposition that 'the mind strives to imagine only those things which posit its power of acting' since Rebecca's desire to be connected to both Anton and Lisette is what ultimately saves her life (1996: 98).

Romance further resolves the binary opposition separating the rational from the irrational by producing the past as a place of desire *and* instruction. *Ruined* and *Coram Boy* represent the past as a seductive and nostalgic fantasy while simultaneously using it to teach readers about the present. *Ruined* opens with a prologue set in New Orleans in the summer of 1853 and describes the effects of yellow fever as it 'ravages' the city. Recalling the grotesquerie and decay of an American Gothic aesthetic, Morris describes 'mass burials' and the 'putrid smell' of 'corpses rotting in piles' (2009: 1). Back in the present, Rebecca shudders thinking of bodies long buried bubbling to the surface, 'corpses peeping out of the wet soil like inquisitive worms' (Morris 2009: 12). However, this fantastic imagery of Gothic decay is framed by instruction. The prologue describes New Orleans as a city shaped by immigration and slavery, describing the fates of the city's migrant and black communities. This lesson about New Orleans's past is then related to the city's present as it recovers from the ravages of Hurricane Katrina. Aunt Claudia tells Rebecca about the city's involvement in the slave trade and its 'huge population of slaves' as well as its Haitian community, adding that 'there are still more black people than white in New Orleans' (Morris 2009: 15–17). Later, Rebecca will see for herself the homes in black neighbourhoods left to ruin by a city that continues to treat its black citizens differently to its white population. In its attempts to educate the reader (through Rebecca) about New Orleans's past and present politics, *Ruined* continues a tradition of presenting romance as educational. Writers and readers of romance have long defended the genre against the charge that it is indulgent nonsense by arguing that that it has intrinsic educational value. In particular, it is the romance's use of historical fact that allows its defenders to claim that this educational value, arguing that romance reading is a worthy pursuit (Radway 1991: 108).

While *Ruined* engages in an explicitly educational project, it also revels in a sensational representation of New Orleans, drawn as much from the Gothic fiction of Anne Rice as from history. As well as communicating important facts about the city's history, the ghosts of New Orleans are also spectacle for Rebecca's consumption. In fact, Rebecca's interactions with the spirit world reveal Gothic Romance's origins in consumerism and spectacle. E. J. Clery argues that in the eighteenth-century 'supernatural fiction figures as the ultimate luxury commodity' (Clery 1995: 5–7). Clery cites the phenomenon of the 'Cock Lane Ghost' as a precursor to the success of Gothic fiction. Crowds assembled to see the purported ghost and to experience the frisson of terror and the ghost was soon 'caught up in the machine of the economy; it was available to be processed, reproduced, packaged, marketed and distributed by the engines of cultural production . . . levelled to the status of spectacle' (Clery 1995: 16). This consumption of Gothic as a spectacle for the sake of affect alone is not easily co-opted into the service of political or pedagogical utility. Thus, the Enlightenment critique of Gothic was in part a rejection of the commodification of terror and of the indulgence in irrational ideas for mere pleasure's sake. Yet, it is this Gothic spectacle of pure affect that Rebecca experiences in her communion with Lisette:

> The city was thronged with ghosts. Three hundred years' worth of ghosts, all of them wearing the clothes they had died in, many of them bearing – all too visibly in some cases – the injuries that killed them . . . Rebecca could see them all. And this sight was so amazing, so overwhelming, it was all Rebecca could do to keep her mouth from hanging open in surprise. (Morris 2009: 131)

Holding Lisette's hand, Rebecca sees a smorgasbord spectacle of ghosts, from 'nineteenth-century dockworkers with rope burns' to 'a gaggle of brassy prostitutes', 'an eighteenth-century fop', an 'Asian guy in green hospital scrubs [with] a small wound in his chest – stabbed during a car-jacking', 'the Sicilian guys from the market',

'Spanish-speaking soldiers' and 'a sallow-faced man in a frock coat clutching a duelling pistol' (Morris 2009: 134–6). The various periods of the city appear here as theatrical settings, the ghosts become actors in costumes presenting themselves for Rebecca's horror and delight as she partakes in a literal 'ghost walk', more spectacular than any experienced by New Orleans's many tourists.

Coram Boy also offers a double image of the past. In the foreword, Gavin explains the historical details that inspired the novel and gives important background information about the eighteenth century. The foreword offers a pedagogical frame for the novel and it imagines that its readers need some instruction about the past, facts through which to interpret the fiction. Gavin's foreword functions as a gesture of authentication, positioning Gothic Romance within the discourse of real, serious history, which offers truth and instruction through the presentation of real events and real people. Gavin jettisons the playful metafictional fakery of Walpole's *Otranto* in her recourse to real historical fact, presenting Gothic Romance as rational and educational. In her blog, Gavin argues that historical truths are 'hidden away, embedded in folk tales, fairy tales and nursery rhymes' and that 'old folk stories and legends containing the most appalling horrors' are not simply 'titivation', but contain 'ancient truths' and 'moral lessons' (Gavin 2011: n.p.). Yet, by drawing on Romance, Gavin interweaves fantasy with history, licensing a fantastic, indulgent representation of the past. Her factual history of the Coram Hospital quickly becomes a fantastic Gothic narrative about a barbaric and terrifying past in which 'the highways and by-ways of England were littered with the bones of little children' (Gavin 2011: n.p). Gavin borrows from eighteenth-century Gothic and nineteenth-century sensation with her description of 'brutalised' children and orphanages that were 'no more than dying houses' (2011: n.p.). The preface recasts historical personages as Gothic characters, describing how 'miserable women' abandoned their children to the self-interested villainous imposter, known as the 'Coram Man' (2011: n.p.).

Gavin's eighteenth-century England is a sensual, nostalgic fantasy as much as a real, historical location. *Coram Boy* doubles the past, presenting it both as a *lesson* and as gothically transgressive; a 'darkly-imagined counter-world, embracing the less avowable regions of psyche, family, and society' (Botting 2001: 22). Like Rebecca's ghost tour of New Orleans, this Gothic version of eighteenth-century England is also the 'symptom of a voraciously consumeristic commercial culture' offering 'pleasure, sensation, and excitement' (Botting 2001: 22). This barbaric past location manifests trauma in the form of ghosts, 'demons' and 'nightmares' populating the 'dark, deep, dripping' landscape through which Meshak travels: 'Everywhere he looked, he saw tiny hands and fingers clawing at the sky, he heard wailing voices and choking cries' (Gavin 2000: 221). The frisson of terror offered by this tour of England's decaying woodlands gives way to a Gothic urban landscape, equally characterised by sensation. Aaron experiences the

> stench, smoke and smells of city streets and houses and hovels. The noise of the capital began to gather and roar like a distant wave and they could no longer walk a straight path, but had to dodge and swerve and battle with a sea of people. (Gavin 2000: 213)

Gavin's description of Gothic London is indebted to novelists like Charles Dickens as much as it is to historical fact, and her intentions to offer a mimetic representation historical fact gives way to nostalgic *pastness*. For Frederic Jameson, nostalgia approaches the 'past' through stylistic connotation, conveying 'past-ness' that creates 'pseudo-historical depth in which the history of aesthetic styles displaces "real history"' (Jameson 1991: 71). My reading of Gothic Romance rejects Jameson's elitist dismissal of nostalgia as empty pastiche. Rather, Gavin's fictionalised past reveals that Gothic's relationship with the past is necessarily one with images and aesthetics. These images are not empty, though. They are replete with affectivity. Gavin's educational use of the past can thus be reconciled with her nostalgic invocation of 'past-ness' as Romance maps a doubled location that performs a rational educational purpose supported by a Gothic affectivity, mobilised by a desire to see, feel and consume the spectacle.

Existing critical readings of Romance, even those that offer a positive explanation of its cultural function, argue that Romance indulges desires that contrast with real material, social or political realities affecting readers. Radway, for example, sees the ending of romantic novels as offering a 'miraculous' resolution of the anxieties that lead readers to Romance in the first place (1991: 148). Crawford argues that *Twilight* articulates 'an entire suite of extravagant wish-fulfilment fantasies, presenting a world in which pure desire has sufficient power to stave off . . . *unavoidable realities*' (2014: 226; my emphasis). Crawford defends *Twilight*'s indulgence of excessive desire, noting that though Bella's desires 'are mad, illogical, amoral, impossible, anti-social, wildly excessive . . . by the end of the fourth book every single one of them has been fulfilled. For many readers, anxious about what and when and to what extent they may be permitted to desire at all, this is clearly exhilarating stuff' (2014: 172). Echoing Radway's analysis of the way adult Romance magically resolves the anxieties and lack felt by women in the patriarchal family, Crawford argues that *Twilight* offers an appealing fantasy in which all the contradictions surrounding love and sexual desire are 'magically resolved' (2014: 217). Though Radway and Crawford seek to account for the positive effects of Romance, their conclusions uphold a binaristic formulation of irrational desire versus rational logic. They imply that the 'dream logic' of *romantic* wish fulfilment defies the *realities* faced by readers (Crawford 2014: 172).

This opposition is resolved by Gavin and Morris in their recourse to a Spinozan ethical schema in which indulging in desire and imagination is a rational and virtuous act. Braidotti argues that 'the desire to reach an adequate understanding of one's potentia is the human being's fundamental desire' and that since desires arise from our passions, 'they can never be excessive – given that activity is the power that activates our body and makes it want to act' (2011b: 312). Thus, *Coram Boy* allows Alex to become a musician, to marry Melissa and to be reunited with his friend Thomas, and his son, Aaron, revealing that his passions and desires are all, ultimately, productive rather than destructive. In *Ruined*, Rebecca solves a mystery that brings the corrupt elite of New Orleans to account while getting to ride in their prestigious parade. She sets Lisette's ghost to rest and gains the adoration of the handsome Anton, and even prompts her new friends to start up a renovation project to rescue New Orleans's dilapidated houses and decaying neighbourhoods. Both texts provide the reader with horror and gore, hauntings and nightmares, indulgent nostalgia, a history lesson and the sensual pleasures of romantic desire. These 'affects' are not mutually exclusive, but constitutive of an affirmatory nomadic subjectivity.

The Nomadic Romance: Becoming Together

Finally, I want to trace the ways that *Coram Boy* and *Ruined* figure desire as transformative, as an outward facing process that leads the nomadic subject into productive relationships with others. In her ambivalent formulation of Romance, Radway maintains that its 'narrative structure embodies a simple recapitulation and recommendation of patriarchy and its constituent social practices and ideologies' (1991: 210). In contrast, Lutz maintains that gothically inflected

Romance offers an 'anarchical rebelliousness' that undercuts any didactic project (2006: 2). Characterising Romance as radically transgressive, Lutz's analysis leads to the aporia of deconstruction as she formulates love as a death drive, propelling inward towards 'the edge of silence . . . fragmentation, and . . . disintegration' (Lutz 2006: 2). Caught up in a binary of containment versus transgression, neither Radway nor Lutz's analysis of Romance offer a satisfactory explanation of how Romance might, in its contradictory nature, offer a productive figuration of subjectivity. *Ruined* and *Coram Boy* offer a way out of this polemic by representing romantic desire as transformative. The characters of Romance indulge their fantasies *and* achieve autonomy while maintaining positive and outward-looking relationships with others. The seeming contradiction of this is resolved in Spinoza's *Ethics* which states that subjects are most useful to one another when each one seeks their own advantage, but that seeking one's own advantage means acting in the interests of other subjects too (Spinoza 1996: 132–3). The characters' indulgence in romantic desire allows them to positively influence each other and their communities, revealing desire as a force that works towards change and transformation.

Though both novels draw on the trope of the exiled lover, these are not stories of othering and isolation. The romantic hero is not a Gothic exile, trapped on the outside of the home, nor is the female heroine confined within. In Ferguson Ellis's formulation, the heroine of 'feminine' Gothic 'marries and creates a happy home, while the hero of the masculine Gothic dies or roams the face of the earth eternally' (1989: 220). For Ferguson Ellis, this 'ritual' maintains the separate spheres even as it critiques them. However, as my analysis has demonstrated, there is no neat spatial separation of male hero and female heroine in these texts. Rather, the characters come together across a variegated landscape of desire, negotiating pathways between entrapment and liberation. In this landscape, desire is not figured as a death-drive as it is in Lutz's analysis, leading to fragmentation and disintegration (Lutz 2006: 2). Nor do these books hold up Botting's formulation of desire as vampiric, reproduced in Romance as an unsatisfying aporia: 'In never being able to satisfy or kill off desire, romance reproduces the incompletion required for more' (2008a: 25). Essentially negative and unsatisfying, these deconstructive accounts of Romance suggest that the subject is unable to move beyond the void of its own lack. In contrast, Morris and Gavin's Romances align more with Deleuze and Guattari's account of love, which is a process whereby the subject finds the other person's packs, 'the multiplicities he or she encloses within himself or herself which may be of an entirely different nature', and joins them to their own (2013: 40). To put it simply, these books develop a romantic plot that describes love as a process of mutual relationality and transformation; these are stories of interconnectedness and positive becoming.

Romance is another location for the development of nomadic subjectivity, then, one that emphasises its potential for empathy and compassion. Building on Deleuze and Guattari's descriptions of love, Braidotti notes that the 'disappearance of firm boundaries between self and other, in the love encounter, in intense friendship . . . is the necessary premise to the enlargement of one's fields of perception and capacity to experience' (2011b: 167). This disappearance of boundaries is modelled by Alex and Melissa in *Coram Boy* when they consummate their love for the first time. Gavin describes the lovers lying in

> each other's arms . . . not knowing where affection ended and passion began, or which was the child and which the adult. They hardly knew what happened or how; just that feelings and sensations and emotions beyond their understanding overwhelmed them, and carried them outside the boundaries of anything they had ever experienced. (2000: 142)

As they indulge their desire, the borders between Melissa and Alex become porous. Though Gavin's depiction of sex is coy, typical in children's and teen fiction, it presents the lovers as undergoing transformation, a sexual maturation caused by a deeply felt connection with another person. Though it initially causes pain when they are separated, this union propels the characters forward on paths that will eventually fulfil their desires and affirm their identities. When Alex and Melissa are reunited towards the end of the novel, Alex has been transformed. He can visualise Aaron's birth and feel Melissa's broken heart as he reconnects with her (Gavin 2000: 317). This is a romantic reunion, but more importantly is a reunion that produces empathy and mutual understanding. As Alex looks back over the events of the novel, 'it sometimes seemed that he was his own son and that somehow they had fused into one person' (Gavin 2000: 317). Alex's non-unitary vision of his subjectivity through his connection to Melissa and Aaron recalls Spinoza's proposition that 'we can think of none more excellent than those which agree entirely with our nature . . . two individuals of entirely the same nature are joined to one another, they compose an individual twice as powerful as each one' (1996: 125). This multiple reunion of lovers, of mother and son, of father and son, revitalises the broken Ashbrook family and looks forward to the future.

Stories of romantic love are stories of productive relations with other subjects. Lynne Pearce argues that 'romantic love is frequently characterized by a profound need/desire to benefit the other' that is all too often interpreted negatively, through psychoanalysis, as 'the subject's need/desire to dissolve/transcend his or her own ego' (Pearce 2006: 8). Pearce draws on an essay by Jean-Luc Nancy to argue that romantic desire is 'experienced by both the lover and his/her beloved as an *outward motion*' (Pearce 2006: 8; emphasis in original). This outward motion is transformative even when it ends with a broken heart. Pearce explains that 'through the "event" of love, the subject is so transformed that s/he can no longer return to the self s/he was' (2006: 11). This redemptive and transformative model of romantic love counters both to the tragic model of subjectivity offered by psychoanalysis and to the self-contained, stable model of the mature subject found in ego-relational psychology. Romance produces a subject that is not contained, but always in process. However, this is not a self tragically split by an identification with the Other. Alan Soble affirms that 'whatever desire is or is not, it is clearly a *relational* function: a conclusion that concurs with Descartes's conception of love as an "outward motion"' (1990: 1). Radway also notes this outward motion in her assertion that 'the fairy-tale union of hero and heroine is in reality the symbolic fulfilment of a woman's desire to realise her most basic female self in relation with another' (1991: 155). I would add, however, that this outward motion is expressed not only through romantic relationships, but in the model of multiple relationality offered in these children's texts.

Coram Boy and *Ruined* are not only concerned with romantic love, but with friendships and familial bonds. Rebecca is mobilised and affirmed through her relationship with Lisette, while Melissa finds comfort in her connection to Alex's sister, Isobel. The multiple friendships in *Coram Boy* reveal that Romance can forge multiple productive connections with others, and is not about a nihilistic desire to lose oneself in another. Melissa and Isobel's deep friendship is mirrored in that between Alex and Thomas, and later, by Aaron and Toby. The novel closes by framing all these relationships through Meshak's outsider perspective, reminding the reader of his unseen connection to all of the characters and the ways he has facilitated their bonds. He looks down upon Ashbrook, thankful that his 'angels', Melissa, Aaron and

Toby, have been reunited (Gavin 2000: 323). The bonds between the characters in *Coram Boy* offer a model of virtue found in Spinoza's *Ethics*. The novel imagines its characters living 'an ethical life . . . which enhances and strengthens the subject without reference to transcendental values but rather in the awareness of one's interconnection with others' (Braidotti 2011b: 313). The desiring subject is not an isolated individual, but occupies 'complex and mutually dependent corealities' (Braidotti 2011b: 312).

In *Ruined*, the ethics of interconnection and codependence manifests in the novel's closing pages, which turn away from the romance between Rebecca and Anton to the story of Lisette. Lisette's haunting and exorcism becomes emblematic of New Orleans and Rebecca and Anton become anonymous actors in a ritual that might transform the city:

> The girl reached forward, leaning the wreath against the door. 'Goodbye,' she said, and took a step back. The boy reached for a hand, and they stood for a moment in silence . . . One of the city's oldest curses had ended. At long last, one of the thousands of ghosts in New Orleans was resting in peace. (Morris 2009: 309)

Morris's decision to strip Anton and Rebecca of their names in this final scene recalls Deleuze and Guattari's claim that 'every love is an exercise in depersonalisation' (2013: 40). Braidotti's manifesto of nomadic subjectivity draws on this idea, suggesting that desire results in 'a depersonalisation of the self in a gesture of everyday transcendence of the ego' (2011b: 167). Here desire becomes 'a connecting force, a binding force that links the self to larger internal and external relations' (Braidotti 2011b: 167). Returning to Lisette's story, Morris recasts Romance as transformative not only of the two lovers, but for a wider network of connections. Lisette's ghost is released, the Bowman family's sins are redeemed, and Rebecca and Anton's union provides a possible model for the ways in which the city might begin to heal itself of the traumas of its ancient, and more recent, past.

In these books, desire transforms lovers from exiles to members of a rejuvenated community. Braidotti argues that 'desire is located transversally, in the . . . immanent interrelations among subjects collectively engaged in the expression and actualization of their power of becoming' (2011b: 205). Accordingly, both novels end with an image of a traumatised community in the process of being rebuilt.

In *Ruined*, this rebuilding is literal as well as figurative as Rebecca leads a project to restore houses left to rot after the hurricane. They start with Lisette's former home, connecting New Orleans's past to its present:

> With the help of a local charity, and a group of enthusiastic volunteers ... they'd managed to gut the house, clear out all the rubble from its collapsing roof, and give the exterior a fresh coat of pale blue. Work on the renovation would continue throughout the summer, even after the girl returned to her hometown, New York City. (Morris 2009: 308)

The renovation productively links the past with the present and looks forward to Rebecca's continued mobility, noting her return to New York. Rebecca's transformative effect on New Orleans will continue after she leaves, and her connection with the city remains.

In *Coram Boy*, desire positively transforms a traumatised community by connecting the past to the present, depicting a scene of family reunion in the cemetery where Alex and Melissa have gathered to say goodbye to Melissa's mother and Alex's friend, Thomas. Alex looks over the Gloucestershire landscape from which he has been exile for so long:

> two boys emerged from the undergrowth and came to the stile. One white. One black. Alexander's heart stopped beating. Everything ceased; even the birds in their flight seemed suddenly suspended. The children of the crying wood faded away. One boy, the white boy, came forward slowly and stood before him. 'Mr Ashbrook,' said Aaron. 'I think I'm your son.' (Gavin 2000: 318–19)

Aaron's homecoming is not simply a family reunion, but it sees the formation of a new family network, containing different classes and races. Melissa is poor, Toby is black, but they both make their home at the rejuvenated Ashbrook Hall. The landscape surrounding them is also transformed. Though the locals still talk about the ghosts that used to haunt the 'crying wood' where so many babies were once buried, children now 'plunge in and fill their willow baskets' during the blackberrying season (Gavin 2000: 323). The close of the novel thus sees the healing of a wider community trauma and the exorcism of its ghosts, looking forward to a possible future in which the class and racial divides that split the Ashbrook family, as well as the horrors of the slave trade that shaped England's middle classes, might be healed. In both novels, then, desire is a force of propulsion and transformation. Following the path of their desire, the subject of Romance navigates their entrapment and exile, returning eventually to a transformed community space. Here, Romance remaps the past as a newly possible world that contains newly possible patterns of becoming.

Note

1. 'Category Romance' refers to mass-market romance fiction that rose to popularity in the US and UK in the 1950s when publishers such as Harlequin, Silhouette and Dell and Fawcett, who had been taken over by large conglomerates, sought to construct a guaranteed audience of middle-class women by producing romance titles to a particular formula, then distributing these titles as cheap paperbacks through supermarkets. Initially, publishers sought to reproduce the reprint success of Gothic titles such as *Rebecca* by commissioning 'Gothics' following a set formula. However, the field rapidly diversified into various subgenres. See Janice Radway, *Reading the Romance* (1991), pp. 25–31.

Chapter 4

Relocating the Mainstream in *Frankenweenie* and *Paranorman*

Rethinking Gothic 'Margins'

In this chapter, I want to move on from books and explore further the transformative impulses of twenty-first-century children's Gothic as it manifests in other media. The nomadic subject is not only produced within the pages of literature and pulp fiction, but also onscreen in a multitude of Gothic television programmes and films made for children and teen audiences in the twenty-first century. I will examine one particular example of such cultural production, the Gothic film parody. I am interested in Gothic film parody because, on the surface, such cultural products seem to confirm critics' worst fears about the proliferation and deterioration of Gothic in a commodified postmodern culture. As I have argued, some critics within Gothic Studies seem keen to dismiss pop-cultural or postmodern forms of Gothic, particularly those aimed at children. Such critics are concerned that through dispersal into such cultural products, Gothic has been emptied of its power to shock, disturb and critique. This idea is rooted in subcultural and modernist notions of cultural production, with their attendant snobberies towards mass and mainstream cultural products. Children's Gothic film parodies offer a means to counter these rather gloomy assessments of contemporary Gothic and cast doubt on evaluative distinctions critics have drawn between 'authentic' and 'inauthentic' works, and between the supposed radical cultural 'margins' and a conservative or commodified 'mainstream'.

Frankenweenie (written and directed by Tim Burton) and *Paranorman* (written and directed by Chris Butler and Sam Fell), both released in 2012, are feature-length children's animated horror films that stage a parody of older Gothic works, employing 'trash' aesthetics and playful pastiche to produce humour as well as horror. *Frankenweenie* and *Paranorman* belong to a tradition of Gothic film parody in Hollywood, which Kamilla Elliott argues goes beyond 'simple mockery to reveal inconsistencies, incongruities, and problems in Gothic criticism' itself (2008: 24). Elliott notes, for example, how Hollywood parodies such as *Young Frankenstein* (1974) and *Abbott and Costello Meet Frankenstein* (1948) mock Freudian and deconstructive theoretical criticism of Gothic (2008: 26, 27). Following these parodies, *Frankenweenie* and *Paranorman* stage and interrogate Gothic criticism's elitist dismissal of popular culture. The films dismantle the idea of 'authenticity' upon which such elitist critiques are founded, revealing a constructed aesthetic of 'authenticity' composed of artifice and fakery. However, these children's films do not employ parody *only* to anticipate and deconstruct critical judgment. *Frankenweenie* and *Paranorman* employ parody to foreground Gothic intertextuality, transforming Gothic tropes and calling attention to new ways of reading them. Like Braidotti's nomadism, this use of parody constitutes 'neither a retreat into self-referential textuality nor . . . apolitical resignation', but a dynamic mode of fiction that imagines new ways of reading, learning and being (Braidotti 2011a: 11).

Parody is a transformative mode that makes full use of self-aware intertextuality to relocate and reconfigure older Gothic works and familiar tropes. Moreover, it imagines an agile viewer able to negotiate its double-voiced nature. Dan Harries argues that parody always says 'one thing whilst saying another' because the borrowed words and images from the target text retain their original meanings and intentions even when the parody text holds them up to mockery (Harries 2000: 5). Linda Hutcheon also asserts that parody is double-voiced; it allows for multiple pragmatic effects, including provoking humour at the expense of the target text as well as reiterating its original meanings (1985: 32, 37). The result is a 'transformational synthesis' between old and new (Hutcheon 1985: 38). Building on the theories that Harries and Hutcheon have put forward about parody, I want to suggest that *Frankenweenie* and *Paranorman* relocate and transform Gothic horror film tropes for a newly imagined audience, able to both deconstruct *and* enjoy the scares. The kind of parody employed in these films offers a counter to critiques of postmodernism that identify its primary modes as empty, imitative simulacra. This critique is central to Frederic Jameson's account of postmodern pastiche as 'blank parody', for example (1991: 17). Jameson's critique of postmodernism, along with Baudrillard's formulation of simulacra (1994), has influenced assessments of pop-cultural Gothic as repetitive, empty, nostalgic commodification. For example, Botting argues that postmodern Gothic reproduces tropes 'beyond exhaustion' so that its once transgressive monsters have become 'normal, domesticated, commodifiably differentiated, serialized' (Botting 2014: 501, 500). Though both *Frankenweenie* and *Paranorman* play with this image of the domesticated monster, in the form of monstrous pets and harmless zombies, their rewriting of Gothic horror cinema does not constitute empty nostalgia or commodification, but a complex double response to the popular proliferation of Gothic in contemporary culture. They synthesise a genuine homage to a traditional canon of Gothic horror cinema with a critique of the very idea of 'authenticity' upon which this canon is based. These films employ parody not as blank reproduction, but instead as a strategy that Deleuze and Guattari call 'following'. Deleuze and Guattari insist that 'one never follows to reproduce' but rather to initiate and partake in a 'continuous variation of variables' (2013: 433–4). Put simply, parody in this nomadic formulation is neither inert mimicry, nor does it aim to reduce Gothic to a set of stock tropes. Negotiating homage, nostalgia, irony and critique, these films posit new reading strategies for Gothic, locating a new audience whose naïvety (rather than cynicism) allows them to experience pop-cultural Gothic products as authentic, even though this 'authenticity' is only temporary and performative.

Frankenweenie and *Paranorman* employ the double-voicedness inherent in parody to locate new readings of Gothic that draw on the transformative power of naïvety. In so doing, these films locate a viewer who is able to recognise Gothic artifice but also experience it affectively. This viewer is not a 'real' child but rather a 'conceptual persona' constructed within and by the text. A conceptual persona is 'a theoretical navigational tool that evokes and mobilizes creative possibilities in order to change dominant subject positions' (Braidotti 2011a: 12). A position from which to theorise and think through philosophical propositions, Braidotti's 'conceptual persona' allows her to 'innovate philosophical form and content' (2011a: 22). Likewise, these children's films innovate the Gothic form through the construction of a conceptual persona able to decode parodic intent while simultaneously remaining open to the affective power of Gothic horror cinema. This conceptual persona is figured foremost through the films' protagonists, both of whom model a naïve suspension of disbelief in the face of the Gothic irruptions into their world. Victor expresses an innocent, though macabre, desire to resurrect his beloved pet, Sparky, while Norman insists that he can speak to ghosts even though his parents and peers mock him. In both cases, the children's naïve and outlandish beliefs transform their cynical communities, allowing members of that community to forge new relationships. These child protagonists may be outsiders, but they are not cynics, and their transgressions against their communities are constructive rather than destructive. The model of productive naïvety offered by Victor and Norman is echoed in the conceptual persona the texts imagine exist outside the narrative: a viewer who does not have to be *in the know* to get the joke, and whose appreciation of parodic humour does not preclude being frightened by the Gothic horror tropes being parodied.

Paranorman explores the affectivity of commodified and trash horror aesthetics via its protagonist, Norman, a horror nerd who loves zombie films and has a bedroom full of horror merchandise. Blithe Hollow, Norman's home, is a dilapidated New England town that trades cynically on a famous witch trial from its early Puritan history. Townsfolk sell key chains and 'Witchy Wieners', exploiting the town's macabre history to draw in tourists. The cynicism of Blithe Hollow is contrasted with the innocent Norman, whose relationship with the dead of Blithe Hollow is empathetic rather than exploitative. Reworking the conceit of M. Night Shyamalan's *The Sixth Sense* (1999), combining it with the trash aesthetics of zombie horror, *Paranorman* celebrates the figure of the nerd, whose insights into the supernatural save the town from destruction. Norman also brings about reconciliation through his interactions with the town's dead, including the zombie corpses of the town's Puritan founders and the spirit of the witch whom they sentenced to death. Much like Tim Burton's earlier animated film, *The Corpse Bride* (2005), *Paranorman* enacts a reconciliation between the dead and the living, the past and the present, and sets the town on a more hopeful trajectory. The film recycles horror tropes from various subgenres and makes explicit reference to a variety of Gothic and horror films – such as *Sleepy Hollow* (1999), *Witchfinder General* (1968), *Young Frankenstein* (1974), *Suspiria* (1977), *Halloween* (1978), *Friday the 13th* (1980) and *Dawn of the Dead* (1978) to name a few. This explicit intertextuality produces both comedy and horror, while the trash aesthetics of the film suggest that 'authentic' horror is not necessarily to be found in modern ultra-mimetic film genres, such as the *Paranormal Activity* series, whose title *Paranorman* playfully mocks.

Frankenweenie is the remake of an old Tim Burton project, originally shelved by Disney in the 1980s. In this 2012 remake, Burton affirms his own brand of 'Disneygothic' in which, much like *Paranorman*, trash aesthetics and horror cinema references abound. This film also literalises Botting's critique of 'postmillennial monsters', which argues, drawing on Derrida, that as monsters become familiar and recognisable they are domesticated to the point of becoming pets (Botting 2014: 500; Derrida 1995: 386). Evoking the monsters of classic Hollywood horror and the trash aesthetics of low-budget science fiction, Burton retells Shelley's *Frankenstein* as the story of isolated schoolboy, Victor, who resurrects his beloved pet dog as part of a science project. A cat, hamster and tortoise are all brought back to monstrous un-life in a monster-mash up reminiscent of the 1950s *Godzilla* and *Gamera* franchises. The protagonist of *Frankenweenie* is an isolated child, whose innocent desire to believe that he can bring 'Sparky' back to life contrasts with the cynicism of the adults around him who desperately wish he could be 'normal'. Reimagining the moral debate at the heart of Mary Shelley's novel, *Frankenweenie* sets the cynical disbelief of the adult in opposition to the naïve conviction of the child. Also like *Paranorman*, this film employs stop-motion animation and draws attention to the construction of a DIY, 'trash' Gothic horror aesthetic. Thus, the battle between cynicism and naïvety that the film stages thematically is also staged at the level of visual aesthetics. *Frankenweenie*, too, resurrects well-worn tropes from classic horror, borrowing from films such as *Frankenstein* (1931), *The Mummy* (1932), *Godzilla* (1954) and *Dracula* (1958), affirming their affective power for a reader who, like Victor, is willing to suspend cynical disbelief.

Frankenweenie and *Paranorman* exemplify a twenty-first-century trend for animated Gothic horror that, for some critics, might seem to confirm Gothic's move from the margins of cultural production to its mainstream.[1] *Paranorman* was produced by the relatively small production studio Laika following the success of their stop-motion adaptation of *Coraline* in 2009, directed by *Nightmare Before Christmas* director Henry Sellick. *Frankenweenie* affirmed Tim Burton's return to the Disney fold following the live-action remake, *Alice in Wonderland* (2010), which Burton also directed for Disney. The current trend for animated Gothic horror is traceable to the influence of both Sellick and Burton, whose earlier Disney production *The Nightmare Before Christmas* (1993) became a cult classic before being revamped and reissued by Disney first in 2000, and then again in 2006 and 2007 to popular and critical acclaim. Other Hollywood studios soon followed suit with the release of a number of animated horror films aimed at children, including Burton's

The Corpse Bride (2005, for Warner Bros), Gil Keenan's *Monster House* (2006, for Sony), Genndy Tartakovsky's *Hotel Transylvania* (2012, for Sony), which was followed by a sequel in 2015, and, more recently, Graham Annable and Anthony Stacchi's *Box Trolls* (2014, for Laika).

Critics who argue that Gothic has moved from the 'margins' to the 'mainstream' of cultural production offer a binaristic map of the development of Gothic since 2000. Separating cultural 'margins' from the 'mainstream' upholds a nostalgic fantasy that Gothic was once an 'authentically' 'marginal' form, rather than, at least in part, the product of a burgeoning publishing market aimed at a mass audience. Drawing a distinction between the 'margins' and the 'mainstream', critics also imply that Gothic's proliferation in the twenty-first century constitutes a lamentable 'gushing up' of a marginal cultural form to a mainstream context, echoing elitist subcultural discourse (Thornton 1995: 5). For example, Jeffrey Weinstock asserts that *Frankenweenie* places Burton firmly at the centre of Hollywood film production, marking the 'ascendency of the Gothic mode in American culture' (Weinstock 2013: 25).

> Whereas the *Frankenweenie* of 1984 was too dark for Disney, the *Frankenweenie* of 2012 is perfectly acceptable Disney fare. It seems that it is not Burton who has changed, but rather the world around him. The Burton twist, however, is that . . . what Burton primarily offers is not Gothic, but rather 'Gothic'. (Weinstock 2013: 25–6)

Weinstock suggests that Hollywood has become more accepting of Gothic's darkness, but he seems discomfited by this shift. The word 'dark' contrasts with the more dismissive phrase, 'perfectly acceptable Disney fare', betraying Weinstock's nostalgia for Gothic's once 'dark', marginal position represented by the failure of the 1984 *Frankenweenie*. For Weinstock, the popularity and success of *Frankenweenie* (2012) suggests it has lost its 'darkness'. For Weinstock, Burton's recent films 'substitute' 'humour', 'sentimentality', 'hope', 'euphoria', 'nostalgia' – all decidedly 'non-Gothic' emotions – in place of horror (2013: 26, 27). The move from margins to mainstream is, for Weinstock, a move from 'authenticity' to 'inauthenticity', seen in his distinction between Gothic and 'Gothic'. In Weinstock's analysis, Burton's mainstream Hollywood works lack the 'affective punch' of Gothic (2013: 27). Thus, Weinstock's initial claim that *Frankenweenie* (2012) transforms Hollywood, reshaping it through Burton's Gothic imagination, dissipates in his concern about the loss of 'authenticity' attendant in the move from margins to mainstream, leading Weinstock, finally, to dismiss the film's monsters as 'more silly than scary' (2013: 25, 27).

My nomadic approach maps the relationship between the 'margins' and 'mainstream' of cultural production in these texts rather differently. Both *Frankenweenie* and *Paranorman* open up a space *within* the mainstream that makes room for difference and critique, revealing productive interconnections between marginal and mainstream locations. Braidotti notes that difference usually carries a negative, pejorative charge: 'the concept of difference has become poisoned and has become the equivalent of inferiority' (2011a: 20). Both the logic of subcultural capital and the modernist aesthetic attempt a reversal of the status of difference, marking difference from the norm, or the mainstream, as an escape from a tyrannical and oppressive, and increasingly commodified, logic of the same. However, the reappraisal of difference as transgression does not adequately produce what Braidotti calls 'positive difference' (2011a: 20). This is not a concept of difference that might bring the 'margins' of culture and society into a more productive dialogue with its 'centre'. Moreover, this reassessment of difference as radical transgression glosses over the fact that Gothic has always located itself between the mainstream and margins of culture, revealing them not as separate locations, but interconnected spaces. *Frankenweenie* and *Paranorman* draw attention to the fact that Gothic texts are neither straightforwardly 'marginal', nor obviously 'mainstream' in their mash up of references to literary culture, popular culture, and 'cult' or 'subcultural' texts, blurring the distinctions between these designations. They mobilise the pedagogical potential of parody to reconstruct a Gothic film canon that brings together so called 'cult' or 'marginal' film texts with mainstream Hollywood production, blurring the boundaries between the 'margins' and the 'mainstream' erected by critics.

Frankenweenie and *Paranorman* map the interrelated connections between the 'margins' and 'mainstreams' of culture through their stories of an outsider's return to the centre of their community. Both films dramatise not a 'gushing up' of Gothic to the mainstream, but a mutual transformation of both spaces as the naïvety of the outsider transforms the cynicism pervading the mainstream community. Victor's neighbours come together to save Sparky and Norman achieves recognition for his part in ending the witch's curse. These shifts in the communities' perspectives offer an image of the centre transformed by its connection with the margins. However, the films also chart the movement of the outsider towards the centre, as both Norman and Victor are reincorporated into their families and their communities. Thus, the films deploy Gothic as a transformative force acting on both marginal and mainstream locations. My reading rejects the idea that Gothic parody is a cynical, deconstructive mode often targeted at mainstream nostalgia and sentimentality. This is the binary Weinstock's commentary on *Frankenweenie* upholds, for example. However, what Weinstock dismisses as *Frankenweenie's* mainstream appeal (Victor's 'childish disavowal of death', the celebration of imagination and innocence, the film's 'faith in the possibility of plenitude' and its drive towards the 'restoration' of family) are not evidence of Gothic's dissipated affectivity, as he asserts, but rather evidence of its transformative power (Weinstock 2013: 23). *Frankenweenie* and *Paranorman* do not position Gothic 'in an oppositional mode of negation' against the 'mainstream', but offer its 'transformative and inspirational' imaginative force to bring together seemingly separate cultural locations (Braidotti 2011a: 14). Thus, Gothic parody contributes to the ongoing project of nomadic subjectivity, which works 'to compose significant sites for reconfiguring modes of belonging' and locates places from which subjectivity can be reconstructed (Braidotti 2011a: 11).

Rejecting 'Authenticity', Reconfiguring 'Disneygothic'

Gothic criticism of 'mainstream' texts, such as these children's films, expresses an anxiety over the 'authenticity' of postmodern cultural production and of popular Gothic more generally. Weinstock does not seek to denigrate Burton's work, or to preclude *Frankenweenie* from serious academic discussion, but his conclusions about the film nevertheless invoke 'authenticity' by drawing a distinction between Gothic and 'Gothic'. Thornton argues that 'distinctions of this kind are never just assertions of equal difference; they usually entail some claim to authority and presume the inferiority of others' (1995: 10). 'Authenticity' forms the background to taste judgments and the logic of subcultural capital opposes the 'authentic' with the 'phony' as it strives to maintain a separation between the subculture and the mainstream (Thornton 1995: 3). Weinstock's equivocations over the status of Burton's Gothic exemplifies Virginia Richter's assertion that authenticity remains – in literary criticism – an unarticulated category, often addressed obliquely rather than overtly expressed (Richter 2009: 59).

Anxieties over 'authenticity' inform some criticism that seeks to reproduce Gothic as a marginal form, aligning it with a left-wing academic tradition of critique as well as with the marginal status of Goth subculture, fashion and music. Elliott argues that Gothic is one of the devalued aesthetic forms 'recuperated by various late twentieth-century humanities theories, serving in return as proof-texts for these theories in their battles against formalism, high-art humanism, and right-wing politics' (2008: 25). The myth of Gothic's subversive or marginal status and its subcultural 'authenticity' is evoked in the opening of Botting's *Limits of Horror*, which begins its critique of postmodern Gothic with a description of a Goth music gig. In Botting's account, The Birthday Party's performance of 'Release the Bats' stages the loss of Gothic's 'bite' in late twentieth-century postmodern culture (Botting 2008b: 1). Aligning himself with the post-punk, subcultural milieu of the early 1980s, Botting locates his critique of postmodern culture in an 'authentic' position, a 'marginal' vantage point from which he can critique the 'inauthentic' proliferation of Gothic that follows in the late twentieth and early twenty-first centuries.

An investment in 'authenticity' also leads some scholars in Gothic Studies to dismiss the 'surfaces' of Gothic in favour of its 'depths', mirroring children's literature criticism's psychological reading of Gothic that I considered in Chapter 1. Both Botting and Beville, for example, find the surface 'trappings' of Gothic problematic. Beville, in particular, distinguishes 'authentic' Gothic texts from 'phony' ones by rejecting pop-cultural texts that only have 'superficial gothic veneers' (2009: 8). Beville's suspicion of the surface trappings of Gothic suggests that 'authentic' Gothic texts are defined by the depth of meaning they offer and by their radical deconstructive power. She concludes that 'authentic' postmodern Gothic 'uncovers the negation of postmodern cultures [and] catharses the terrors of the dissolution of reality and subjectivity that lie at the heart of the postmodern condition' (2009: 200). Beville premises her definition of Gothic postmodernism on the assumption that its trappings are in themselves 'inauthentic', and that 'authentic' Gothic reveals the dissolution at the heart of subjectivity. 'Authentic' Gothic depths are thus not productive of subjectivity, but deconstructive. In Botting's analysis, it is the *repetition* of Gothic tropes that points to postmillennial Gothic's inauthenticity. He seeks texts able to produce a depth of meaning lacking in the banal surface repetition of Gothic tropes found in pop-cultural Gothic, which have become 'already too familiar' (Botting 2014: 500). In these accounts, Gothic's generic tropes are rejected in favour of a definition of Gothic as 'abstract, psychological, metaphorical, and ideological' (Elliott 2008: 26). That is, 'authentic' Gothic derives its charge from the depths it represents, not from its tropes. In this psycho-symbolic reading, Gothic serves a deconstructive psychoanalytic critique of postmodern subjectivity.

'Authenticity' is, however, a paradoxical social and discursive construct and Gothic Studies has not paid sufficient attention to its constructed nature. Elsewhere, critics in other fields are beginning to turn their attention to problematising 'authenticity'. Sociologist David Grazian explains that 'authenticity' 'pervades popular culture and public arenas . . . [and] refers to a variety of desirable traits: credibility, originality, sincerity, naturalness, genuineness, innateness, purity, or realness' (Grazian 2010: 191). 'Authenticity' thus legitimises some cultural objects while devaluing others that are not seen to carry these traits. It is also a deeply paradoxical construct that mediates and commodifies that which it labels as precisely unmediated and uncommodified. As Wolfgang Funk, Florian Gross and Irmtraud Huber argue, 'authenticity itself turns into a quality of mediation and is thus conditioned by what it seems to deny' (Funk, Gross and Huber 2012: 10). For Grazian, this is most obvious in the 'underground' blues scene in Chicago, US, where 'authenticity' is staged very consciously. Grazian also claims that the desire for 'authenticity' in popular culture is premised on a paradoxical logic, since the more one searches for 'authenticity', the further away it seems (Grazian 2005: 11). While Grazian locates 'authenticity' as a commodity of consumer capitalism, comparative literature scholar Jochen Mecke rejects 'authenticity' as a category devoid of meaning in fragmentary, postmodern times (Grazian 2010: 192; Mecke 2006: 114, cited in Funk, Gross and Huber 2012: 11). However, Funk, Gross and Huber counsel critics to not be too swift in dismissing 'authenticity', noting 'authenticity' remains one of the 'guiding values' of our times whether it is constructed, or not (2012: 11–12, 20). Likewise, Richter maintains that 'authenticity' remains a pervasive and important category of reference in terms of negotiating identity in popular culture, literature and critical discourse and, as such, it cannot simply be 'done away with' (2009: 73). A non-essential definition of 'authenticity', one that recognises its constructed nature, can be adopted by those texts usually discredited by discourses invested in 'authenticity'. Funk, Gross and Huber argue that texts *are* capable of creating new forms of 'authenticity' (2012: 19). Such texts may take their status as always already mediated into account and recognise the paradox at the heart of any claim to 'authenticity', but they do not content themselves with this insight and instead attempt to move beyond postmodern deconstruction, 'establishing a kind of paradoxical third-order authenticity' that is explicitly performative (Funk, Gross and Huber 2012: 19–20). 'Authenticity' may not really exist, but simply deconstructing it belies its continued power in popular culture and critical discourse alike. Reconfigured as temporary and performative, 'authenticity' allows texts usually discredited to claim some of its power.

Gothic film parody provides a fitting space in which to reconfigure 'authenticity' as temporary and performative because it reveals that Gothic has, since its inception in the cardboard crenulations of Horace Walpole's Strawberry Hill, been a form in which the artifice of aesthetics is foregrounded. Despite the fact that Gothic critics often acknowledge the fakery of Gothic, there remains an implicit investment in an 'authentic' Gothic in the dismissal of texts (particularly those for children) that employ fakery and pastiche. In *Limits of Horror*, for example, Botting notes 'the artifice accompanying all Gothic productions from Walpole's fake original and fabricated castle, Twain's dismissal of Southern Gothic shams, to *Rocky Horror* camp and beyond' (2008b: 2). Despite this, Botting goes on to dismiss many forms of modern Gothic pastiche, from *Count Duckula* to *Buffy the Vampire Slayer*, as evidence of the pervasion, normalisation and dissolution of a once authentic Gothic now evaporated into 'simulations' (2008b: 9–10). Yet, Gothic's fakery, including its constant repetition of tropes and an emphasis on the production of aesthetics, is the means by which a critical investment in 'authenticity' can be revealed and contested. I contend that *Frankenweenie* and *Paranorman* make a strong claim for their 'authenticity' as Gothic while also revealing this claim as performative, showing the aesthetic practices necessary to its staging. This has the twofold effect of claiming *some* of the discursive power of 'authenticity', and allowing viewers the opportunity to experience the text as authentic, while at the same time acknowledging that this experience is performative and temporary.

Frankenweenie and *Paranorman* challenge the charge of 'inauthenticity' levelled at pop-cultural Gothic by offering a counter to the pejorative critical terms, 'Disneygothic' and 'candygothic'. As mass-market children's cultural products, these films are apt to be included along with dolls and breakfast cereal in Botting's list evidencing the shift that Gothic has made away from the 'cultural margins' to become the 'standard if not dominant form of aesthetic expression'

(2008b: 37). Botting's notion of 'candygothic' attempts to account for the new function of Gothic in the face of its rapid circulation in a postmodern economy. In its original context, 'candygothic' accounts for the ways in which Gothic texts provide both pleasure and pain, romance and trauma, and describes how Gothic might function in a cultural context that has erased limits and taboos as consumers move swiftly on to the next thrill (Botting 2008b: 9, 47–8). However, 'candygothic' is used by other critics to support dismissive value judgments about twenty-first-century Gothic texts. In Beville's analysis, 'candygothic' denotes a work which is 'not really Gothic' in which terror is 'obviously a novelty . . . created by stereotypical Gothic tropes' (2009: 9, 38). Similarly, though Weinstock does not use the term, 'candygothic', his accusation that *Frankenweenie* is 'Gothic lite' echoes the same value judgment.

If 'candygothic' has struggled to remain a judgment-free term, Botting's other contribution to this debate is even more problematic. 'Disneygothic' signals a shift into an 'anything goes' pervasion of Gothic, a Gothic of pure simulacra (Botting 2008b: 3). 'Disneygothic' constitutes a damning critique, which largely follows Baudrillard's account of postmodernism, one that tells of the degeneration of an 'authentic' Gothic into mere artifice and simulation. The use of the word 'Disney' refers to arguments made by Baudrillard about American culture, but also has far wider connotations in the academy, pejoratively denoting sanitised commodification (Baudrillard 1994: 14. See also: Walz 1998: 51; Wasko 2001: 113; Ross 1999: 51). 'Disneygothic' has thus become a pejorative critical term that constructs a polemic between a mass of texts denoted as popular, frivolous, childish and inauthentic – texts that offer empty simulation – and a precious few that may still manage to elicit feelings of the uncanny, offer moments of radical transgression or 'reflect critically and culturally on modernity' (Botting 2008b: 12). The binaries erected in this term between the modernist and the postmodern, the 'authentic' and the 'inauthentic', between literary value and mainstream appeal are not easily escaped.

As the latest in a series of collaborations between Tim Burton and Disney, *Frankenweenie* embraces and redefines 'Disneygothic'. Here, Disneygothic becomes a label that identifies with both terms equally, privileging neither. I do not wish to claim that Gothic Disney films did not exist before *Frankenweenie*, nor that Disney films more generally are not open to Gothic readings. The latter is evidenced in a number of popular and critical discussions about the 'darker' side of Disney (see, for example, Swan 1999; Oxberry 2006). However,

I do contend that *Frankenweenie* is the moment when 'Disneygothic' emerges as a self-identified form, overtly *both* Disney *and* Gothic. *Frankenweenie* arrives at a pertinent moment for Gothic Studies and intersects in striking ways with critical anxieties circulating what Gothic has become in the new millennium.

Botting's concern about the domestication of Gothic monstrosity is also expressed in popular terms as a 'disneyfication' of horror film and reflected in popular commentary on *Frankenweenie*. For example, the name of the film, a specifically American reference to a cute domestic pet, puts some critics off, while others find Burton's association with Disney renders the film 'tame and compromised' (Scott 2012; Bond 2012). While individual Disney films may contain Gothic elements, explore dark themes or potentially terrify children, the Disney brand itself is promoted as a purveyor of wholesome, innocent fun, and continues to be perceived that way. The studio did not release the first version of *Frankenweenie* (1984) because they considered it too macabre. Soon after they pulled the film, Disney fired its creator, the apprentice animator, Burton, for spending time and money on projects that were too 'dark and scary' (Adams 2012; Vincent 2012). Burton's view on Disney during this period, that it was boring and not innovative, is one that is still shared by many film critics and is apparent in the response to his recent collaborations with the studio. Crucially, Burton represents eccentricity, a 'quirky aesthetic', positioning himself as the 'rebellious outsider', while Disney is held to be mainstream and conservative, its characters and themes reinforcing 'the key elements in mainstream US culture' (Weinstock 2013: 2; Wasko 2001: 2). The Disney brand, represented by the Walt Disney signature and enchanted castle logo, also connotes consistency, uniformity and familiarity. Disney scholars point out that the company is 'notoriously protective of its brand' and maintains 'a carefully regulated self-image' (Wasko 2001: 3; Doherty 2006; Pallant 2011: ix).

The 2012 remake of *Frankenweenie* is significant because it appears to undermine both this sacred self-image cultivated by Disney and the distinction between an eccentric outsider director and a mainstream studio. This move is apparent from the opening few seconds of the film, before the story gets underway. Everything begins as expected: the camera pans down over a familiar twilight landscape, with its snaking river and twinkling lights rendered in a soft colour palette of blue, purple and pink; colourful fireworks appear as the iconic enchanted Disney castle logo comes into the foreground; the familiar 'wish upon a star' theme music plays out, almost to completion. However, in the last bar, the music shifts into a minor key and the gentle melody is replaced with crashing organ chords and spooky choral voices. Suddenly the magical scene switches into black and white and the fireworks are occluded by a stormy night sky. Briefly, a lightning flash illuminates the now shadowy and clearly Gothic Disney castle. Only the Walt Disney signature that materialises in the foreground retains its familiar appearance. The transformation takes place in a matter of seconds and is onscreen for the briefest of moments, but it is significant for the way in which it juxtaposes and thus recontextualises the conventions of both Disney animation and classic Hollywood Gothic cinema. There is a brief and unstable shift into the Gothic mode that disrupts the connotations a viewer might associate with the usual opening Disney logo screen. Usually, these few seconds of animation prior to a film are unlikely to gain any sustained viewer attention, since the Disney logo is so familiar. It is only when the logo is placed in direct contrast with a Gothic cinema aesthetic that the viewer is encouraged to consider what associations it conjures. Recontextualised in this way, the Disney logo is implicitly all that is inimical to Gothic, saccharine sweetness and fairy-tale enchantment, and the initial effect of the 'Burtonesque' transformation is to assert the dominance and value of horror over the Disney brand. This might be termed a 'reverse Disneyfication'.

'Disneyfication' is widely conceived of by critics in the liberal arts and humanities as a negative process that reduces potentially interesting or subversive content into something sanitised, homogenous and conservative – the perceived parameters of the Disney brand. Typically, 'Disneyfication' is described as 'that shameful process by which everything the studio later touched, no matter how unique the vision of the original from which the studio worked, was reduced to the limited terms Disney and his people could understand' (Schickel 1997: 225). Elsewhere, 'Disneyfication' denotes the bowdlerisation of literature, myth and history in a simplified, sentimentalised, programmatic way (Walz 1998: 51). The modal shift in the opening of *Frankenweenie* is in part as a self-conscious response to this negative perception of Disney. It is as though the film resents the implication that Disney is not qualified to produce the eccentric, creepy or quirky Burtonesque.[2] In this opening sequence, the collaboration between Burton and Disney is represented as a takeover of the brand, albeit temporary and sanctioned, with the enchanted castle and all it represents being hijacked by the Gothic director. Yet, the shift is also more complex than my term 'reverse Disneyfication' accounts for, since it offers up both the values of Disney and the aesthetic conventions of Gothic cinema as targets for parodic recontextualisation. In addition to playful parody, the transformation of the Disney logo is also a way of legitimising the studio as a producer of horror, lending it the cultural authority and canonical knowledge required to make an authentic Gothic horror film. Another reading of the sequence might also suggest that *Frankenweenie* simply appropriates the conventions normally associated with classic horror studios – notably Universal, American International Pictures and Hammer – for sanctioned Disney use, and constitutes a straightforward Disneyfication even as it appears to undermine the brand. My own reading, however, sees the modal shift as a double quotation, which stylises both elements – Disney through Gothic and Gothic through Disney – in a way that leaves both open to transformation. Is this a Disney film or a Gothic film? The opening credits suggest that *Frankenweenie* legitimately is both. Thus, *Frankenweenie* stages its critique of 'Disneygothic' and counters the distinctions this term has come to denote, between authentic and inauthentic, and between marginal and mainstream cultural production.

Home-Made Aesthetics

Frankenweenie and *Paranorman* draw attention to their own production techniques and so complicate notions of 'authenticity' by revealing the artifice inherent in the production of an 'authentic' home-made, 'trash' aesthetic. Both films open by screening a film within a film that celebrates a low-budget aesthetic. In the opening of *Frankenweenie* Victor screens his own short *Monsters from Beyond!* to his parents. Victor's film is a reference both to Burton's own *oeuvre* – including his animated short *Stalk of the Celery Monster* (1979) and the feature film B-movie homage *Mars Attacks!* (1996) – as well as to the low-budget horror and science-fiction films from the 1950s and 1960s. *Monsters from Beyond!* features a conventional monster plot, involving Victor's dog Sparky (sporting a home-made costume) heroically fending off a (plastic model) pterodactyl as his (cardboard box) town is engulfed in (fake) flames. The low, sonorous brass music and clunky voice-over of Victor's film provide the diegetic sound opening for *Frankenweenie*, briefly merging the two films, and associating the latter with low-budget, B-movie monster horror, evoking nostalgia for a 'lost' era of horror film. However, this is not the mournful nostalgia implied by the 'Disneygothic' critique circulating in Gothic Studies, but rather a celebration of a fake visual aesthetic, represented in Victor's cardboard sets, plastic models, and home-made costumes. Everything looks fake, but the fakery is neither weary nor cynical. *Monsters from Beyond!* is Victor's triumph, opening *Frankenweenie* with a celebration of pop-cultural, pastiche horror film.

Paranorman also begins by screening a film within a film, in this case a low-budget zombie horror with appalling special effects and acting, which Norman is watching on his television. Again, *Paranorman* seems to invoke nostalgia for a 'past' era of film-making and offers low-budget film production techniques as more 'authentic' than the new methods favoured in Hollywood horror. The aesthetics showcased here deliberately present themselves in opposition to mimetic film-making techniques such as digital imaging technology and the 'found footage' style of modern horror. *Paranorman*'s film within a film begins with the shot of the heel of a shoe squishing a brain. The brain becomes stuck to the heel, rhythmically squelching as the screaming victim attempts to flee from a zombie. As with *Frankenweenie*, the nostalgia evoked in this trash aesthetic differs from that expressed by Gothic critics, since the 'past' texts evoked are not critical of mass culture, but products of it. Universal Studios and Hammer, for example, made films to maximise profit, reusing sets, stories and actors in a bid to capitalise on the success of previous films. *Paranorman* and *Frankenweenie*'s reference to 'pastness' through 'trash' aesthetics revels in the affective possibility of repetition, rather than decrying repetition as the death of Gothic. In these films, the naïve repetition of cliché tropes marks, rather than precludes, their 'authenticity'.

Both films stage a paradoxical claim to home-made 'authenticity' through the production of a fake 'trash' aesthetic that reveals their big-budget production and mainstream release. Stop-motion animation emphasises an 'authentic' DIY, or home-made, aesthetic that is implicitly pitched against 'inauthentic' 'modern' film production techniques. This 'authenticity' is located in the obvious physical labour involved in producing and animating the clay models. The artistry and labour of stop-motion is emphasised, even though the visuals simulate trashy, cheap production techniques. Victor's efforts, as amateur film auteur, stand in for Burton's own, referencing a DIY aesthetic in Victor's use of a cardboard set, toy soldiers, a costumed pet dog and a plastic pterodactyl. The audience can see both the string and the stick to which the pterodactyl is attached in shot, as well as Victor's hand moving the models. Attention is drawn to the home-made aesthetic further when Victor's father comments 'isn't that your grandmother's table-cloth?' The hand in shot also shows the auteur's presence in the work and codes film-making as a labour of love, while the home-made props signal the auteur's control over production. Victor's film uses a mixture of stop-motion animation, live manipulation of objects, voice-over and diegetic screams, as well as title cards normally associated with silent film. This patchwork of styles produces a pointed failure of mimesis. Nothing in Victor's film looks real or convincing. 'Authenticity' is thus located not only within DIY aesthetics, but also in the aesthetics of failure, or 'trash' cinema. Similarly, the film within a film that opens *Paranorman* uses the clay models of stop-motion animation to ham up the trash aesthetics of the (live-action) horror genre it is referencing. Though this type of horror is characterised in both cases by a failure to create mimesis, especially in its fake-looking props, it is nonetheless presented as having an 'authenticity' that, by implication, modern horror does not.

The use of stop-motion animation in both films also signals that this trash, DIY aesthetic is a fake aesthetic. Stop-motion animation requires time, money and the indulgence of a big studio to be viable. The original *Frankenweenie* from 1984, for example, was not produced in stop-motion because the cost was too prohibitive. As Rob Latham argues, big budgets recreate DIY aesthetics better than DIY aesthetics (2013: 140). Though it is at pains to produce a low-budget aesthetic, *Frankenweenie*'s homage to the artistry of 'trash' cinema reveals the indulgence of its mainstream studio, Disney. Similarly, though the trash aesthetics of the zombie film Norman watches are heavily exaggerated, this trash aesthetic contrasts with the seamless, professional animation of the parent text. In both cases, the 'authentic' DIY, home-made, 'trash' aesthetic appears firmly in quotation marks as a camp (re)construction.

This first portion of *Frankenweenie* is concerned with foregrounding kitsch, outdated and thus, 'authentic', film-production techniques in order to reveal the paradox behind claims to 'realness' and 'authenticity'. After Victor's short finishes, he rushes to his attic-cum-editing suite to fix a portion of broken film. The attic, transformed into a Gothic laboratory, is where Victor makes his films, and contains a handmade rolling scenery contraption and editing desk with a stapler, rolls of film and some scissors. Here, Burton further validates 'home-made' techniques and Victor's skills at the editing table draw attention to the skill and effort required in a stop-motion animation, which for Burton 'shows the artist's work more' (Burton, quoted in Griffiths 2012). The conflation of 'authenticity' with artistry and home-made production techniques is reflected overall in the choice to film in black and white: 'I just felt it was more emotional in black and white than in colour, and more real in a strange way' (Burton in Griffiths 2012). Black and white film is 'real in a strange way' because it pretends to realness even as it fails at mimesis compared to shooting in colour. In *Frankenweenie*, 'realness' is achieved by foregrounding the artificiality of film production and by drawing attention to the processes whereby the film is made.

This focus on the process of production becomes thematic when Victor's attic film studio becomes a Gothic laboratory. Here *Frankenweenie* suggests contiguity between Gothic's mad scientist and the film auteur. Both work with whatever materials they can gather, cobbling together their creation in the isolation of their romantic garret. To prepare for the experiment, Victor collects a bizarre assortment of banal household items. The result is a replica of the original laboratory used in James Whale's 1931 production of *Frankenstein*. This laboratory film set was reused in Mel Brooks's *Young Frankenstein* (1974), itself a parody of the original film, and its reappearance here in *Frankenweenie* further emphasises it as a kitsch cliché. Nonetheless, the laboratory is not offered up for ridicule. Rather, the fact that it is cobbled together from items such as bicycle wheels, a kitchen whisk, an ironing board, a desk fan and a toy robot has a potentially dual effect: alleviating the horror on the one hand, and increasing it on the other, by making everyday items strange and grotesque. Burton's emphasis on the home-made conditions of Sparky's resurrection reveals that all monsters from Gothic horror cinema are in some way DIY creations, artificial and fake, but nonetheless 'authentic'. The other monsters created in *Frankenweenie* are all home-made in some way, too, resurrected using home or garden products in a cobbled-together DIY experiment. The crucial difference between these creatures and Sparky, however, is that their production process lacks 'love'. *Frankenweenie* thus locates 'authenticity' in the loving investment of the auteur and in the labour of the production process. Burton's comments on his love for the trash director, Ed Wood, whose works influence *Frankenweenie*, similarly site 'authenticity' within trash aesthetics because of the love and 'artistry' they reveal having gone into the creation: 'they are bad, but they're special . . . there's a certain consistency to them, and a certain kind of weird artistry' (Burton and Salisbury 2006: 130–1).

Frankenweenie's monster creation scene also reveals that 'authenticity' is a staged performance, not an essential, inherent quality of the text. The laboratory is very clearly a film set, not only because it contains Victor's props and film-production equipment, but because it is a fabricated reproduction of a famous Gothic film set. The scene's 'authenticity' is also located in Victor's frenetic actions as he brings Sparky back to life. These are not very scientific, rather the scene is staged in order to be a Gothic spectacle and the processes Victor engages in are aesthetic, rather than obviously functional. The performance is also a *re*production, a *re*staging of the already familiar spectacle – mad scientist creates monster – suggesting that 'authenticity' does not have to emerge from originality, that it is open to revision and reinvention. That is, 'authenticity' always involves a renegotiation of values and meanings. In *Frankenweenie*, this struggle inheres in Victor's performance of the mad scientist role, which recombines fragments of previous iterations of the monster-creation scene in new ways. The result is a staged performance of Gothic 'authenticity' rather than a cynical, weary pastiche of well-worn tropes and images.

Paranorman likewise establishes its 'authenticity' through references to previous Gothic performance in a way that reveals the constructed nature of its fake 'trash' aesthetic. The earlier parody, *Young Frankenstein* (1974), cited in *Frankenweenie*, also appears in *Paranorman* in a scene where Norman must prise a book from the hands of a corpse. In the original scene, a locked box is prised to humorous effect from the hands of the desiccated body of 'Baron von Frankenstein'. When *Paranorman* restages this scene – celebrating it as a worthy cliché of Gothic film history – it underscores its own painstaking production techniques. The scene presents a heavy physicality not present in the original: Norman struggles to remove the book from his uncle's hands and he ends up stuck with the corpse in a number of humorous and uncomfortable positions. It takes far longer for the scene to play out than in *Young Frankenstein* and the clay models are manipulated repeatedly to produce a number of detailed close-ups that display the model corpse's bloated face and grotesque facial features. The details and artistry of the models, as well as time-consuming filming process are emphasised. All of this is to remind the viewer that trash aesthetics and 'fakery' require skill and money to produce. The zombies who menace Blithe Hollow, for example, evoke low-budget zombies with their green skin and comically squishy body parts, but minute detail in the models is required to achieve this trashy effect. On the one hand, then, clay models and stop-motion animation emphasise artistry and skill. On the other hand, they constitute a further level of fakery beyond the original trash aesthetics they reference: *Paranorman*'s zombies are, paradoxically, both faker than the B-movie zombies they reference, since they are miniature dolls, but 'authentic' since they are the result of a particularly labour- and skill-intensive animation style.

Stop-motion animation draws more attention to the fakery used in Gothic horror film aesthetics and appears, paradoxically, as both more 'authentic' and more fake. As such, stop-motion animation offers an apt embodiment for 'authenticity' itself. This is significant since live-action Gothic parody films already 'heighten awareness of their constructedness and, by extension, the constructedness of the Gothic [adding] further layers of fakery to the Gothic re-faking of fakery' (Elliott 2007: 224–5). In live-action Gothic parody, such as *Young Frankenstein*, these additional layers of fakery draw attention to the real costumes, actors and make-up used to create the original fakes (Elliott 2007: 225). In the references that *Paranorman* and *Frankenweenie* make to these earlier parody films, the stop-motion animation adds yet another layer of fakery. While making a claim for their own 'authenticity', *Frankenweenie* and *Paranorman* highlight the inauthenticity of their production techniques, their aesthetic choices and their characters: the refaking of fakery at the heart of their visual aesthetic. Contesting the subcultural binary of 'authentic' versus 'phony' reproduced in critiques of postmodern Gothic, both *Paranorman* and *Frankenweenie* point to the fact that 'authenticity itself can never be authentic, but must always be performed, staged, fabricated, crafted or otherwise imagined' (Grazian 2010: 192). The films represent the integral role of staging in the production of 'authenticity' and both make a strong claim for their 'authenticity' as Gothic while also arguing that this is a claim that must be performed, at pains to reveal the aesthetic practices necessary to its staging. Both films also position themselves within a network of Gothic and horror texts, parodically recontextualising Gothic literature and film. In this way, they employ similar strategies to *Coraline* since they foreground their intertextuality and code it as part of their Gothic aesthetic. These films' relationship with their intertexts is characterised by irony and humour and both films employ parody not only in their aesthetic mode (utilising visual quotation and pastiche), but also in the way they construct their viewer in relation to these intertexts. It is this pragmatic dimension of parody I want to explore next.

The Pedagogical Pragmatics of Parody

Parody is the critical term that best communicates the double-voiced intertextual pragmatics of *Frankenweenie* and *Paranorman*, since it is a mode that neither cynically deconstructs nor plays faithful homage to its target texts, but rather synthesises them into something new. For Hutcheon, parody is the repetition of a target text with critical distance, marking difference from, rather than similarity to, an 'original' (Hutcheon 1985: 6). Though this critical distance is often achieved through irony, parodic texts do not necessarily mock their target texts and, as Hutcheon points out, parody can 'cut both ways' (1985: 37). For Hutcheon, parody is a 'bitextual' form, 'bouncing' the reader between complicity with and distance from a target text, a process that produces a new text (1985: 32, 38). In his analysis of film parody, Harries argues that parody oscillates between similarity to and difference from its target in a way that is more equalised than in Hutcheon's account, though still results in the synthesis of a new text (2000: 6). This oscillation of parody, between similarity to and difference from the intertext, is employed in *Frankenweenie* and *Paranorman* to establish and connect to a 'tradition' of Gothic horror film, but also to open up this 'canon' to new readings and innovation. This pragmatic dimension of parody likewise constructs an agile, nomadic reader who swiftly negotiates the different responses parody provokes.

Parody's complicity with past forms, its conservative preservation of past works, suggest that it is, in part, a nostalgic mode. However, through their parodic recontextualisation of prior works, *Franken-weenie* and *Paranorman* do not construct an exclusive 'canon' of Gothic film for a select, knowing audience, but open up into a broad intertextual network of Gothic and horror film texts for exploration by an imagined audience of *new* viewers. *Frankenweenie*'s allusions and references include Universal Studio's monster pictures of the 1930s, notably James Whale's *Frankenstein* (1931), *The Mummy* (1932), *Bride of Frankenstein* (1935) and *Son of Frankenstein* (1939); early German expressionist cinema, notably *Nosferatu* (1922); Roger Corman's Poe films of the 1960s, starring Vincent Price; Christopher Lee's Hammer Horror films of the 1950s and 1960s, notably *Dracula* (1958) and 1950s 'trash' science fiction, notably *Godzilla* (1954), *The Beast from 20,000 Fathoms* (1953), *Rodan* (1956) and *Gamera* (1965). *Paranorman* extends its canon a little later into the twentieth century, with references to an era of splatter and 'slasher' films from the 1970s and 1980s, notably *Suspiria* (1977), *Halloween* (1978), *Friday the 13th* (1980) and *Dawn of the Dead* (1978). In *Frankenweenie* and *Paranorman*, the reference to these past, 'classic' works does not function to exclude viewers' participation. The films' construction of a Gothic film canon is not dependent on the audience spotting every citation. Instead, they celebrate a broad and inclusive Gothic horror film aesthetic. Trash aesthetics, small-budget films, recurring characters, reused costumes and sets, and low-tech monsters are elevated to the status of a canonical, or 'classic' Gothic cinema. This act of recuperation not only elevates 'trash' cinema, but also relocates 'cult' cinema to a mainstream context, for a mainstream audience.

In part, *Frankenweenie* and *Paranorman* deploy parody pedagogically to teach viewers about Gothic film and to promote genre literacy. Harries notes this aspect of parody in his assertion that it functions to teach the 'logonomic system' of the target text (2000: 104). The logonomic system is the broad genre or mode, which guides the viewer by explicitly drawing their attention to particular textual norms and conventions. Hutcheon also notes the 'didactic value of parody in teaching or co-opting the art of the past by textual incorporation and ironic commentary' (1985: 27). She claims that parody texts can aid readers in the difficult process of decoding by sharing cultural codes, reminding or educating readers, so that they can become competent decoders (1985: 27). The Gothic transformation of the Disney logo in the opening credits of *Frankenweenie* begins this pedagogical process, drawing attention to a number of Gothic clichés that recur throughout the film. Later, Burton's representation of New Holland's pet cemetery offers further opportunities for promoting Gothic literacy in its exaggerated *mise en scène* of a stormy, ruined graveyard. As Sparky moves between the looming headstones, lightning illuminates the laughably cute names of the deceased pets inscribed upon them, and a bunny carved in stone sits atop as memorial in place of a grimacing gargoyle. Here, the gentle parodic humour targets Mary Lambert and Stephen King's *Pet Sematary* (1989) as well as the broader literary and filmic trope of the Gothic graveyard. Yet, the humour of the scene does not function as deconstructive mockery, but works to draw attention to the referenced conventions. The parody simultaneously asks its audience to become familiar with, to understand, and to enjoy, the generic codes of Gothic film.

Frankenweenie constructs a 'canon' of Gothic horror film and argues for the continued importance and affectivity of the works in this canon. In one scene, Christopher Lee as Dracula appears on Victor's parents' television screen. Victor's parents are rapt by Lee's performance, as Victor sneaks back into his house with the freshly exhumed corpse of Sparky the dog. Non-diegetic music from *Dracula* accompanies Victor's entrance, functioning as diegetic sound in the context of *Frankenweenie*, with the swells and accents of the original film score marking the points at which Victor risks detection. The double function of the music gives viewers untutored in horror film conventions a quick lesson in the logonomic system, marking the affective points of the music through Victor's actions. More importantly, the Hammer Horror film is not rendered in clay stop-motion animation. Its jarring appearance as a live-action visual marks it as special and important. Though it is recontextualised, with its musical score providing a more comedic function in the diegesis of *Frankenweenie*, *Dracula* is presented as a piece of affective Gothic horror: Victor's parents shudder in delight as they watch the film. Furthermore, the inclusion of *Dracula* in its original format – a direct, rather than oblique, reference – marks this parodic reference as a specific quotation, which acts itself as an invitation to viewers unfamiliar with the Christopher Lee text to seek it out.

Throughout *Frankenweenie*, the names and faces of key figures from a canon of 'classic' Gothic film are echoed in the names and faces of characters. Elsa van Helsing, Victor's neighbour, references Elsa Lanchester, while the shock of white hair on her pet poodle, Persephone, visually recalls Elsa's role as the *Bride of Frankenstein* (1953). Vincent Price's visage is recreated in clay in the features of Mr Rzykruski, Victor's science teacher. Here the reference to previous horror films is doubled in that this relationship also echoes Burton's autobiographical short, *Vincent* (1982), in which a young boy forms a bond with Vincent Price through his love of horror film, a relationship replayed in the relationship between the eponymous trash-cinema director and Bela Lugosi in *Ed Wood* (1994). The climactic scene of *Frankenweenie* is another double quotation, reprising the windmill scene in *Frankenstein* (1931) and Burton's *Sleepy Hollow* (1999). Without mockery, the scene plays out along the same affective lines as the 'original(s)', rather than with ironic detachment or distance. In all these cases of specific, marked references, *Frankenweenie* makes a claim for the repeatability and continued affective power of those texts it constructs as 'classic' Gothic horror cinema.

Paranorman uses parody to teach the 'logonomic system' of Gothic horror film by employing clichéd conventions. These clichés are not parodied for the purposes of mockery, but in order to restage their affective power. Early in *Paranorman*, the clichés of zombie cinema are marked comedically in Norman's morning routine. A zombie alarm clock wakes Norman with an electronically generated groaning noise, and a plastic zombie arm reaches out of its base. Norman's arm likewise reaches up into the shot, waving around aimlessly, much like a poorly coordinated zombie limb, as he makes a similar groan, though this time resulting from his early morning grogginess. In the next scene, Norman brushes his teeth in front of the bathroom mirror with a zombie-themed toothbrush. The tooth-paste foams as Norman opens his lips, grimacing, giving him the appearance of a slack-jawed zombie. Again, Norman's early morn-ing grunts and groans accompany the scene. These sounds, gestures and facial expressions are all later repeated by the actual zombies who pursue Norman through the town. In the first instance, the cliché is marked as humorous, and also linked to the commodifica-tion of horror through the branded alarm clock and toothbrush. In these sequences, the groans, flailing limbs and facial grimace are not marked as scary, but their connection with zombie films is made clear through the zombie-themed products. Thus, as the clichés are parodied they also serve as an example preparing viewers for their repetition. The second iteration of the cliché occurs in the context of a more typical zombie film narrative: the protagonist flees for his life from undead attackers. In this second iteration, the events elicit fear in the fleeing Norman. Their previous iteration as humorous not-withstanding, the zombies' movements and sounds are represented as retaining the power to terrify.

The fact that the clichés appear more than once in *Paranorman* allows the audience to gain a lesson in the logonomic system of Gothic in advance of the cliché's second appearance. The movements of the zombie in the film within a film that opens *Paranorman* work similarly to Norman's morning routine as an amusing introduction to the conventions of zombie films. In the film within a film, the zombie's advance upon the screaming victim is marked as silly. Nonetheless, when zombies advance upon Norman as he raids his Uncle's house for clues about the curse, they are marked as threatening and terrify-ing. Norman rifles through piles of books in his Uncle's study when he hears banging at the door. Immediately, the soundtrack of *Paranor-man* plays the music of the earlier zombie film within a film, signalling to viewers what to expect. Again, music is the means through which the film teaches its logonomic system as the soundtrack anticipates the appearance of the zombie. Repeating the television movie from the opening of *Paranorman*, the zombie's hand punches through the door and bursts it open. Interestingly, this cliché is repeated a third time, but recontextualised again, when Norman and his friends are trapped inside the town hall by an angry mob of townsfolk. This time, it is the hands and arms of the townsfolk punching through the walls, attempting to grab the children trapped inside. The repetition of the convention marks the town mob as monstrous, and their aggressive attempts to get Norman and his friends are genuinely frightening. In *Paranorman*, then, each iteration of a cliché renders the narrative situation more threatening, not less. The townsfolk's murderous intents towards Norman are scarier than the early zombie advance, which was scarier than the zombie advance Norman watched on his television screen in the opening scene. Each time, the cliché reiterates the rules of a zombie film, simultaneously upping the potential affectivity of the cliché.

As I state in the introduction, pedagogies of the Gothic often imagine an unequal power relation between an authoritative text and an untutored child reader. This hierarchy is resisted by *Frankenweenie* and *Paranorman*, which reject didactic forms of education. School educators in particular, with the exception of the eccentric science teacher Mr Rzykruski in *Frankenweenie*, are brutish fools who terrorise rather than encourage their pupils. The initial plot conflict in *Paranorman* is the failure of a patronising act of education, designed to keep a young girl docile. Every year, Norman's uncle reads a 'bed-time story' to the spirit of the witch, actually a little girl, so that she will 'go back to sleep for another year' and not cause trouble in the town. When Norman's uncle fails to carry out this duty, the witch wakes up and takes her revenge on Blithe Hollow. Instead of taking up his uncle's role, Norman rejects the tradition of placating the witch because it fails to engage with the town's real history and only leads to a disastrous build-up of resentment and fear. Norman's intervention offers a message: children should not be patronised or fobbed off with cynically motivated acts of 'education'. The film further condemns the patronising fairy tale in the depiction of Ms. Henscher's school play, which Norman and his classmates are forced to take part in. The play is a heavy-handed retelling of the witch trial and it is roundly dismissed by the school children who recognise it as an inaccurate and stereotypical depiction of a witch. Ms Henscher dismisses the pupils' concerns. She tells them that the play is not supposed to be accurate; it is supposed to sell key-chains to tourists. Norman's school fails its children because it does not offer the right sorts of learning experiences. Knowledge is vital if the town is to survive, as Norman's independent investigations into the town's history demonstrate, but this is not knowledge he will learn in school. Likewise, *Frankenweenie* presents the school environment and school educators as offering little in the way of valuable learning experiences for the protagonists. The school's response to Mr Rzykruski's unconventional science lessons, which is to sack him, is represented as small-minded and anti-intellectual. The school replaces Mr Rzykruski with a bullish and uninspiring gym teacher, who removes the chance of creative expression by reducing the school science fair to the lowest common denominator, giving the prize to the least imaginative experiment.

Paranorman and *Frankenweenie* position Norman and Victor as outsiders in small-minded and limiting educational institutions. However, this outsider status allows them to model new types of knowledge for their peers. They possess the right sort of knowledge, developed out of their geeky love of Gothic horror, to save their dull suburban communities. In *Paranorman*, Norman's supernatural abilities save the town from destruction by the witch's curse. His expertise is emphasised in his empathy with and understanding of the zombies, which allows him to work out the truth behind the story of the witch's curse. This expertise upsets the hierarchies fostered by school, and Norman's sister, a popular cheerleader, is initially disgusted that 'the geeks are in charge'. However, she later defends her brother to a jeering mob of townsfolk, exclaiming 'I really think he knows what he is talking about.' In *Frankenweenie*, the learning experience is rather different, since the experiments initiated by Victor, later copied by the other elementary-school pupils, lead to chaos and destruction in the town. Nonetheless, Victor's creative use of science and the supernatural inspires his peers far more than the dull textbook lessons foisted upon them by the replacement science teacher. Victor, who is initially isolated, is validated as an expert. Later, Victor's Gothic expertise saves the day as he and Sparky use their ingenuity and knowledge gleaned from monster movies to fight the other monsters rampaging at the town fete. In both films, the protagonists use their unusual expertise to become heroic, educating the town in new forms of knowledge, combating the cynicism and patronising didacticism of adult-sanctioned forms of learning.

In their pedagogical use of Gothic parody, promoting genre literacy and constructing a canon of Gothic horror cinema from which viewers can learn the 'rules' of the system, *Frankenweenie* and *Paranorman* would seem to employ parody didactically. Yet, within the narratives themselves, the hierarchies of teacher and student, adult and child, expert and amateur are consistently undercut. In *Paranorman*, for example, Norman is far more literate than the foolish adults, who are not able to understand the supernatural events in Blithe Hollow. Yet, it is not only Norman's Gothic literacy that marks him as more capable than the adults, it is his lack of cynicism and naïve engagement with supernatural events. Similarly, in *Frankenweenie*, Victor's naïve attempts to carry out a science experiment based on the unreal and fantastic conventions of Gothic horror exhort the disenfranchised adults to have more faith in their children's understanding of the world. Contrary to the logic of subcultural capital, Norman and Victor are not cynical outsiders. Rather, their unusual expertise and naïve faith in Gothic horror marks it as a potentially transformative force and works to resolve the films' anxiety about the pedagogical function of parody. Both films construct a 'canon' of Gothic horror film and use parody to promote genre literacy to an audience of children, constructed as untutored and ignorant of 'classic' Gothic texts and conventions. However, within both narratives, this marginal Gothic material is actually best understood by naïve child protagonists, who are the only ones able to deploy its transformative and affective power. Frankenweenie and Paranorman imagine a new viewer, a nomadic subject able to negotiate the multiple meanings offered by their parodic recontextualisation of Gothic tropes.

A Sophisticated-Naïve Reader

Frankenweenie and *Paranorman* construct a nomadic 'conceptual persona' whose response to Gothic testifies to its continued affective power. The conceptual persona is not necessarily representative of a real viewer, nor can it account for the myriad of ways various real viewers might read the parody. Rather, the conceptual persona offers a position from which to consider the pragmatic effects of parody without making unverifiable assumptions about the way viewers might read a film. In Hutcheon's formulation of parody the intention encoded into the parody text by its producer and the recognition of the intent by a reader are both required for the successful *énonciation* of parody. This formulation depends on readers recognising the inferred intent and so requires readers to have the requisite genre, linguistic and ideological competencies, 'an ability' to decode the intended parodic meaning (Hutcheon 1985: 22). Harries views Hutcheon's model as culturally 'elitist' because it infers that an ideal reading of parody is possible when a 'sophisticated subject' matches competencies with the producers of a text in order to decode it in the preferable way (Harries 2000: 109; Hutcheon 1985: 94). Harries contends that parody texts offer a wide range of readings and that this ideal model of reception rarely, if ever, emerges. I agree that a range of readings of a parody text will always be available since an almost limitless host of factors might contribute to the context of reception. However, the notion of a 'conceptual persona' allows me to consider how these recent parody films construct a particular viewer whose response acts as a catalyst for the innovations presented in the filmic text.

Typically, commentary on children's film echoes Hutcheon's hierarchical formulation of the pragmatic effects of parody. Reviewers often put forward a 'different levels' account of reception, claiming that children and adults read films on different levels. Rohrer Finlo notes that parodic references in animated films are 'missed' by children, and only register with the adult audience (2009). This 'different levels' argument is clear in Angie Errigo's review of *Frankenweenie*, which notes that the references to classic Hollywood horror in the film 'sadly will go over a lot of oblivious heads these days' (2012). Jeffrey Weinstock likewise notes that *Frankenweenie* has been made 'for those with the requisite Burton and Hollywood "literacies"' and Edwin Page suggests that Burton's pop-culture references are not likely to be recognised by children but can be enjoyed by the adults accompanying them (Weinstock 2013: 2; Page 2006: 231). In this hierarchical formulation, critics construct two viewers: those with competencies (adults) who can decode the text, and those without (children) who respond naïvely. However, *Frankenweenie* and *Paranorman* resist this binaristic hierarchy and demonstrate faith in the competency of their imagined readers, whether child or adult.

Paranorman constructs a viewer in whom it has complete faith, building the competencies required to decode its parody into the text. *Paranoman*'s viewer does not need knowledge of extratextual material or prior genre literacy. Chris Butler acknowledges that the film includes several 'eye-winking' references 'for horror movie fans'.

Although those references may go over the heads of most children, Butler argues that they work for a range of reader competencies:

> What's interesting is that . . . when Neil wears the hockey mask [from *Friday the 13th*], children squeal with laughter just because Neil himself is funny. I don't think that you need to get that it's a reference to *Friday the 13th*. I think it works on multiple levels. (Butler, quoted in Laws 2013)

Though Butler still offers the 'different levels' argument to account for the effects of this reference to slasher movie horror, I argue that the material needed to decode the parody is provided within the narrative. In providing this material, the film imagines a viewer who can decode its references to slasher horror, even if they might not know the specific films in question. The target for the parody here is what is referred to, by a character in the film, as a 'slasher movie vibe'. Neil's brother Mitch uses this description to refer to the old house out of town that Norman investigates for clues about the curse. The house looms menacingly above Norman as he approaches and its interior is filthy and threatening. Norman creeps about the house anxiously, frightened to disturb the piles of clutter and strange objects that litter the grimy surfaces. Here, *Paranorman* establishes its 'slasher movie vibe' through its *mise en scène*, regardless of whether a viewer has seen or even knows what a 'slasher' movie is. Within this *mise en scène*, the subsequent specific references to *Halloween* and *Friday the 13th* are thus marked as belonging to a logonomic system of 'slasher' movies.

In one scene, the theme music from *Halloween* plays on Norman's phone, making the character jump briefly before he realises the source of the noise. The staccato soundtrack music of *Halloween* is sufficiently at odds with the diegesis of *Paranorman* that it is significant both within the diegesis – through Norman's reaction – and extra-diegetically, through its contrast with the non-diegetic sound in this scene. The realisation that it is simply a ringtone that has spooked Norman works to create comedy through incongruity, regardless of whether it is noted as a reference or not. However, the viewer has access to enough material within the narrative to understand that the ringtone is likely a further reference to Norman's love of horror film, demonstrated by his collection of horror movie memorabilia. Moreover, the ringtone echoes the staccato rhythm of the soundtrack of the trashy zombie flick that opens the film, and *Paranorman* has subsequently demonstrated how horror soundtracks work to emphasise climactic scary moments. In this context, the ringtone can be identified by the viewer as belonging to a horror film, even if the viewer is not familiar with *Halloween*. This familiarity with the slasher genre is further cemented when Neil – Norman's friend – appears below the bedroom window, wearing Jason's infamous hockey mask from *Friday the 13th*. *Paranorman* invites an affective response in its viewer, as well as one of ironic detachment. First, the *mise en scène* is focalised through Norman, who looks down out of his window at this strange faceless figure. Neil looks spooky and comical at the same time; the mask blots out his facial features, yet his rotund figure and ginger hair are visible. Here, *Paranorman* oscillates between horror and humour, but marks that shift for the viewer, who is invited to empathise with Norman's fear while also laughing at Neil. Neil does not remove the mask, but his muffled voice comes through after a few seconds, dispelling Norman's momentary fear. The logonomic system of the 'slasher movie' is coded into the narrative through a series of references, musical, visual and verbal. The way these references are linked together in sequence codes into the narrative opportunities for any viewer to 'pick up' the parody as they go.

Paranorman does not teach the rules of the genre in a didactic way, interrupting the narrative diegesis to signal a particular moment as parodic. Instead, the logonomic system is coded into the narrative without disrupting the suspension of disbelief or affectivity of events. Harries' notion of the 'sophisticated naïve' reader is a useful way to think about how these films construct a reader that is neither 'adult' nor 'child', neither genre savvy nor illiterate, but one who is able to access genre literacy to decode the parody and, at the same time, enjoy the texts naïvely as genuinely frightening. For Harries, this 'sophisticated naïve' reader gets a 'quick lesson' in the parody as they watch, learning as they go, and, perhaps accessing different readings if they view the text multiple times (2000: 110). Harries follows Derrida, who claims that 'parody always supposes a naivety withdrawing into an unconscious, a vertiginous non-mastery' (Derrida 1979: 79). Derrida's suggestion is that language is incalculable but that parody allows some kind of access to it because it presumes a position of naïvety. Robert Phiddian elaborates upon this by claiming that Derrida treats notions such as 'language' and 'truth' as though they were in a play of parody, and so parody is itself a form of deconstruction since it foregrounds the processes that exist within language itself (1997: 673). The idea that parody encourages a naïve reading, and that a reader can be simultaneously naïve and sophisticated, has a particular resonance in these children's films. I would go further than Harries' notion of the 'quick lesson', and suggest that parody here functions to create a space for the naïve reader's enjoyment, and, more than this, celebrates naïvety itself as the ideal reading position.

Even in texts where Gothic parody appears to deflate expectations and subject the naïve reader to a lesson in rationality, pretensions to mastery may still be lampooned. Jacqueline Howard argues that Jane Austen's Gothic parody, *Northanger Abbey* (1817), pits the naïve and inexperienced enjoyment of Catherine Morland against the detached irony and knowing pretensions of Henry Tilney. Henry tutors the naïve Catherine, whose love of Gothic novels is tempered by his calm rationality. Nonetheless, Howard claims that the final lesson comes at Henry's expense. Austen has Henry 'overstate his case' when rubbishing Gothic novels and

> treats such blinkered avowals of an ordered society and security from threat with some irony. Furthermore, Henry's pleasure in feeling superior to Catherine, whom he loves for her freshness, honesty, teachability, and 'very ignorant mind' both undercuts and limits his perceptions. (Howard 1994: 167)

Catherine's naïvety is anything but ignorant as she is well versed in the conventions of the books she loves: 'I know it must be a skeleton, I am sure it is Laurentina's skeleton. Oh! I am delighted with the book!' Catherine effuses to a friend about her enjoyment of Radcliffe's *The Mysteries of Udolpho* (Austen 1995: 36). Her expectations of the genre are based on extensive reading, as her comment about the skeleton suggests, but neither her knowledge nor the repetitiveness of the tropes have lessened Catherine's enjoyment or suspension of disbelief. Catherine's enthusiastic enjoyment of Gothic is echoed in the enjoyment that *Frankenweenie* and *Paranorman* encourage in Gothic film conventions. These children's films utilise some of the techniques of parody, not to inculcate a cynicism about the parodied texts in their implied naïve viewers (children who are unlikely to have seen James Whale's 1931 *Frankenstein*, for example), but to imply that naïve enjoyment of Gothic remains available to all. This enjoyment exists in spite (or, perhaps, because) of the fact that Gothic tropes reveal themselves as recycled citations made out of inauthentic materials. Naïvety is the preferred reading strategy because it allows continued belief in and enjoyment of pop-cultural Gothic, a form that is elsewhere dismissed as having been emptied of affectivity and meaning. The films construct a naïve, but agile reader, opening up a Gothic 'canon' to renewal and innovation, rather than monumentalising it, or rendering it inert. As Elliott argues in relation to the representation of Dracula in an earlier Gothic film parody, *Abbott and Costello Meet Frankenstein*, 'Gothic, film, and parody remain in excess of prior ideological uses, ready for new uses, ready for new narratives, new films and, of course, new parodies' (Elliott 2008: 40).

Naïvety as Transformation

Frankenweenie and *Paranorman* tell the stories of protagonists who are initially marginalised and isolated within their communities. Victor spends most of his time alone in his attic, while Norman escapes the scorn of his peers and parents by watching trashy horror films. Though Victor and Norman are marginalised, their engagement with Gothic is presented as productive, not destructive. The climax of each film stages a triumph of naïvety and belief, reversing the logic of subcultural capital and a cynical account of postmodern Gothic cultural production. Relocating from the margins to the mainstream, these Gothic outsiders transform their communities. Throughout the films, 'authenticity' is equated with naïvety and innocence, evoked through the use of toys. Toys feature prominently in Victor's home-made film as props, and, later, in his laboratory. Toys based on Gothic horror also fill Norman's bedroom: there is an alarm clock, dolls and figurines, posters, even a pair of zombie slippers. Victor's toys may mark him as a film producer, while Norman's mark him as a consumer, but their prominence indicates that making and watching Gothic must be an innocent pleasure if it is to be 'authentic'. This innocent enjoyment experienced by the child protagonists contrasts with the gloomy cynicism of the adults in the films. Norman's parents, especially his father, berate the trashy film and Norman's 'weird' hobbies. A similar conflict emerges between Victor and his father. It is Victor's father's insistence on making 'compromises' that leads Victor to take part in the fateful baseball game in which Sparky is killed by a passing car. In both cases, the child wins this conflict: naïvety overcomes cynicism; idealism overcomes pessimism; and narratives of loss are overturned as the living and the dead are reconciled; belief in the supernatural trumps disbelief as the insights of the once marginal outsider come to be valued by a community utterly transformed. The films reinvest a supposedly exhausted textual world with wonder and delight. Both films flirt with a kind of utopianism, too, since they offer lessons about community, about the integration of social outsiders and the most beneficial and transformative types of education.

The conclusion of *Frankenweenie* demonstrates the triumph of naïvety over cynicism as Victor's love for his undead companion, Sparky, wins over first his father, then the other townsfolk. Though the rampaging (pet) monsters are defeated by Victor's ingenuity, they are swiftly replaced by a rampaging mob of townsfolk, eager to punish Victor and his undead creation for bringing this evil upon their town. As in *Paranorman*, the townsfolk appear monstrous because of their fear, hatred and cynicism. The mayor – the most brutish and visually ugly of all the adults in the film, accidentally sets the windmill on fire with his niece Elsa inside. The adults must learn their lesson accordingly, and look on helplessly as Victor and Sparky save the girl. Sparky functions in this scene as a reminder of the faithful, heroic dog narratives once popular in sentimental US television and film, made famous in *Lassie* (1954), *The Littlest Hobo* (1963) and *Bingo* (1991). Burton's use of Gothic, then, brings together sentimental narrative with Gothic fear and monstrosity, confounding the separation of the forms imagined in Mark Edmundson's account of late twentieth-century American culture (1999).

Frankenweenie structures its ending in stages and, at each stage, threatens to foreclose on Victor's naïve idealism. Earlier in the film, Victor's father chides his son, rather comedically, for 'crossing the boundary between life and death, reanimating a corpse . . . it's very upsetting!' Victor's suburban parents cannot believe that their son has resurrected the family's deceased pet dog. Victor's response is one of naïve confusion: 'you said it yourself: you'd bring back Sparky if you could!' Victor's father's reply is typical of a cynical adult attitude that pervades Burton's fictional town of New Holland: 'It's easy to promise the impossible', he scoffs. Burton codes cynical disbelief as the province of adults, and naïve conviction as the privilege of the child. As the film reaches its climax, it seems as though Victor will have to learn the lesson of compromise and loss. A firefighter emerges from the ashes of the ruined windmill, Sparky's corpse in his arms. As Victor leans over the dog, sobbing, a pause suggests Victor's time with his faithful childhood friend has ended. However, this foreclosure stalls when Victor's father begs the townspeople to start their car engines. Shocked, Victor reminds his father, 'you said I had to let him go'. Here the relationship between father and son transforms, as Victor's father learns from his son's conviction and idealism: 'Sometimes adults don't know what they are talking about.' The angry mob relinquish their burning torches and encircle the boy, using their car engines to revive Sparky. The community gesture seems futile, and, for a few moments, it seems as though Victor will have to learn the hard lesson of loss after all. 'It's OK boy; you don't have to come back', Victor whispers to the unmoving corpse. However, *Frankenweenie* rejects foreclosure one last time when Sparky – at the last moment – revives. Not only is one boy's naïve idealism justified here, and the innocence of childhood promised eternal existence in the revived body of Sparky, but a whole community is transformed by the events initiated by Victor's experiments. From the margins to the centre, Victor relocates from the position of weird outsider to the centre of his community.

The resolution of *Paranorman* likewise sees the action of a vilified outsider transforming the community, placing himself at its centre in the process. The ending stages reconciliation between past and present, and between adult and child, through the healing of the trauma suffered by the child witch, Agatha, at the hands of the adult townsfolk who feared her. Norman solves the problem of the witch's curse by finding the spirit of the 'little girl' hiding inside the vengeful witch. Again, this film positions the innocence of the child against the cynicism of the adult. It posits forgiveness, rather than punishment, as the solution to the community's problems. The idealised ending even sees the vicious bully, Alvin, recuperated as a positive character when he tells a reporter that Norman is his best 'buddy', and that they write a paranormal investigation blog together. Norman's conversation with Agatha at the climax of the film reiterates its message: 'you're not alone'. Naïvety is celebrated through the emphasis on the importance of 'happy endings'. 'Aggie' relinquishes her hatred and revenge, as she recalls the place that her 'mommy' used to take her as a child: 'We sat under the tree and she told me stories. They all had happy endings.' Even though the themes of *Paranorman* are markedly dark, dealing with persecution and the murder of a child, a 'happy ending' is both possible and necessary. As Agatha fades into bright light and melts away, the scene switches to a view of the trashed town of Blithe Hollow, with a close up on the severed head of the town's warty-faced witch statue. The townsfolk mill around, clearing up and talking to the press. As in *Frankenweenie*, Norman's father awkwardly embraces his son, saying 'well done'. Everything returns to normal in Blithe Hollow in a narrative of comic restitution rather than Gothic disintegration, but it is a renewed and transformed normality. Finally, *Paranorman* transforms the domestic space of the home, which is figured in the opening not only as drab, but marked by familial conflict and mistrust. The film ends just as it opened, with Norman seated in front of his television, watching a trashy horror film. This time, however, he is joined by the whole family, who have a new-found appreciation for Norman's favourite film genre. They are also reconciled to the presence of the ghostly grandmother who haunts the house. With the dead and the living finally reunited, the family follow Norman's example and sit down to enjoy Gothic horror together.

Paranorman and *Frankenweenie* also pit belief against disbelief, echoing earlier Gothic film parodies that resist critical *disbelief* in Gothic. According to Elliott, Gothic parody film texts resist criticism's attempts to map onto them critical readings that assert that Gothic narratives are representative of something else (Elliott 2008: 24, 27, 37). Elliott argues that twentieth-century Gothic parodies, such as *Abbott and Costello Meet Frankenstein* and *Love at First Bite* 'always already [subject] any deconstructive operations upon themselves to parody' and 'laugh at critical formulae' as much as they do Gothic clichés (2008: 27, 30). Though Gothic film parodies seem to 'diminish the power of literal manifestations of the Gothic supernatural to terrorise and horrify, representing them as mere metaphors' in lines such as 'you've gone bats', they also parody the way criticism makes Gothic monsters into mere metaphors, by rendering these critical metaphors themselves as conventional clichés (Elliott 2008: 31). Elliott's account of the reduction of critical formulae to harmless cliché works for films such as *Love at First Bite* and *Young Frankenstein*, which in particular parody Freudian psychoanalytical accounts of Gothic. The resistance to critical disbelief is rather different in *Paranorman* and *Frankenweenie*, though. Like these earlier texts, they use parody to mark Gothic clichés, metaphors and tropes as repetition and artifice, thereby resisting a 'depth' reading of Gothic. However, their resistance to critical acts of deconstruction does not render the Gothic trope harmless and empty, but imagines a reader that will reinvest in the narrative of the film as it presents itself on the surface.

Elliott argues that some Gothic novels, such as those by Jane Austen and Ann Radcliffe, chart a character's 'journey from terrified belief in the Gothic supernatural to rational disbelief', while in others, like *Dracula*, 'characters journey in the opposite direction: from scoffing disbelief into awestruck belief' (2008: 37). In contrast to a pervasive critical disbelief in the supernatural narratives of Gothic fiction, Gothic parody encourages audience investment in the supernatural, requiring a 'willing suspension of disbelief' (Elliott 2008: 37). In *Abbott and Costello Meet Frankenstein*, for example, the rational sceptic Abbott contrasts with the terrified believer Costello. Elliot argues that 'Abbott becomes a parody of those menacing monsters, their rational, quotidian, bullying, delimiting double' (2008: 38). Ultimately, it is Costello's affirmation of belief ('I saw what I saw what I saw what I saw') that represents, for Elliott, the role of Gothic film parody in undermining critical disbelief. It 'serves as a slogan for how what one sees at first continues to construct what one sees thereafter [and] critiques pervasive tendencies to see only what one has seen before, to discover only what one already knows, and to affirm only what one always already believes in recent Gothic criticism' (Elliott 2008: 39). In *Paranorman* and *Frankenweenie*, the relocation of the naïve child from the outside to the centre makes a similar claim for resisting disbelief in Gothic. The naïvety and willing belief manifested by Norman and Victor triumphs over the disbelief of the rest of their community. Norman's wish that everyone 'could see what I see' has, to some extent, come to pass by the end of the film. While his family cannot see the ghost of their grandmother, they now accept that she is there rather than reading her manifestation as a bizarre bid for attention by a disturbed little boy. The 'child' believer occupies the position of mastery at the film's close, a narrative outcome that is echoed in the way these texts make room for a sophisticated naïve viewer within the text, someone who can come to the film without the 'requisite literacies', and yet is nonetheless able to decode and enjoy the parody.

In summary, *Paranorman* and *Frankenweenie* counter claims made by some Gothic critics that postmodern and pop-cultural Gothic has exhausted itself through repetition, that it has become diluted through pervasion in popular culture. These films embrace the negative term 'Disneygothic', identifying as both 'Disney' *and* 'Gothic' in a way that subjects both terms to mutual transformation. These films also foreground the production of 'authenticity' in such a way as to contest discourses that mark mainstream popular culture as 'inauthentic', while simultaneously providing ways in which 'authenticity' can be reconfigured as a temporary and performative designation, rather than as an elitist value judgment. Finally, parody functions in these three films as an alternative pedagogy, one that posits naïvety as the ideal reading position. Naïvety allows viewers to approach pop-cultural Gothic with enchantment, rather than with wary cynicism. Moreover, the nomadic reader constructed by these parodies initiates interaction between territories separated by the elitist logic of subcultural capital and modernist accounts of cultural production. In these films, the naïvety of the child is also the outsider's perspective, providing an opportunity for defamiliarisation not only with conventional Gothic narratives, but also with attitudes about learning and being. These texts use parody to promote self-reflexivity, but this self-reflexivity does not lead to deconstructive emptiness. Rather, as in Braidotti's nomadic theory, with increased self-reflexivity comes defamiliarisation: 'a new critical distance is established between oneself and one's home grounds – a sense of estrangement that is not painless, but rich in ethical rewards and increased understanding' (2011a: 16). The films chart a move from the 'margins', represented by Victor's attic and Norman's bedroom, to the 'mainstream', represented by the town square and the family living room. In this relocation the centre is 'set in motion toward a becoming minoritarian [requiring] qualitative changes in the very structures of its subjectivity' (Braidotti 2011b: 20). In Deleuze and Guattari's account, 'there is no becoming-majoritarian; majority is never becoming . . . All becoming is minoritarian' (2013: 123). That is, if there is to be a universal or central figure that represents subjectivity, it is the minoritarian, or, the outsider, who represents everybody. Following this logic, it is not only that the centre is transformed through its contact with the margins, but that the margins become central. Gothic parody enacts a mutual transformation that connects rather than isolates cultural spaces.

Notes

1. Angela Carter's statement 'we live in Gothic times', originally articulated in the afterword to *Fireworks* (1974), is often repeated in Gothic Studies to support the idea that in Gothic proliferates in the contemporary moment, though the effects of this proliferation differ depending on the critic. In Carter's afterword the statement sits alongside her insistence that Gothic's function is to 'provoke unease', suggesting Gothic times are uneasy times (Carter 1981: 133). The sentiment is echoed

in Mark Edmundson's *Nightmare on Main Street*, which argues that Gothic novels and films proliferate in late twentieth-century American culture, and that Gothic despair more generally informs the images and narratives of news media and reality television (Edmundson 1999: xii, xiii). However, in Fred Botting's influential analysis of contemporary Gothic, 'Gothic times' indicates instead a proliferation of the form no longer able to provoke unease, since the pervasion of Gothic strips it of its depth and affective power (Botting 2008b: 37, 40).

2. While Disney may still hold immense influence and popularity in popular culture, this is not the case in the academy. Disney studies, as Doherty points out, seems to be primarily concerned with defacing the pristine image of Disney, deconstructing its politics and demythologising its history, with an increasing socio-economic focus (Doherty 2006: 57).

Chapter 5

The 'Great Outdoors' in the Weird Fiction of Derek Landy and Anthony Horowitz

Nomadic Encounters with the Weird

The final iteration of twenty-first-century children's Gothic I want to consider is Weird fiction, focusing on two series of books by Anthony Horowitz and Derek Landy. The *Skulduggery Pleasant* series by Landy (2007–16) and *The Power of Five* series by Horowitz (2005–14) combine Weird horror fiction (a style typified in the works of H. P. Lovecraft, first published in the pulp magazine *Weird Tales* in the 1920s) with pop-cultural appropriations of Lovecraft's 'Cthulhu Mythos', within the narratives of extended fantasy. The Weird sits uneasily alongside both Fantasy and the Gothic, particularly as the two forms have been typically deployed within children's literature. Foremost, the ontological and epistemological horror aimed at by Weird fiction rejects the mastery and transcendence offered by heroic fantasy narratives.[1] There are no heroes: everybody dies or goes insane. So, too, does the Weird run contrary to the concept of Gothic as a means of catharsis in which terror is evoked to be expelled or assimilated.[2] Weird monsters are not manifestations of repressed psychological material or cultural anxieties and so cannot be assimilated or expelled from experience. Rather, Weird monsters gesture to a material realm beyond human perception, what Lovecraft terms the 'chaos and the dæmons of unplumbed space' (1927: 3).

Through an encounter with the Weird, children's Gothic pushes to its limits a nomadic project that unhomes the child and refigures it outside the bounds of pedagogical and psychoanalytical narratives. Opening out into a Weird universe that is both incomprehensible and indifferent to human subjectivity, Landy and Horowitz propel their protagonists into epistemological anxiety and potential ontological oblivion. In this way, these books stray further from the traditional terrain of children's literature than any of the works I have discussed so far. Yet, despite their seeming incompatibility, the Weird and children's fiction are mutually transformed in *Skulduggery Pleasant* and *The Power of Five*. The injection of ontological horror into the terrain of children's fantasy undermines and complicates the matura- tion and mastery the form promises, and, furthermore, challenges psychoanalytic and humanist accounts of the 'I'. In its new figuration within children's literature, the Weird denotes a space beyond the self, in which the nomad encounters what recent speculative philoso- phy designates the completely 'foreign territory' of the material realm (Meillassoux 2009: 7). Here, the nomad flirts with the pleasures of oblivion, or, rather, with the feeling of being 'entirely elsewhere' (Meillassoux 2009: 7). This is not the 'realm of non-signification' described by Rosemary Jackson, nor a world of dark 'Things' imag- ined in Botting's deconstructive psychoanalytic account of the Weird, but rather a territory of non-human materiality in which the nomad may (indirectly) engage with objects that lie beyond the borders of the self (Jackson 1981: 25; Botting 2012b: 283). This, is the '*great outdoors*' (Meillassoux 2009: 7).

The Weird aims to produce both ontological and epistemological horror in its revelation of what Lovecraft terms 'spheres of existence whereof we know nothing and wherein we have no part' (1927: 2). Lovecraft biographer and scholar, S. T. Joshi suggests that the Weird deals in '"supernormal" phenomena' that lie outside human under- standing but *within* material reality (1990: 8). For Joshi, these super- normal phenomena prompt epistemological horror because they reveal 'our ignorance of certain "natural laws"' (1990: 7). Interpret- ing the Weird slightly differently, writer and critic, China Miéville argues that the horror of Weird fiction is specifically *ontological*:

> The Weird is not the return of any repressed: though always described as ancient, and half-recalled by characters from spurious texts, this recruitment to invented cultural memory does not avail Weird monsters of Gothic's strategy of revenance, but back-projects their radical unremembered alterity into history, to en-Weird ontol- ogy itself. (Miéville 2008: 113)

In Miéville's account, the Weird rejects a Gothic, or uncanny, 'return of the repressed' for an encounter with a material world made radically strange. According to Miéville's focus on the ontological, the problem of the Weird is not epistemological (that is, a problem to do with *how* we know about the world), but a fundamental problem with *what* we know. This is ontological horror because it confronts characters and readers with a world they no longer recognise; it remakes the very fabric of the world.

Skulduggery Pleasant and *The Power of Five* evoke *both* ontological horror and epistemological anxiety in their revelations of a hidden world of Weird magic and creatures existing alongside everyday reality. This is not the 'sword and sorcery' magic of traditional fantasy, but a dangerous power employed by and against monstrous entities from an 'outer' realm, beyond human existence. Recalling Lovecraft's 'The Call of Cthulhu', *Skulduggery Pleasant* posits the existence of god-like beings from another plane of existence, 'The Faceless Ones', while Matt in *The Power of Five* discovers the existence of 'The Old Ones' lurking behind the quotidian world (Lovecraft 1963: 57). The protagonists are tasked with protecting the oblivious inhabitants of the human world from these terrifying outer beings who seek to reclaim dominance on earth. In the first *Power of Five* novel (*Raven's Gate*) Matt confronts the a priori nature of the Weird. He describes it as 'living on one side of a mirror: you think there is nothing on the other side until one day a switch is thrown and suddenly the mirror is transparent' (Horowitz 2005: 214). Initially, Matt is horrified by the epistemological error humanity has made: 'The Christian church talks about Satan, Lucifer and all the other devils. But these are just memories of the greatest, original evil: The Old Ones' (Horowitz 2005: 214). However, as the series progresses, this epistemological error opens out into a Weird universe that replaces the ontology of the human world. For Stephanie, in *Skulduggery Pleasant*, the adjustment to a Weird world is also destabilising: 'Bit by bit, she was seeing how close magic had been to her when she was growing up, if only she had known where to look. It was such a strange sensation . . . *Better get used to that feeling*' (Landy 2007: 187; emphasis in original). As in *The Power of Five*, Stephanie's encounter with this other world forces her to view all aspects of her world anew, and Weirdness increasingly permeates even her own home, undermining the quotidian and retroactively rendering it strange.

Though they evoke the sanity-blasting power of the Weird, Landy and Horowitz reject the aporia and dissolution offered in deconstructive psychoanalytic accounts of the Weird and Gothic.

The deconstructive psychoanalytic criticism I have so far traced throughout accounts of the Gothic is itself an expression of the 'linguistic turn', a mode of thought that 'glori[fies] the aporetic' (Braidotti 2011a: 77). It is against this deconstructive linguistic turn that Braidotti positions nomadism (2011b: 5). Weird fiction complements Braidotti's project because it too is implicated in a response to the 'linguistic turn' through the speculative writing of philosophers such as Quentin Meillassoux and Graham Harman. This 'speculative turn' in philosophy seeks to examine 'reality in itself' as an alternative to humanist correlationist thought, drawing on the writings of Lovecraft as an expression of a speculation about material reality (Bryant, Srnicek, and Harman 2011: 1, 3). Briefly, correlationism follows Kant's *Critique of Pure Reason* (1781) with the thesis that there is no possible access to things-in-themselves except by way of a correlation between objects and perceiving subjects. That is, objects cannot be thought of without subjects. Kant's philosophy designates objects in themselves 'noumena', a term most often considered in its 'negative sense' as an object outside the subject's 'mode of intuition' (Kant 2007: 259). Kantian correlationism prompts the 'linguistic turn' of theorists such as Lacan and Derrida, in which there is effectively no access to reality outside language. That is, Kant's 'noumena' have become the 'aporia', or black holes, of deconstruction. The seductive aporia of the 'linguistic turn' informs Fred Botting's account of the relationship between horror and materialism in his recent discussion of Weird fiction. In Botting's analysis, Kant's noumena become the dark 'Things', or black holes, of a Lacanian Real: 'the Thing lying outside categories of sense, knowledge, reason; it intimates a realm of horror, revulsion, nausea, dissolution, a place where names do not apply and speech fails in heart-rending screams or strangled silence' (2012b: 283). Through this lens, the Weird leads only to dissolution, to silence, to nothing.

However, Botting's recourse to Lacanian 'Things' belies the more affirmative account of reality offered by speculative realists. Graham Harman uses Lovecraft's writing to argue that 'reality is object-oriented ... made up of nothing but substances – and they are *weird* substances with a taste of the uncanny about them, rather than stiff blocks of simplistic physical matter' (Harman 2008: 347). In Harman's 'weird realism', Lovecraft's writing draws attention to the 'gaps' between objects and perception, between reality and language, but also provides a speculative and indirect access to those weird objects lying just outside perception (Harman 2012: 5).

Harman asserts that 'the absent thing-in-itself can have gravitational effects on the internal content of knowledge, just as Lovecraft can allude to the physical form of Cthulhu even while cancelling the literal terms of the description' (2012: 17). Whereas Botting links impossible noumena, or 'Things', to horror, Harman argues that the Weird substance of reality itself is not necessarily horrifying (Botting 2012b: 283; Harman 2012: 4). Harman's account of Lovecraft allows for the possibility that Weird writing might affirm a material world beyond perception, rather than lead to the melancholic aporia of deconstruction.

My reading of *Skulduggery Pleasant* and *The Power of Five* proposes a synthesis of Braidotti's nomadic materialism and Harman's weird realism. In nomadic thought, the materially embodied subject can assert itself outside the 'master code or single central grid' imagined by linguistic and constructivist accounts of subjectivity (Braidotti 2011b: 5). Moreover, this embodied subject entails the dissolution of the humanist, universal 'I', and so functions for Braidotti as a potentially feminist body (Braidotti 2011a: 15). That is, the nomad is inclusive of a multiplicity of subjectivities, locations and positions. Finally, nomadism's 'ontology of presence replaces textual or other deconstruction' (Braidotti 2011b: 132). In other words, Braidotti's nomadic body is a material presence: it exists in relation to an external material reality and is mobilised by encounters with other material objects. It is not a black hole of dissolution and silence. Harman's philosophy, which attempts to trace the force real objects exert on the phenomenological world, forms a useful counterpoint to Braidotti's 'enchanted materialism' (Harman 2008: 336; Braidotti 2011b: 5). Harman questions the reductively materialist reading of Lovecraft expressed by Michel Houellebecq, who asserts that Cthulhu is simply an 'arrangement of electrons, like us' (Houellebecq 2008: 32). For Harman, material objects are more than this. Material objects assert themselves on the sensual realm of human perception, deforming it, making it Weird. Likewise, the objects we access within the phenomenal world of sensual perception are more than simply (co)relational, more than our perceptions of them. Objects have a reality beyond that phenomenal world. In its encounter with these objects, the nomadic subject affirms its own material force and potentiality. *Skulduggery Pleasant* asserts the empowerment available in this encounter through its protagonist, Stephanie. Stephanie's discovery of the Weird universe is, in part, an affirmative experience. Breathless, she exclaims, 'I've seen a world I never even knew *existed*' (Landy 2007: 64;

emphasis in original). Though Skulduggery insists on returning Stephanie to her 'normal life', Stephanie refuses to go home, and insists that Skulduggery shows her more. Soon, Stephanie discovers that she possesses magical abilities and learns to assert her own material force upon the world of sense and perception through the mastery of Weird energies. Thus, although Landy's exploration of the Weird evokes Lovecraft's 'atmosphere of breathless and unexplained dread', it also produces wonder, delight and power (Lovecraft 1927: 3). Stephanie's delight and eagerness allows the Weird to become playful.

Skulduggery Pleasant and *The Power of Five* also appropriate the Weird in an act of intertextual nomadism that figures the reader as agile and active. Like the parody films of the previous chapter, *Skulduggery Pleasant* and *The Power of Five* engage in postmodern playfulness and metafictional self-reflexivity, connecting different forms of culture in what Henry Jenkins calls 'an impertinent raid on the literary preserve' (Jenkins 2014: 26). This playful Weird fiction marks a shift in the cultural status and function of a form that was, until recently, not very visible in popular culture. In the past decade Cthulhu has emerged from the shadows of pulp magazines and role-playing games into the mainstream. Initially, this was confined to adult texts such as Comedy Central's *South Park*.[3] Cute and cuddly versions of Cthulhu have also become visible in merchandising, comics and online culture. These often-comedic versions of Weird monsters indicate a change in the way the Weird is being read and appropriated. For example, a recent episode of the children's animated series *Scooby Doo! Mystery Inc.* (2010–13) pits Scooby and the gang against a tentacle-faced monster, 'Char Gar Gothakon', whose other-worldly shriek renders his victims gibbering wrecks (Cook 2010). The episode playfully lampoons writers and works from the Weird tradition in a parodic homage, inviting child and adult viewers alike to get in on the joke. Moreover, the episode title, 'the Shrieking Madness', recalls not only Lovecraft's hysterical protagonists, but Botting's description of Weird horror as 'a place where . . . speech fails in heart-rending screams or strangled silence, where bodies shudder and collapse, and minds spin in delirium or shut down in utter vacancy' (Botting 2012b: 283). *Scooby Doo!* represents a popular form of the Weird that rejects the cynicism of such criticism. *Scooby Doo!* suggests that the Weird is no longer a signifier of what Miéville calls 'crisis-blasted modernity', but opens the form up to playfulness and pleasure (2008: 128).

Playfully poaching past works, these children's fictions reject both the literary critic and Lovecraft himself as authorities on the Weird. Embracing popular culture and mass-market audiences, the Weird fiction of Landy and Horowitz counters Joshi's attempts to police the borders of the form. In his insistence that the Weird is an *epistemological* rather than *ontological* form, Joshi privileges a modernist aesthetic over postmodern forms of fiction (1990: 7). Drawing this distinction, Joshi follows Brian McHale's assertion that modernist fiction is epistemological in character and postmodern fiction, which supersedes it, is ontological (McHale 1987: 9–10). Like the Gothic critics I discuss in Chapter 4, Joshi expresses an elitist and nostalgic desire to maintain a modernist and marginal status for Weird fiction that is at odds with its pulp origins and current popularity. His insistence that good Weird fiction comprises 'a small modicum of genuine literature' read by a 'discriminating audience' further echoes the subcultural investment in 'authenticity' and distaste for 'mainstream' audiences expressed by the Gothic critics Botting and Beville (Joshi 2001: 3). Though Joshi's monographs on Weird fiction, *The Weird Tale* (1990), *The Modern Weird Tale* (2001), and *The Evolution of the Weird Tale* (2004), come at the very beginning of a postmillennial explosion of Weird fiction in popular and literary culture, and so cannot account for its later proliferation, they attempt to establish a modernist, cult, literary status for Weird fiction that precludes the inclusion of popular works. Like Beville, Joshi dismisses the surface features of genre in his assertion that the Weird is 'an inherently philosophical mode' (1990: 11). Joshi laments that 'the amount of meritous Weird fiction being written today is in exactly inverse proportion to its quantity' and suggests that contemporary Weird is reduced to 'a body of conventionalized scenarios and tropes from which authors can draw and upon which they can, as it were, hang a tale' (2004: 1; 2001: 2). Through these evaluative manoeuvres, Joshi sets Lovecraft's works as a standard against which later fictions are judged, and appoints himself as the judge. Though Joshi's work on Lovecraft is responsible for drawing the academy's attention to Weird fiction, it reproduces a hierarchical model of reading in which the critic is positioned as a 'sanctioned interpreter . . . working to restrain the "multiple voices" of popular orality, to regulate the production and circulation of meanings' (Jenkins 2014: 26). Counter to this, popular twenty-first-century Weird appropriates Lovecraft's mythos according to the model of reading suggested by Michel de Certeau in *The Practice of Everyday Life*, in which the reader is not passively moulded by a text, but makes it their own through an act of reappropriation (1984: 166).

Both *Skulduggery Pleasant* and *The Power of Five* (re)appropriate the Weird within pop-cultural, mass-market series fiction, a form that itself spawns yet more versions. The first novel in Horowitz's series was recently adapted as a graphic novel, with the others soon to follow, and a *Skulduggery Pleasant* film is in development. As pop-cultural works, *Skulduggery Pleasant* and *The Power of Five* incorporate the irreverence and playfulness that can be seen in *Scooby Doo!* yet also manage to retain the ontological horror of the Lovecraftian Weird. The reader of this mass-market Weird is nomadic, 'migrating and devouring its way through the pastures of the media' (de Certeau 1984: 165). De Certeau's formulation of the reader as a nomadic poacher influences Henry Jenkins's accounts of fan culture, which perceives fans and readers as 'active producers and manipulators of meaning' (Jenkins 2012: 22). As fans of Lovecraft, Landy and Horowitz reappropriate Lovecraftian tropes to initiate their adolescent *protagonists* into a Weird universe. At the same time, they employ reflexivity and metafictional play to figure the *reader* as an initiate into the cult of Lovecraft. In so doing, Landy and Horowitz counter the logic of subcultural capital I have identified in some criticism of pop-cultural or postmodern fiction by conferring subcultural capital upon a newly imagined mainstream audience. Discovering a canon of Weird fiction through Stephanie, Skulduggery and Matt, the child reader imagined by Landy and Horowitz is included in the Lovecraft cult, able to embody subcultural capital through 'being in the know' (Thornton 1995: 12). De Certeau and Jenkins's nomad, who reads by 'poaching their way across fields they did not write', also presents a challenge to the authority of the writer and academic critic because they do not read for authorial meaning, but instead engage in the production of new meanings (de Certeau 1984: 174). Landy and Horowitz imagine a nomadic reader able to negotiate the intertextual threads of their work, creating new meanings through juxtapositions between different cultural texts. This playfulness remakes the Weird into an affirmative space that imagines a child reader capable of agency and mobility.

Rewriting Epistemological Horror

In a typical Lovecraftian tale, knowledge of the Weird universe inevitably results in madness and death. Through its concern with epistemology, the Weird suggests that human knowledge is woefully inadequate. Joshi notes that Lovecraft provokes horror by inserting 'many horrible events into the real history of the ancient and contemporary world . . . what Lovecraft seems to be suggesting is that *more* things have happened in history than we suspect' (Joshi 1990: 194). In these revelations of secret histories, real world places coexist with imaginary towns, real and imaginary dates and events jostle for our attention, and 'lost' artefacts and manuscripts are discovered among actual historical facts. Miéville notes that these Weird insertions into accepted history produce a horror not of intrusion, but realisation: 'The world has always been implacably bleak; the horror lies in our acknowledging that fact' (Miéville 2005: xiii). Both *Skulduggery Pleasant* and *The Power of Five* draw on this epistemological anxiety. In *Skulduggery Pleasant,* the Faceless Ones are consigned to myth, initially dismissed by the characters as nonsense. Skulduggery scoffs at the stories, telling Stephanie, 'it's a legend. It's an allegory. It didn't really happen' (Landy 2007: 82). However, throughout the course of the first book, Skulduggery and Stephanie untangle a knot of history and legend to uncover the terrible truth: the Faceless Ones are real. Both epistemological and ontological horror are produced here. Not only must the protagonists accept that *what* they know about the world is wrong, but they also come to question *how* they know.

In *Skulduggery Pleasant* and *The Power of Five* epistemological anxiety centres on the validity of sources and the textual documentation of history. Repeatedly, in both series, texts that document important 'truths' are inevitably lost, destroyed or turn out to be useless. Much of the action of *The Power of Five* is dedicated to finding an important manuscript that supposedly reveals important information about the Old Ones' return, the diary of a mad monk, Joseph of Cordoba. However, when the characters finally get their hands on this tome, they find it is written in a language they do not understand, 'and anyway his handwriting was almost illegible' (Horowitz 2009: 117). The one character that might have been able to translate the text is killed before he has a chance to read it. Thus, the text that the children had thought to be a prize turns out to be of no use whatsoever. In *Skulduggery Pleasant*, the fabled *Book of Names*, a powerful tome listing everything and everyone that ever has or will exist, is disintegrated. The book has been protected under a powerful spell for centuries, thought to be indestructible: 'it can't be torn; it can't be burnt; it can't be damaged by any means we have at our disposal' (Landy 2007: 148). Yet, by the end of the novel it has 'disappeared in a cloud of dust' before it can give up any of its secrets (Landy 2007: 359).

Skulduggery Pleasant and *The Power of Five* suggest that it is not only records of the past that cannot be trusted to provide knowledge, but that all potential future instances of recorded knowledge are likewise questionable. Joshi notes how Lovecraft not only inserts events into historical record, but also obliterates them too, often simultaneously (1990: 195). This strategy appears in *The Power of Five* when Matt discovers that Raven's Gate, one of the portals used to let the Old Ones into the world, is the site of the very first stone circle ever built, though its name doesn't appear in any records. Following the events at Raven's Gate, in which Matt successfully prevents the Old Ones from breaking through into the human world, all textual records are obliterated: 'Nobody ever spoke of it again. It was as if Raven's Gate had never existed' (Horowitz 2005: 213). In this novel, any sense of resolution experienced in Matt's success at closing the gate and banishing the Old Ones is undercut by the erasure of the whole episode from written record. Matt's journalist friend, Richard, is not able to get his story printed, and the heroes and villains, including the chief villain, Sir Michael Marsh, simply disappear:

> Here was a man who had once been an influential government scientist, who had received a knighthood. Yet there were no obituaries, no comment, nothing. He might as well have never existed. (Horowitz 2005: 237)

The erasure of the episode from recorded history has two important effects. Firstly, written records are revealed as false and worthless. Truth is only ever glimpsed in fragments, between the lines of print, in what is not recorded. As such, Horowitz follows Lovecraft in his suggestion that any grasp on knowledge is slippery at best. Secondly, events at Raven's Gate are not reported because the Weird cannot be integrated into reality; it remains impossible. Richard notes, 'this is the twenty- first century and the one thing that people cannot live with is uncertainty . . . We live in an age where there is no room for the impossible' (Horowitz 2005: 280). In this sentiment, Richard echoes Joshi's analysis of the scepticism at the heart of Lovecraft's writing: 'Better . . . actively to conceal certain things in the past than to come face to face with our own fragility' (Joshi 1990: 198).

The scepticism inherent in Weird's epistemological horror disrupts a maturation narrative premised on the protagonist's eventual triumph over darkness or mastery of knowledge. In the past two decades the 'felix culpa', or innocence-to-experience, narrative can be seen in a number of popular children and Young Adult fantasy texts, such as Garth Nix's *Sabriel* (2002), J. K. Rowling's *Harry Potter* series (1997–2007) and Philip Pullman's *His Dark Materials* (1995–2000). Though Landy and Horowitz borrow the framework of these adolescent fantasies, their use of Weird fiction posits knowledge as disastrous rather than empowering. In 'The Call of Cthulhu', Lovecraft famously asserts:

> We live on a placid island of ignorance in the midst of black seas of infinity, and it was not meant that we should voyage far . . . but some day the piecing together of dissociated knowledge will open up such terrifying vistas of reality, and of our frightful position therein, that we shall either go mad from the revelation or flee from the deadly light. (Lovecraft 1963: 47)

Such pronouncements suggest Lovecraft is an anti-Enlightenment writer, sceptical of the reach of human knowledge. Certainly, Lovecraft's stories do not glorify a human quest for knowledge since characters following this path always suffer a spectacular doom. Joshi argues that in Lovecraft's Weird universe 'knowledge, which in itself is morally neutral, can cause profound psychological trauma' (1990: 207). The trajectory of the Weird tale thus works in the opposite direction to adolescent fantasy, such as *His Dark Materials*, which chart a fortunate 'fall' into knowledge and the growth of the protagonist.

This notion of knowledge as trauma is echoed in *The Power of Five* and *Skulduggery Pleasant*. Here knowledge of the Weird universe is corrosive, a taint that the protagonists will never be rid of. In *Skulduggery Pleasant*, Stephanie is increasingly isolated from her family as she learns more about the Weird world. Her Uncle Fergus is frightened and disgusted by the 'filthy magic' she is learning and orders Stephanie to stay away: 'I don't want you teaching my daughters anything' (Landy 2011: 361). Fergus's fierce care of his daughters highlights Stephanie's isolation: she is forced to keep most of her life secret from her own parents. Early on in *Raven's Gate*, Matt too realises that he carries the taint of Weird knowledge that excludes him from normal life. His neighbour shuns him: 'I'll never forget the look on her face. She was horrified. More than that. She was actually sick . . . She was horrified and sick because of me' (Horowitz 2005: 184). None of the children inducted into the Weird universe in *The Power of Five* feels blessed by the knowledge they have. Throughout the series, characters repeatedly wish that they had never heard of the Old Ones. When, at the close of the first novel, Matt learns of a second portal that he needs to close, he implores, 'I don't want to *know* any more' (Horowitz 2005: 282; my emphasis).

Yet, Landy and Horowitz also reframe the anti-Enlightenment tendency of Weird fiction, countering Lovecraft's scepticism by making other forms of knowledge available to their protagonists. Even as the Weird isolates and taints the protagonists, it also marks them as special and confers upon them status denied those characters who remain in the quotidian world. The protagonists' initiation into the Weird is as much a celebration of Geek culture as it is an expression of epistemological anxiety. Lovecraft's increasing popularity in recent decades is down to the rise in visibility and popularity of Geek culture, participation in which can confer subcultural capital on the previously uninitiated. Numerous pop-cultural spaces have opened the Weird up to this increased participation, including websites such as *The Onion*'s 'Gateways to Geekery'. This website, which aims to demystify Geek culture for a 'mainstream' audience, notes the existence of 'a real world cult of Lovecraft that's been dissecting, debating, and expanding on his legacy for decades' (Heller 2009). Landy and Horowitz not only evoke a Weird universe *within* their narratives, but also open up this *extratextual* 'real world cult' to readers.

Again, I find Thornton's theorisation of subcultural capital as the means by which young people negotiate and accumulate status helpful in understanding the gesture made in Landy and Horowitz's fiction (1995: 163). Thornton argues that subcultural capital allows members of a subculture to 'assert their distinctive character and affirm that they are not anonymous members of an undifferentiated mass' (1995: 5, 10). In *Skulduggery Pleasant*, Stephanie gets to be *in* on a subculture that is far more out there than wearing black, listening to metal or quoting obscure science fiction. She is simultaneously initiated into a universe of Weird magic *and* the cult of Lovecraftian fiction, as the novel's playful references to 'Mr Howard L. Craft' illustrate. Within the narrative, uncool characters do not get the reference, but Skulduggery and Stephanie invite the reader to be in on the joke, giving just enough background information for readers to follow up the reference (Landy 2007: 300). In this way, *Skulduggery Pleasant* constructs its own Weird subcultural space, membership of which entails 'being in the know' as well as gaining magical powers. Stephanie saves the world *and* makes witty quips as she does so. Here, the construction of a Weird universe is not simply about inspiring epistemological horror; it also expresses the desire to transmit subcultural knowledge (and status) to new audiences. Landy follows 'Gateways to Geekery', and other pop-cultural manifestations of the Weird, in opening up its fictional worlds to a mass-market, mainstream audience.

The Power of Five also makes playful use of existing Weird fiction, partaking in the ongoing production of the Weird as cultural and literary text in process. In an interview, Horowitz discusses Lovecraft's 'mythos' as though it were real, and describes 'a strange, sixth century text called the *Necronomicon*' (Horowitz 2011). With a metafictional nod, Horowitz inserts his books into the 'Cthulhu Mythos' by employing a device used by Lovecraft and other Weird writers, who deliberately include references to one another's fictional mythical texts as 'real' sources in their stories. Horowitz's 'mad' Spanish monk, St Joseph of Cordoba, is also a knowing nod to Lovecraft's invented occultist and author of *The Necronomicon*, Abdul Alhazred. While I cannot comment on what Horowitz does or does not believe, it is tempting to read his reference to the grandfather of these fake occult tomes – *The Necronomicon* – as a playful gesture that contributes to the wider Cthulhu fan culture. Horowitz does not only borrow from Lovecraft; he also takes material from fan-authored sources, poaching fragments from the many fake versions of the *Necronomicon* available on the Internet. The symbol used by the Lesser Malling witches in *Raven's Gate*, for example, is identical to a symbol taken from one such Internet source (see Ottinger 2014). These borrowings from official and unofficial sources suggests that Horowitz is not only paying his dues to a literary Weird tradition, but also contributing to a fan culture that 'constructs its own identity and artefacts from resources borrowed from already circulating texts' (Jenkins 2012: 3). Jenkins's assertion that texts accumulate meaning through use is evident in the way new meanings of the *Necronomicon* are possible when this fictional work is recycled in a new fictional setting. A body of writing 'constantly in flux', the Weird is an open text no longer requiring the authentication of Lovecraft, or a sanctioned interpreter, but becomes available to a community of fans who themselves become writers (Jenkins 2012: 23).

The Power of Five's intervention in this wider Weird text is complex. On the one hand, Horowitz's insistence on the *Necronomicon* as real, uncovered by his research and utilised in his stories, maintains a status quo whereby the text subordinates readers to the author, who becomes the privileged holder of knowledge and meaning. On the other hand, Horowitz's borrowings from unofficial sources counter author-centred accounts of the Weird, like Joshi's, which judge subsequent contributions to the field by how they hold up to a standard set by the originator. Horowitz's playful references to Mythos elements resist this hierarchy that values the author over the reader, allowing the field of Weird fiction to expand into new territories where readers become participants. In interview questions reprinted at the back of *Necropolis*, Horowitz tells readers he will print a portion of the *Necronomicon* at the beginning of the book for them, which in turn initiates much fan activity over the Internet as readers share with one another their attempts to translate this strange excerpt: 'Ia sakkath. Iak sakkakh, Ia sha xul' (Horowitz 2009: 395, 14). The phrase is meaningless, based on nonsense phrases used in the various *Necronomicon* texts available online. Though Horowitz's game playing positions the adult author as holder of arcane knowledge, this fragment works to disintegrate the validity and authority of source documents. Since it is undecipherable, its meaning becomes available to multiple interpretations and reappropriations. Landy and Horowitz are writers as fans, opening up Lovecraft's tales to create new texts, seeking to welcome a new generation of readers into a subcultural space that they do not need to be 'discerning' to enjoy.

Weird Monsters: Encounters with Objects

In its depiction of impossible monsters that elude description in language, Weird fiction figures a space beyond the limits of the 'I' and points to a territory beyond the phenomenological. De Certeau argues that reading is 'an impertinent absence' that removes the reader 'elsewhere, where they are not, in another world' (1984: 173). De Certeau's nomadic reader creates a space beyond the social 'checkerboard' that limits and structures subjectivity in a rebellious act of 'deterritorialisation' (de Certeau 1984: 173). In Weird fiction, this nomadic reader-in-exile finds an 'elsewhere' that gestures not only beyond social structures and constraints, but beyond human perception itself, to the realm of material, or 'real', objects. In Weird fiction these real objects manifest as monsters, terrifying in part because they mark the limits of language and sensory perception. Lovecraft's hysterical description of Cthulhu notes 'the Thing cannot be described – there is no language for such abysms of shrieking and immemorial lunacy, such eldritch contradictions of all matter, force, and cosmic order' (Lovecraft 1963: 95). However, these monsters do not simply mark an impossible space beyond language, denoting the emptiness found in deconstruction or Lacanian psychoanalysis, but exert a strong physical force on the phenomenological world. In their bulk and cosmic size, Weird monsters are excessively, materially real, not aporetically 'Real'. In *Skulduggery Pleasant* and *The Power of Five* monsters oscillate between functions as they phase between appearance and retreat, manifesting as spectacularly material in one moment, disappearing from perception in the next. The protagonists of the novels deftly negotiate these tricky encounters with the Weird objects of reality, navigating an object-oriented ontology that mobilises the force of the nomadic subject.

Foremost, the Weird monster represents a catastrophic event that destabilises the traditional narrative schema of children's fantasy, which demands monsters be defeated or banished to effect closure and restitution. For Joshi, the emergence of Cthulhu from the Pacific depths in 'The Call of Cthulhu' is 'an unprecedented union of horror and science fiction unlike anything that went before . . . it embodies the quintessential phenomenon of the Weird tale – the shattering of our conception of the universe' (1990: 190) Likewise, Miéville posits the Weird monster as 'the narrative actualisation of the Weird-as-novum, unprecedented, Event' (2008: 110). The Weird monster as 'Event' is most obvious in the excessive bulk and size of the creatures who appear in *Skulduggery Pleasant* and *The Power of Five*. In *Skulduggery Pleasant* the arrival of 'The Faceless Ones' creates a series of massive shockwaves. Stephanie cannot comprehend the cosmic dimensions of the creatures she sees 'passing behind the tree, five times as tall, a towering, changing beast' (Landy 2009: 352). The monsters defy Stephanie's senses; she can only view them from the 'corner of her eye' rather than confront them with a totalising gaze. This fragmented vision, denoting incomprehensible, cosmic size, also features in *Raven's Gate* when Matt first glimpses the Old Ones:

> The blackness welled up, blotting out the red, thrusting it aside in a chaos of swirling bubbles. A brilliant white streak seared across the surface of the pool. The black thing brushed it away and with a shudder Matt saw what it was: a huge hand. The monster that owned it must have been as big as the reactor itself. He could see its fingernails, sharp and scaly, and he could make out the wrinkled skin of its webbed fingers. (Horowitz 2005: 248–9)

This creature is clearly other-worldly, but its physicality is depicted in sharp fingernails and webbed fingers. These monsters are not 'material' beings in a reductive sense, but nor are they completely outside sensory perception. As Harman notes, the 'strangeness of . . . objects comes from the fact that they can never be exhaustively described or defined', but nonetheless constitute a chunk of 'obstinate reality' within the phenomenological realm (Harman 2008: 355). Weird monsters are objects in this sense; they straddle the gap between a perceptual realm in which material objects exert their force, but also mark a noumenal space beyond perception. The whole of the monster retreats beyond what it is possible for Matt and Stephanie to process or describe.

The Faceless Ones and the Old Ones constitute a break with the types of monsters usually found in children's fantasy, since they upset one of the traditional functions of the monster as bogeyman. For Marina Warner, the bogeyman is a vehicle through which cultures magnify menace, courting 'fear and dread' in order to produce 'catharsis' (Warner 2000: 9). Weird monsters interrupt this process because they refuse to be fully captured in language, constituting an impasse in the process of signification itself. For Miéville, Lovecraft's 'regular insistence that whatever is being described is "un-describable", is, in its hesitation, its obsessive qualification and stalling of the noun, an aesthetic deferral according to which the world is always-already un-representable' (2009: 511–12). Harman argues that this aspect of Weird writing points to a 'vertical gap' between the real world and sensual perception and reveals the 'crippled descriptive power of language' to capture real objects (2012: 27). Stephanie's description of a 'Faceless One' suggests this inadequacy. Though the monster's image 'burns' its way into her mind, she is only able to express it as 'the hint of an idea, or the memory of something she'd never known' (Landy 2009: 353). Fleeting, uncertain, the Faceless Ones are 'impossibility made manifest, the formless given form' (Landy 2009: 353). Stephanie's articulation of what she does not properly see draws attention to a gap in the power of language to describe and contain, but also attempts to bridge this gap by giving form to the formless. Harman notes that:

> Reality itself is weird because reality is incommensurable with any attempt to represent or measure it. Lovecraft is aware of this difficulty to an exemplary degree, and through his assistance we may be able to learn about how to say something without saying it . . . When it comes to grasping reality, illusion and innuendo are the best we can do. (2012: 51)

Likewise, Landy does not allow the monster to completely retreat beyond the reach of sensory perception and language, but imagines ways in which fragments of it may be encountered. However, this encounter cannot produce the catharsis imagined in Warner's account of the bogeyman, since the object always remains partially elusive.

The *Power of Five* also describes indescribable monsters and likewise refrains from gesturing to the aporia beyond language. Chaos, the king of the Old Ones, is described as 'a black hole in outer space' with 'no face' and 'no features of any sort', erasing reality as he moves (Horowitz 2007: 290). Chaos appears at a climactic moment in the fantasy narrative, at the peak of a battle between the heroes and the Old Ones, but the description given fails to definitively articulate what the Old Ones are. Like Landy, Horowitz utilises a typical Lovecraftian trope, deferring articulation in his assertion that Chaos is 'too gigantic to be seen, too horrible to be understood' (Horowitz 2007: 337). Rosemary Jackson's Lacanian reading of Lovecraft describes Weird monsters, such as Chaos, as 'thingless names . . . mere signifiers without an object . . . indicating nothing but their own proper density and excess. The signifier is not secured by the weight of the signified: it begins to float free' (1981: 40). In Jackson's deconstructive account, Weird monsters become only signifiers, not objects, 'superficially full' names that open out into 'a terrible emptiness' (1981: 40). However, Horowitz's evocation of the Weird resists this deconstructive account through its insistence that the monster is an object, not an empty signifier. Chaos 'cuts' his way through the phenomenological world, in a 'twisting or torsion' of human perception (Horowitz 2007: 290; Harman 2012: 360). Though the object is difficult to register in the human sensual realm, it nonetheless feels real. Harman asserts that the term 'black hole' is suitable for the 'allusive, withdrawn object that Lovecraft so often loves to establish', but that even as objects appear 'absolutely distant', they are also 'near to us insofar as they inscribe their distance in directly accessible fashion' (2012: 239).

As well as pointing to a gap between human sensory perception and reality beyond, Weird monsters also reveal a gap between the object as a whole and its myriad surfaces. Harman designates this a 'horizontal gap' located within the phenomenological realm that marks the subject's inability to fully account for the many qualities of the objects it encounters (2012: 25). Harman argues that Lovecraft points to this gap through his 'cubist' style in which language is 'no longer enfeebled by an impossibly deep and distant reality . . . [but] overloaded by a gluttonous excess of surfaces and aspects of the thing (Harman 2012: 25). Miéville also alludes to this cubist aspect of the Weird in his assertion that its monsters constitute 'a radical break with anything from a folkloric tradition . . . agglomerations of bubbles, barrels, cones, and corpses, patch-worked from cephalopods, insects, crustaceans, and other fauna notable precisely for their absence from the traditional Western monstrous' (Miéville 2009: 512). Not only are Weird monsters ontologically horrifying because they manifest a bizarre teratology, but this teratology is made up of an excess of surface features. The Old Ones in *The Power of Five* display a fragmented excess of such features, including tentacles, pincers, eyes on stalks, teeth, beaks, scales, feathers and claws. Horowitz describes the Old Ones as 'an infestation . . . a horde with no shape or formation, just an oozing mess of nightmarish creatures . . . a crazy mixture of arms and teeth and beaks and scales and feathers and claws, all brought together to create unimaginable monsters' (2007: 288–9). Horowitz's Weird monsters are not empty signifiers, nor are they manifestations of social anxieties or psychoanalytic 'depths', but rather an expression of the surplus surfaces of objects, the many 'qualities, planes, or adumbrations, which even when added up do not exhaust the reality of the object they compose' (Harman 2012: 3).

Horowitz's blending of the visual spectacle of fantasy and horror fiction with the 'unrepresentable' monsters of the Weird suggests a desire to exceed, or outdo, the sense of unprecedented 'Event' marked by Cthulhu's appearance from the Pacific waves. The emergence of the Old Ones from the opened portal in the second book, *Evil Star*, prompts a frenzied description spanning five pages. Horowitz begins with the horrific bulk of a huge hummingbird and gigantic spider, invoking disgust and terror through their insectoid features, the 'glistening fangs', 'black and brilliant' eyes and 'twitching' bodies (Horowitz 2006: 334). The description progresses from this into the realms of the grotesque, drawing attention to the 'buzzing' of a 'swarm' of 'flies with fat black bodies and beating wings' (2006: 335). The creatures form and reform as Matt looks on, becoming degenerate 'strange freakish shapes' 'stretching' and 'bulging', 'part animal, part human', 'dirty yellow pus dripping' from their gaping wounds (2006: 335–6). Horowitz describes monsters as bizarre and tortuous experiments, each one 'more deformed, more horrible' than the last (2006: 339). Horowitz's excessive descriptions point to the heightened visibility of the Weird monster evident elsewhere in popular culture. From board game miniatures and fan art to cartoons and cuddly toys, a multitude of images celebrate the bizarre forms of Weird monstrosity. As well as horror, this increased visibility suggests possibilities for fun and enjoyment, allowing these children's texts to incorporate the bleak cosmic vision of the Lovecraftian Weird, while simultaneously indulging in gleeful spectacle.

In its gluttonous excess of surfaces, the Weird is a spectacle that provokes more than ontological horror. Just as the monster as object exerts its force on the phenomenological realm, so the protagonists' encounter with the monster allows them to, likewise, exert force in return. Both *Skulduggery Pleasant* and *The Power of Five* stage a (temporary) defeat of Weird monsters in a way that would be unthinkable in a Lovecraft story. *The Faceless Ones* climaxes in a chapter titled 'Killing Gods', in which the heroes discover a weapon that will banish the monsters from the human world. Stephanie fires the 'Sceptre of the Ancients' as though it were a gun, the black lightning it emits functioning as a bullet 'hitting the Faceless One in the chest':

> It staggered, and even though it had no mouth, it shrieked, an inhuman scream of pain and rage. The black lightning curled around its body . . . The skin dried and cracked . . . and the body emptied into a cloud of dust . . . Skulduggery ran over, 'What happened? Are you alright? What was that scream?'
> 'That was the sound of a god dying.' (Landy 2009: 375)

Despite the initial paralysis of her encounter with the Faceless Ones, Stephanie here occupies the position of triumphant hero, and, briefly, the Weird monster is dispatched. Horowitz offers the same spectacle in *Nightrise*, staging a fantasy battle scene reminiscent of Tolkien rather than Lovecraft:

> Chaos . . . seemed to explode outwards, completely losing his human shape, becoming nothing more than a huge shadow, a sort of living night that was at last being torn apart by the coming of the day. He screamed one last time and his servants knew, right then, that the battle was lost . . . Every evil being in the universe heard it and knew that the end had come . . . Jamie looked up and saw that at last the clouds had parted and the sun had been allowed to show its face. (Horowitz 2007: 308–11)

In this blending of Weird with high fantasy, Landy and Horowitz borrow from pop-cultural and fan-authored Cthulhu fictions in which Weird monsters are reimagined as monsters to be faced in battle. The most notable of these reinventions are Chaosium's table-top role-playing games and the more recent Fantasy Flight *Arkham Horror* board game series, both of which pit players directly against Shoggoths, Hounds of Tindalos and even Cthulhu himself. With the roll of a dice, and a bit of luck, players might send the Weird monster back to the abyss.

At the intersection of Weird excess, pulp horror and fantasy game-playing, *Skulduggery Pleasant* and *The Power of Five* construct a Weird monstrous that is able to embody a number of competing functions, imagining a reader able to deftly navigate these shifts in the image of the monster. In *Skulduggery Pleasant*, for example, crisis and ontological horror blend with playful mockery. Many of the novels carry a humorous tag line. The cover of *Skulduggery Pleasant: The Faceless Ones* jokes, 'Do Panic. They're Coming', suggesting that not even the unimaginable horror of the Weird is immune to playful mockery. Both *The Power of Five* and *Skulduggery Pleasant* continually oscillate between possibilities for what Weird monsters can mean. On the one hand, they posit the Weird monster as crisis, but one that can be laughed or shot at, effectively dispatched with violence or humour. On the other hand, they continue to provoke ontological horror in their revelation of 'outer, unknown forces' utterly inimical to humanity (Lovecraft 1927).

The oscillating function of the Weird monster manifests as a series of encounters with and retreats from the objects of Weird reality. Neither *Skulduggery*'s humour nor the fantasy heroics of *The Power of Five* results in complete expulsion of the Weird monster. In *Nightrise*, Horowitz suggests that the defeat of Chaos is merely temporary, since time is 'circular' and 'the whole thing will begin again' (Horowitz 2007: 330–1). After the novel's epic battle scene, the spectacular visibility of Horowitz's Weird monstrous rapidly dissipates as the Old Ones retreat to the edges of the story and to the dark corners of perception. In *Necropolis*, the monsters are face-less, haunting the city crowds, but never revealing themselves. The protagonist notes, 'they were here, in Hong Kong . . . The Old Ones were toying with her. They were the ones who were controlling the crowd' (Horowitz 2009: 237). Here, the Weird monster retreats from the field of vision, where it can be diminished and dispatched, to a space beyond human perception.

The Weird monsters of *Skulduggery Pleasant* also remain an unsettling presence at the edges of the story. In *Dark Days*, the sequel to *The Faceless Ones*, Stephanie discovers that the defeated monsters lurk on the other side of a portal. They haunt an empty world, never fully manifesting but instead inhabiting the broken, decomposing body of their human victims. Travelling to this world to rescue a friend, Stephanie gains a disturbing reminder of the Weird monster's continuing power to disrupt reality:

> She staggered, feeling the goose-bumps ripple. The inside of her mouth was tight, dry skin and her beating heart was the drum it was stretched across. She stumbled over the body and fell, and now she was crawling. Her head was filled with deafening whispers. The Faceless Ones were coming. (Landy 2010: 97)

Stephanie successfully completes her rescue and returns safely home, though this time she elects to hide from the monsters rather than face them in battle. As she wryly notes, 'there wasn't a whole lot she could do against a Faceless One, except maybe distract it by dying loudly' (Landy 2010: 101–2). Mockery and spectacle have not robbed the Weird monster of its power to disturb. As real objects, Weird monsters are not simply relational, easily dispatched by the exertions of the hero. Nor are they only noumenal, existing beyond sense. Nor are they empty signifiers, pointing to a black hole beyond language. They are something more than these interpretations suggest. The nomadic protagonist propelled into a Weird universe encounters the monster as an oscillating presence, but which remains always to some extent in excess of the text's strategy to describe, contain, defeat and mock.

The Pleasures of Oblivion

Skulduggery Pleasant and *The Power of Five* offer a variation on the usual narrative found in Lovecraft's stories, in which an adult protagonist uncovers the terrifying truth about the universe. In *Skulduggery Pleasant* and *The Power of Five*, the discovery that 'en-Weirds' the universe is made by a child on the cusp of adolescence. Stephanie is twelve; Matt is fourteen and their rite of passage between childhood and maturity involves a shift into the Weird. In *Raven's Gate*, Matt leaves the care of his aunt and enters the LEAF project, a rehabilitation programme for young offenders. As well as struggling to come to terms with his adolescent abandonment issues, Matt has to cope with the discovery that his new foster carers are cultists who want to sacrifice him in order to bring the 'Old Ones' back into the world. The book begins with Matt travelling to Lesser Malling, a village modelled on Lovecraft's dilapidated and isolated New England hovel, Innsmouth, from 'The Shadow over Innsmouth' (1936). The unnatural woodland surrounding the village denotes the shift into the Weird as Matt notes that 'nature wasn't meant to grow like this' (Horowitz 2005: 86), recalling Lovecraft's description of the 'deep woods that no axe has ever cut' in West Arkham where 'the hills rise wild' (Lovecraft 1963: 176). Yet, it is not simply the movement into a Weird landscape that creates ontological horror. Rather, it is Matt's growing understanding that what he encounters in Lesser Malling will transform him forever. There is no escaping the terror of the Weird: 'The darkness was waiting for him. He was like a fly on the edge of a huge web' (Horowitz 2005: 86). Here, the Weird figures as a threshold that must be crossed as part of the maturation process, but crossing the threshold means entering the jaws of the monsters waiting on the other side, with no hope of triumph or return. The irruption of the Weird into these adolescent narratives disrupts the trajectory of growth and mastery typically associated with the adolescent hero. The epistemological horror evoked by the a priori existence of Weird monsters precludes the mastery of knowledge, while the en-Weirding of ontology disrupts the process of becoming and being. Hailed as Harry Potter-meets-Lovecraft, these novels offer a very different hero narrative in which knowledge is destructive and oblivion might be desirable.

Rather than engaging in the construction of identity, these Weird fantasies toy with the obliteration of the self. Weird monsters are predators, 'stalking' humans to obliterate in the void. When the Faceless Ones arrive in Stephanie's world, they immediately seek to possess human hosts. The process of possession is a brutal effacement of physical and psychic identity:

> His hair fell gently out, strand by strand, and his head tilted upwards in time for Valkyrie to see his face melting. The nose and the ears were first to go, sinking back into the skin. The lips congealed, sealing the mouth, and the eyes turned to liquid and dripped from the sockets down either cheek, like tears. The eyelids closed and ran into each other. The Faceless Ones had taken their first vessel. (Landy 2009: 353–4)

Following the depiction of cultists in Lovecraft's stories and in contemporary mythos fictions, those who offer themselves up to the Faceless Ones are consumed by a power that transcends man. One does not even have to be possessed by a Faceless One to be swallowed by the void, a mere glimpse is enough to result in a 'broken' mind (Landy 2009: 373). In *The Power of Five* even the heroes destined to fight the Old Ones can become their prey. Scott's experiences as a prisoner of the Old Ones result in a disturbing change to his personality, manifesting in moments of utter blankness: 'He stood where he was, frozen to the spot. He wasn't even blinking. Matt could see his chest heaving and his whole hands seemed to be locked in place' (Horowitz 2009: 111). As the story climaxes, Matt realises that he cannot trust Scott, seeing in him a growing coldness and cruelty (Horowitz 2009: 128). This function of the Weird monster indicates a concern with the fragility of identity, particularly relevant for texts charting the process of maturation. Thus, unlike other children's texts celebrating a hero's gradual mastery of a magical world (in particular the texts that prefigure the twenty-first-century period I am exploring, including the *Harry Potter* novels and *His Dark Materials*), the formulation of the adolescent's identity is here en-Weirded, corrupted in its encounter with Weird reality.

The Weird creates tension with the developing hero narrative, resulting in a fissured text that will not settle on one definitive trajectory for the hero protagonist. In contrast to the hero narrative, which also informs these narratives, there is no 'boon' for the triumphant hero, here, nor any chance of reintegrating into normal society (Campbell 2008: 29). In *The Power of Five*, Matt occupies the position of hero and fights the forces of the Weird. He is no hapless researcher helpless in the face of his discoveries and is actually able to defeat the Old Ones in the final instalment in the series, *Oblivion* (2012). However, as Matt becomes increasingly heroic, he is *used up* rather than invigorated, losing his drive and fight the closer he comes to the end. At the climax of the novel, Matt surrenders to his fate to be sacrificed (a fate that, in the first novel, he fought bitterly to avoid) in order to finally expel the Old Ones. As his companion notes: 'Matt had changed . . . the two of them were complete strangers. It was as if everything they had been through together had somehow been left behind' (Horowitz 2012: 584). As a character, Matt fades during the second half of this latter book, becoming more like a Lovecraft protagonist: his individual psychology dissipates as he gives himself up in a 'surrender to the ineluctability of the Weird' (Miéville 2009: 512). In terms of fulfilling the conditions of the adolescent hero narrative, Matt actually rejects maturation, finding only oblivion in his last act of triumph. In a postscript, we learn that Matt finds an existence of sorts in a dream world beyond reality. While it is tempting to read in this the consolations of transcendence offered in Campbell's treatment of the hero myth, the dominant maturation narrative is thwarted. Matt never grows up.

Stephanie's fate is equally precarious as the *Skulduggery Pleasant* series progresses. She, too, is engaged in a battle for her sense of self, with an amoral magical being, Darquesse, who intermittently usurps her identity and takes over her body. The threat of dissolution and evacuation of self-hood is constant throughout, brought out by the inclusion of Weird elements into the traditional hero narrative. The threat of oblivion suggests that Landy and Horowitz imagine a child reader who doesn't want happy endings, healing, or a mature sense of self. The series offer neither maturation, nor a fortunate fall, but rather a wilful surrender according with Miéville's view that Weird fiction offers 'radical humility' rather than Promethean power (Miéville 2009: 512). However, Matt and Stephanie's surrender to the Weird also expresses a *desire for* trauma as much as a resistance to it. As her fight with the otherworldly alter ego progresses, Stephanie admits to herself how 'good' it feels to let Darquesse 'take over' (Landy 2013: 62). Other pop-cultural manifestations of the Weird also offer this reading. *South Park*'s Cartman revels in his new-found friendship with Cthulhu, and fake religious tracts can be found online offering advice on how to hasten the demise of humanity by gleefully worshipping Lovecraft's Old Ones (Van Lente and Ellis 2000; Parker 2010). These texts reveal that there is humour and pleasure, rather than humility and dissolution, available in a surrender to the Weird.

Children's Weird fiction is characterised by contradictory impulses and oscillating monsters, creating fissured texts that allows for multiple readings. The narrative's movement towards oblivion competes with a desire for mastery and status. Ontological terror, on the one hand, also produces epistemological wonder and subcultural inclusion on the other. Abject and grotesque horror, denoting the limits of signification, likewise also offers an indulgent spectacle of Weird objects. These texts do not simply recreate the haute Weird of the early twentieth century: they remake it. As the 'shrieking madness' of Cthulhu referenced in *Scooby Doo!* threatens to become a twenty-first-century cliché, Landy and Horowitz develop a new form of Weird that manages to retain its bleak horror alongside new functions. Not least of these is the way the Weird transforms traditional narratives of maturation and mastery, countering the linear narratives popular in earlier children's fantasies. Yet, an encounter with the Weird does not lead to the oblivion, or black hole, of deconstructive psychoanalysis. Rather, it offers a complete deterritorialisation that connects the nomadic subject with the Weird substances of reality. Encounters with these Weird substances imagine a vitalised nomadic subject. Weird monsters connect the self to materiality and serve as reminders of 'the immanent power of corporeality in all matter' (Deleuze and Guattari 2013: 479). Though Weird writing points to the gaps between reality and perception, between objects and their surfaces, this gap is *productionist*, not *deconstructionist*. Weird writing does not aim at a real 'outside', of course, but engages in the production of a fictional space in which the nomad can experience new realities within and beyond the interior of their subjective experience.

Notes

1. Rosemary Jackson argues that the genre of high fantasy, typified in works by J. R. R. Tolkien, C. S. Lewis or Ursula le Guin, offers a nostalgic, humanist vision in which dark 'others' are defeated (1981: 1, 5, 90).
2. As discussed in the introduction, Jackson, Coats and McGillis express this concept of the Gothic when discussing why it is suited to the project of children's literature (2008: 8). Chris Baldick dates this tradition of 'anti-Gothicism' in Gothic back to the eighteenth century, where often writers borrowed the 'nightmares of a past age in order to repudiate their authority' (1992: xiii–xiv).
3. See, for example, the *South Park* episode titled 'Mysterion Rises' in which Eric Cartman evokes Cthulhu and has him kill Justin Bieber onstage during a live performance (Parker 2010).

Francis Hardinge's *The Lie Tree* and Beyond

In the introduction, I suggested that *A Series of Unfortunate Events*, published at the beginning of the twenty-first century, refigured the child in Gothic fiction as a nomad, whose journey across an expansive terrain engages with, rather than rejects, an irredeemably corrupt world. This reading is at odds with Danel Olson's assessment of the series in *21st-Century Gothic: Great Gothic Novels Since 2000*. Olson suggests that *A Series of Unfortunate Events* opens and closes with 'despair', offering only an 'unlikely' hope in its final image of the Baudelaire orphans setting sail (2010: 521, 522). Olson emphasises the melancholic aspects of the series to mark the work as a 'Gothic Goodbye' (2010: 506). This reading echoes many other melancholic and deconstructive approaches dominating contemporary Gothic criticism. In contrast, I suggest that *A Series of Unfortunate Events* marks the beginning of a period of proliferation, of innovation, and diversification in Gothic as it expands productively through the terrain of children's literature and culture. The nomadic impulse of *A Series of Unfortunate Events* asks readers to make a different assessment of the Gothic, suggesting an affirmative function for this darkest of cultural modes in the twenty-first century. These books are an invitation to explore and remap the terrain of Gothic in children's fiction. It is a journey that has taken me from the explicitly 'uncanny' house of *Coraline* to the post-apocalyptic landscape of *Zom-B*; from romantically reconstructed past worlds in *Coram Boy* and *Ruined* to the gleefully inauthentic Gothic stage-sets of *Pararnorman* and *Frankenweenie*; finally, I made contact with the strange material substances of the Weird universe as revealed by *Skulduggery Pleasant* and *The Power of Five*. These diverse Gothic works and locations reimagine the child and challenge critical conceptions of both Children's and Gothic fiction.

Though the works I have explored are still largely ignored by Gothic Studies, children's Gothic continues to attain status and significance in wider culture. The importance and influence of children's Gothic is evidenced by the 2015 UK Costa Book of the Year, which was awarded to Frances Hardinge's *The Lie Tree*, a neo-Victorian Gothic novel written for children and young adults. The only other children's book to win the overall prize is Philip Pullman's *The Amber Spyglass* in 2001, one of the 'dark fantasy' forerunners of twenty-first-century children's Gothic. Hardinge's book echoes many of the themes and concerns of Pullman's fantasy, namely the excoriation of dogmatic religious authority. However, Hardinge's explicitly feminist Gothic tale employs many of the strategies of nomadism identified throughout this book, and eschews the idea that Gothic is solely the cultural expression of anxiety, or else a marginal form that critiques and deconstructs. Hardinge's protagonist, Faith Sunderly, is a mobile, active subject, determined to transform herself and her society. The critical and popular success of Hardinge's novel points to the ascension of children's Gothic, particularly in the UK, as a creative mode that imagines new ways of becoming. At the close of the twentieth century, Mark Edmundson suggested that the Western 'culture of Gothic' functioned as the expression of fear and haunting, providing a counterweight to stories of 'easy transcendence' offered by sentimental cultural narratives (1999: 5, xvii). However, Edmundson's social anxiety reading of Gothic no longer holds as the twenty-first century progresses. In children's fiction, at least, Gothic does not express latent or growing cultural anxieties, but is a creative force through which to imagine positive self-transformation and productive interconnections with others. I want to spend some time briefly exploring Hardinge's novel as the latest manifestation of this creativity. The many tendrils of *The Lie Tree* connect and incorporate the strategies and images of nomadism that I have identified elsewhere in children's Gothic.

The Lie Tree offers an image of the female grotesque in its depiction of Faith and the other women on the island of Vane, where the story is set. The women of the novel perform precarious identities that allow them to push against the constraints of Victorian society.

For example, Faith's mother Myrtle is a practised flirt, a talent that she makes expedient use of when her husband dies leaving the family friendless and without income. Later, Myrtle explicitly acknowledges the performative nature of her femininity, noting that the restrictions of her life have 'made me what I am. When every door is closed, one learns to climb through windows' (Hardinge 2015: 402). Faith recognises that her mother is playing a dangerous game. Another unmarried woman, Miss Hunter, has her house burned to the ground after rumours that she is in league with treasure hunters and thieves reach the islanders. Faith realises that Miss Hunter is defiant, but that there is 'a tightrope beneath her feet' (2015: 404). In this novel, female performances are risky. Faith takes on various roles (grieving daughter, counterfeit ghost, hooded spy) in order to move about the island of Vane and investigate her father's death, but she is continually aware of being 'nothing but a paper girl, and could be torn apart if she was discovered' (2015: 318). Faith's female grotesquerie is not the bodily gross-out of Darren Shan's pulp horror, but it is freakish nonetheless. Her reluctant compatriot, Paul calls her a 'crazy woman . . . You're ripe for Bedlam, but somehow I keep believing what you say' (2015: 343). In fact, Faith's daring performances inspire as well as repulse Paul, who later confesses his desire to create his own 'line of flight' and become a photographer of 'faraway places' (2015: 407). As a female grotesque, Faith is in danger, but she is also 'a bad example' whose line of flight might create opportunities for others.

The Lie Tree imagines subjectivity as contingent, adaptable and continually in process. Throughout, characters take on different identities that allow them to negotiate the restrictions of their social location and the impulses of their desires. Just as Coraline uses the strategy of 'protective coloration' to fool the 'other mother' in the climactic scenes of Neil Gaiman's novel, Faith deliberately performs submissiveness and a lack of intelligence to become invisible among the male scientific community. Such invisibility affords her a degree of mobility. Like Coraline, Faith creeps about at night and listens at doors. She moves between social spaces and temporalities, receiving visions of the recent and ancient past when she consumes the fruit of the Lie Tree. Faith's symbiotic connection to the tree empowers her to break the circumscribed bounds of the territories normally reserved for her in feminine domestic society. Like Rebecca in *Ruined*, Faith finds herself in locations usually barred to those of her class and gender. In one scene she boldy attends a 'ratting' with the working men of the island, feeling 'neither squeamish nor powerless' (Hardinge 2015: 287). Like Rebecca in *Ruined*, Faith is mobile despite the fact she also plays the part of an incarcerated Gothic heroine. In fact, Faith takes on many identities: Faith the detective, Faith the dutiful daughter, Faith the 'madwoman', Faith the avenger. By the close of the story, Faith rejects all of these for a more amorphous and nebulous subjectivity: 'These other selves all seemed lifetimes away. Faith barely knew what she might say to any of them' (Hardinge 2015: 386–7). At the end, she has shed her previous selves like the skin of the snake, revealing 'new colours, vibrant and unabashed' (Hardinge 2015: 403). This new self is nomadic, open to the continual possibilities of change and transformation.

Like other texts I have considered, *The Lie Tree* weaves elements of Gothic Romance and romantic fiction into its narrative, balancing its ostensibly rational, Enlightenment manifesto of social and scientific progress with a dark kernel of supernatural mystery and indulgent romance. Although Faith rejects her father's religion in favour of the discipline of the natural sciences, the powers of the mysterious Lie Tree refuse explanation by either science or religion. Like Rebecca in *Ruined*, Faith must act upon knowledge that is not necessarily rational nor scientifically acquired, if she is to defeat her enemies and solve the mysteries of the plot. The novel also celebrates the interpersonal connections of romantic fiction, asking Faith to open herself to others, including the young photographer, Paul, despite the risk involved. Though Faith feels vulnerable when she places her trust in Paul, she forms a connection with him that extends her ability to act in the world. Here, as in *Coram Boy*, romantic connections might be dangerous and painful, but they are also necessary if the nomadic subject is to push at the boundaries of its surrounding territory. As in *Ruined*, the romance between the male and female characters opens up a connection that lasts beyond the close of the book. Though Faith leaves the island of Vane, she promises to write to Paul, suggesting that their different lines of flight will rely on sustaining their interpersonal connection.

Moreover, *The Lie Tree* embraces the rhizomatic nature of twenty-first-century Gothic intertextuality in the way that it equates telling lies (or stories) to the process of becoming. The novel's treatment of lies and stories recalls both *Haroun and the Sea of Stories* and *A Series of Unfortunate Events*, which I discussed in the introduction. Some lies, or stories, confine Faith, while others expand her territory of becoming, allowing her to try out different identities, to 'shed herself like a snake's skin and slide away to be somebody new' (Hardinge 2015: 309). The Lie Tree grows as Faith tells lies and spreads them across the island. The descriptions of the tree's inexplicably growing tendrils recall Deleuze and Guattari's concept of the rhizome. They assert that a book is rhizomatic, spreading out many roots to produce multiple meanings. The book does not reflect the world mimetically, but converges with multiple other objects, discourses, organisations of power and semiotic chains (Deleuze and Guattari 2013: 10). Similarly, the Lie Tree expands through its cave, a 'mass of writhing black creeper, so dense and dark that it looked like a portal into an abyss. Huge, muscular wooden vines arched and weaved among the black tendrils, like sigils in some vegetable language' (Hardinge 2015: 391). The overlapping tendrils of the tree create an abyss, a portal, into multiple stories. Like the tree, the book is rhizomatic, tracing many tangents and forging many connections to other works and ideas, refusing a totalising reading. Its 'sigils' are not easy to decipher. Echoing the uncanny imagery of *Coraline*, the tree is also likened to a 'many-legged spider', another image that suggests the weaving interconnections out of which the novel is formed (Hardinge 2015: 282). Within the narrative, Faith comes expresses the tenets of intertextuality expressed by Barthes's 'The Death of the Author'. Once her lies are told, they grow outward in ways she does not necessarily expect and certainly cannot control: 'Some lies took hold and spread, crackling with excitement, and no longer needed to be fed. But then these were no longer your lies. They had a life and shape of their own, and there was no controlling them' (Hardinge 2015: 278). If the story is a rhizome, there can be no controlling didactic or pedagogical intent, and its meaning cannot be mapped easily onto a linear narrative of maturation and development.

Finally, like *A Series of Unfortunate Events*, *The Lie Tree* begins and closes on the ocean. Here, the ending is also a beginning as Faith sets sail with her mother, intending to return home. As they stand on deck, looking out to the ocean, the pair discuss their future. In this moment, poised on the edge of the smooth space of the sea, possibilities emerge. Faith voices her desire to become a female natural scientist and though 'the words sounded fragile as soon as they were out in the air' they nonetheless chart a line of flight, mapping a new space of becoming for Faith, and, those who might follow her (2015: 407). In this moment, Hardinge's feminist manifesto is most explicit. Faith wants to 'help evolution' by mutating, so that she may also transform the world around her (2015: 407). The novel recognises that this mutation will be difficult, perhaps painful, forging Faith into something grotesque. However, such 'bad examples' are also necessary if mobility is to be possible. Echoing the affirmative tone of *Frankenweenie* and *Paranorman*, *The Lie Tree* celebrates Faith's naïve desire to become something impossible. It also concludes with a journey home, and with the healing of familial relationships once fraught and fractured. Faith and her mother reconcile, and Faith is now determined to involve herself in a society she once felt she had no place in.

Throughout this book, I have argued that twenty-first-century children's Gothic constructs new and multiple figurations of the child beyond the limiting pedagogical framework of traditional humanist and ego-relational concepts of children's literature. At the same time, the nomadic subject of this Gothic fiction refuses the melancholic cast of much criticism in Gothic Studies, imagining instead vibrant, embodied, desiring subjectivities that refuse the aporia, or black hole, of deconstructive criticism in its various forms. My work in this neglected area of cultural production asks critics to think of new ways of accounting for the Gothic. Though, at times, they seem to express contradictory impulses, children's fiction and the Gothic open a productive space of mutual transformation in our twenty-first-century moment. Where these fictions evoke the Gothic as a transgressive or unsettling force, they imagine a child subjectivity outside the confines of a limiting pedagogical framework. These fictions also subvert the linear teleology of maturation favoured in accounts of children's literature that draw on the theories of ego-relational psychology. However, when Gothic is remapped by playful children's fiction, it becomes an inclusive space that enfolds both the cultural centre and its margins. Such pop-cultural children's fictions call out Gothic criticism's investment in 'authenticity' and subcultural capital, reclaiming previously maligned forms of feminine and popular culture as valid spaces for the nomadic project.

Nomadic subjectivity is particularly apposite for our current social and cultural moment because it defies dualistic and oppositional thinking that divides and distances subjects in an increasingly fragmented social imaginary. Rosi Braidotti notes that the current historical moment is one of upheaval and transition, in which society and culture is in the process of being reshaped by postcolonial politics, by the feminist movement, by the emergence of queer identities and by the flows of globalisation. Her project of nomadic subjectivity aims to give expression to emerging subjects-in-process and new patterns of becoming (2011a: 8). My mapping of the nomadic figurations of the child in twenty-first-century Gothic is a small contribution to this wider cultural and theoretical project. The nomadic subject of children's fiction is just one means whereby writers and readers might negotiate the fragmentary and often contradictory nature of post-modern culture. The children's fiction explored here offers a mode of representation that imagines 'the sort of subjects we are in the process of becoming' (Braidotti 2011a: 11). As I have shown, these Gothic texts reject a modernist aesthetic for culture, finding sites of empowerment and transformation within postmodern commodity culture itself. Through parody, poaching and reappropriation, the nomadic subject mobilises itself within the power relations of contemporary culture. This nomadic subject also resists hierarchical and oppressive pedagogical models, and offers inclusive and expansive modes of reading.

My heterogeneous critical approach traces twenty-first-century Gothic fiction through its multiple manifestations, each offering its own figuration of nomadic subjectivity. These nomadic subjects emerge through intertextual connections and interrelationships between cultural discourse, popular commentary, critical theory and fiction itself. The character of Coraline points to a concept of subjectivity beyond the narratives of psychoanalysis that have dominated accounts of children's Gothic to date. Beyond this explicitly 'uncanny' Gothic, Darren Shan's *Zom-B* offers a subversive figuration of the child in the grotesque body of the zombie. The zombie nomad is not a middle-class, teachable body; it resists the processes of identification as they are currently theorised within children's literature criticism. Where grotesquerie and gross-out characterise this pulp-horror form of children's Gothic, other recent fictions embrace the wish-fulfilment appeals of Romance. In *Ruined* and *Coram Boy*, the vital force of desire propels the nomad to form productive and transformative relationships with others. Parodic Gothic horror film likewise embraces the transformative potential of the Gothic, imagining a naïve viewing child who can respond affectively to the 'inauthentic' recreations onscreen, bringing together the margin and mainstream in a process of mutual transformation. In Weird fiction, the nomadic subject moves beyond the interiority of the 'I' to encounters with material objects of reality. In this Weird space, the linear maturation of humanist accounts of subjectivity become impossible, and oblivion is desirable. In all of these imaginative spaces, the nomadic subject emerges through its relationships with other subjects and other things. This nomad is thus something quite different to the isolated wanderers of early Gothic fiction; it represents the positive potential of engagement with difference and otherness.

What I have presented herein is not a totalising account of twenty-first-century children's Gothic, which is a body of work still very much in process. Nor do I offer a universal argument about the cultural function of this form. Rather, I explore just some of the ways that children's Gothic reimagines pedagogy, reading and subjectivity in the early twenty-first century. Rather like Lemony Snicket's *The End*, I offer this conclusion as an invitation for further explorations of Gothic cultural production for children. As in Braidotti's account of nomadic subjectivity, 'there is no possible conclusion, only more productive proliferations' (2011a: 13). The project of nomadic thought is ongoing and looks to the future as a space of yet more exploration and productive dialogue. Nomadic thought, like the nomadic subject itself, aims for 'a forward-moving horizon that lies ahead . . . between the no longer and the not yet . . . [it] traces the possible patterns of becoming' (Braidotti 2011a: 205–6). In this book the 'no longer' is represented by staid critical approaches such as the monologising account of children's literature offered by psychoanalysis, the aporia of deconstructive accounts of the Gothic and by the melancholic cast of the 'linguistic turn' more generally. The 'not yet' is a space of possibility towards which the nomadic subject travels. Indeed, children's fiction is perhaps the most fitting space in which writers and critics can take up the project of mapping nomadic subjectivity. It is a mode of writing that imagines, both within and without the text, a subject in process. It figures being as becoming without recourse to the teleology of maturation; its movement is future-directed and open-ended.

Works Cited

Adams, Tim (2012), 'Tim Burton: The Love and Life and Death Stuff Was Stewing from the Start', *The Guardian*, 7 October, <http://www.theguardian.com/film/2012/oct/07/tim-burton-frankenweenie-interview> (last accessed 15 March 2017).

Allen, Graham (2002), *Intertextuality*, London: Routledge.

Ariès, Philippe (1973), *Centuries of Childhood*, Harmondsworth: Penguin.

Austen, Jane [1817] (1995), *Northanger Abbey*, London: Penguin.

Bakhtin, Mikhail Mikhaïlovich (1981), *The Dialogic Imagination: Four Essays by M. M. Bakhtin*, ed. Michael Holquist, trans. Caryl Emerson and Michael Holquist, Austin: University of Texas Press.

Bakhtin, Mikhail Mikhaïlovich (1984a), *Rabelais and His World*, trans. Helene Iswolsky, Bloomington: Indiana University Press.

Bakhtin, Mikhail Mikhaïlovich (1984b), *Problems of Dostoevsky's Poetics*, trans. Caryl Emerson, Minneapolis: University of Minnesota Press.

Baldick, Chris (1992), 'Introduction', in *The Oxford Book of Gothic Tales*, ed. C. Baldick, Oxford: Oxford University Press, pp. xi–xxiii.

Banks, Iain (1998), *The Wasp Factory*, New York: Simon & Schuster.

Barthes, Roland (1974), *S/Z: An Essay*, trans. Richard Howard, New York: Hill & Wang.

Barthes, Roland (1977), *Image, Music, Text*, ed. and trans. Stephen Heath, London: Fontana.

Baudrillard, Jean (1994), *Simulacra and Simulation*, Ann Arbor: University of Michigan Press.

Bauman, Bruce (2006), 'Lilith in Wunderland', in *Alice Redux: New Stories of Alice, Lewis, and Wonderland*, ed. Richard Peabody, Arlington: Paycock Press, pp. 109–12.

Becker, Susanne (1999), *Gothic Forms of Feminine Fictions*, Manchester: Manchester University Press.

Berger, John (1972), *Ways of Seeing*, London: Penguin.

Beville, Maria (2009), *Gothic-Postmodernism: Voicing the Terrors of Postmodernity*, New York: Rodopi.

Billson, Anne (2009) 'March of the Zombie', *The Guardian*, 1 June, <http://www.theguardian.com/film/2009/jun/01/zombie-horror-film-doghouse> (last accessed 28 February 2017).

Bishop, Kyle (2009), 'Dead Man Still Walking: Explaining the Zombie Renaissance', *Journal of Popular Film and Television,* 37 (1), 16–25.

Bloom, Clive (1996), *Cult Fiction: Popular Reading and Pulp Theory*, New York: Palgrave Macmillan.

Blum, Virginia (1995), *Hide and Seek: The Child Between Psychoanalysis and Fiction*, Urbana: University of Illinois Press.

Bond, Matthew (2012), 'Dr Burton's Gothic Horror Has a Heart', *The Daily Mail*, 22 October, <http://www.dailymail.co.uk/tvshowbiz/article-2221392/Frankenweenie-movie-review-Tim-Burtons-gothic-horror-heart.html> (last accessed 15 March 2017).

Botting, Fred (1996), *Gothic*, London: Routledge.

Botting, Fred (2001) 'In Gothic Darkly: Heterotopia, History, Culture', in *A Companion to the Gothic*, ed. David Punter, Oxford: Blackwell, pp. 3–14.

Botting, Fred (2002), 'Aftergothic: Consumption, Machines, and Black Holes', in *The Cambridge Companion to Gothic Fiction*, ed. J. Hogle, Cambridge: Cambridge University Press, pp. 277–300.

Botting, Fred (2008a), *Gothic Romanced: Consumption, Gender and Technology in Contemporary Fictions*, London: Routledge.

Botting, Fred (2008b), *Limits of Horror: Technology, Bodies, Gothic*, Manchester: Manchester University Press.

Botting, Fred (2012a), 'Love Your Zombie Horror, Ethics, Excess', in *The Gothic in Contemporary Literature and Popular Culture: Pop Goth*, ed. Justin D. Edwards and Agnieszka Soltysik Monnet, New York: Routledge, pp. 19–36.

Botting, Fred (2012b), 'More Things: Horror, Materialism and Speculative Weirdism', *Horror Studies* 3 (2), 281–303.

Botting, Fred (2013), 'Zombie Questions for Global Gothic: From White Zombie to World War Z', in *Globalgothic*, ed. Glennis Byron, Manchester: Manchester University Press.

Botting, Fred (2014), 'Post-Millennial Monsters: Monstrosity-No-More', in *The Gothic World*, ed. Glennis Byron and Dale Townshend, London: Routledge, pp. 498–509.

Braidotti, Rosi (2011a), *Nomadic Subjects: Embodiment and Sexual Difference in Contemporary Feminist Theory*, 2nd edn, New York: Columbia University Press.

Braidotti, Rosi (2011b), *Nomadic Theory: The Portable Rosi Braidotti*, New York: Columbia University Press.

Brockes, Emma (2011), 'Maurice Sendak: "I Refuse to Lie to Children"', *The Guardian*, 2 October, <http://www.guardian.co.uk/books/2011/oct/02/maurice-sendak-interview> (last accessed 18 September 2016).

Bryant, Levi R, Nick Srnicek, and Graham Harman (2011), 'Towards a Speculative Philosophy', in *The Speculative Turn: Continental Materialism and Realism*, ed. Levi Bryant, Nick Srnicek and Graham Harman, Melbourne: re.press, pp. 1–18.

Buckley, Chloé (2014), 'Gothic and the Child Reader, 1850–Present', in *The Gothic World*, ed. G. Byron and D. Townshend, London: Routledge, pp. 254–63.

Burton, Tim (2012), *Frankenweenie*.

Burton, Tim, and Mark Salisbury (2006), *Burton on Burton Revised Edition*, London: Faber & Faber.

Butler, Chris, and Sam Fell (2012), *Paranorman*.

Campbell, Joseph (2008), *The Hero with a Thousand Faces*, Novato, CA: New World Library.

Carrington, Victoria (2012), 'The Contemporary Gothic: Literacy and Childhood in Unsettled Times', *Journal of Early Childhood Literacy*, 12:3, 293–310.

Carroll, Lewis [1865] (1982), *Alice's Adventures in Wonderland and Through the Looking Glass*, ed. Roger Lancelyn Green, Oxford: Oxford University Press.

Carter, Angela [1974] (1981), *Fireworks: Nine Stories in Various Disguises*, London: Harper & Row.

Chambers, Aidan (1985), 'The Reader in the Book', from *Booktalk: occasional writing on literature and children*, Stroud: Thimble, pp. 34–58.

Chaplin, Sue (2013), 'Gothic Romance 1760–1830', in *The Gothic World*, ed. Dale Townshend and Glennis Byron, London: Routledge, pp. 199–209.

Chilton, Martin (2012), '*Zom-B* by Darren Shan, Review', *The Telegraph*, 28 September, <http://www.telegraph.co.uk/culture/books/children_sbookreviews/9568888/Zom-B-by-Darren-Shan-review.html> (last accessed 25 February 2017).

Christian-Smith, Linda (1987), 'Gender, Popular Culture, and Curriculum: Adolescent Romance Novels as Gender Text', *Curriculum Inquiry* 17 (4), 365–406.

Cixous, Hélène (1976), 'Fiction and Its Phantoms: A Reading of Freud's *Das Unheimliche* (The "uncanny")', *New Literary History* 7 (3), 525–48, 619–45.

Clery, E. J. (1995), *The Rise of Supernatural Fiction, 1762–1800*, Cambridge: Cambridge University Press.

Coats, Karen (2008), 'Between Horror, Humour and Hope: Neil Gaiman and the Psychic Work of the Gothic', in *The Gothic in Children's Literature: Haunting the Borders*, ed. A. Jackson, K. Coats and R. McGillis, New York: Routledge, pp. 77–92.

Cocks, Neil (2004), 'The Implied Reader. Response and Responsibility: Theories of the Implied Reader in Children's Literature Criticism', in *Children's Literature New Approaches*, ed. Karín Lesnik-Oberstein, Basingstoke: Palgrave Macmillan, pp. 93–117.

Cogan Thacker, Deborah, and Jean Webb (2002), *Introducing Children's Literature: From Romanticism to Postmodernism*, London: Routledge.

Cook, Victor (2010), 'The Shrieking Madness', *Scooby-Doo! Mystery Incorporated*.

Coykendall, Abby (2005), 'Gothic Genealogies, the Family Romance, and Clara Reeve's *The Old English Baron*', *Eighteenth-Century Fiction* 17 (3), 443–80.

Cranny-Francis, Anne (1990), *Feminist Fiction: Feminist Uses of Genre Fiction*, Cambridge: Polity Press.

Crawford, Joseph (2014), *The Twilight of the Gothic: Vampire Fiction and the Rise of the Paranormal Romance*, Cardiff: University of Wales Press.

Creed, Barbara (1993), *The Monstrous-Feminine: Film, Feminism, Psycho-analysis*, London: Routledge.

Day, William Patrick (1985), *In the Circles of Fear and Desire: A Study of Gothic Fantasy*, Chicago: University of Chicago Press.

de Certeau, Michel (1984), *The Practice of Everyday Life*, trans. Steven Rendall, Berkeley: University of California Press.

DeLamotte, Eugenia C. (1990), *Perils of the Night. A Feminist Study of Nineteenth-Century Gothic*, Oxford: Oxford University Press.

Deleuze, Gilles (1992), 'What is a *dispositif?*', in *Michel Foucault Philosopher*, trans. Timothy J. Armstrong, New York: Routledge, pp. 159–68.

Deleuze, Gilles, and Félix Guattari [1987] (2013), *A Thousand Plateaus*, London: Bloomsbury.

Dendle, Peter (2007), 'The Zombie as barometer of cultural anxiety', in *Monsters and the Monstrous*, ed. Niall Scott, New York: Rodopi, pp. 45–57.

Derrida, Jacques (1979), *Spurs: Nietzsche's Styles*, Chicago: University of Chicago Press.

Derrida, Jacques (1995), 'Passages – from Traumatism to Promise', in *Points . . . : Interviews, 1974–1994*, ed. Elisabeth Weber, Stanford: Stanford University Press, pp. 372–95.

Dickens, Charles [1853], 'Frauds on the Fairies', in *Household Words*, <http://www.victorianweb.org/authors/dickens/pva/pva239.html> (last accessed 18 September 2016).

Doherty, Thomas (2006), 'The Wonderful World of Disney Studies', *Chronicle of Higher Education* 52 (46), 57.

DuPlessis, Rachel Blau (1985), *Writing Beyond the Ending: Narrative Strategies of Twentieth-Century Women Writers*, Bloomington: Indiana University Press.

Eco, Umberto (1994), *Reflections on the Name of the Rose*, London: Minerva Press.

Edmundson, Mark (1999), *Nightmare on Main Street: Angels, Sadomasochism, and the Culture of Gothic*, Cambridge, MA: Harvard University Press.

Elliott, Kamilla (2007), 'Gothic – Film – Parody', in *The Routledge Companion to Gothic*, ed. Catherine Spooner and Emma McEvoy, Oxford: Routledge, pp. 223–32.

Elliott, Kamilla (2008), 'Gothic – Film – Parody', *Adaptation* 1 (1), 24–43.

Errigo, Angie (2012), '*Frankenweenie*: Tim Burton's Pet (Semetary) Project', *Empire Online*, 17 October, <http://www.empireonline.com/reviews/review.asp?FID=137415> (last accessed 16 March 2017).

Felman, Shoshana (1982), 'To Open the Question', in *Literature and Psychoanalysis: The Question of Reading Otherwise*, Baltimore: The Johns Hopkins University Press, pp. 5–10.

Ferguson Ellis, Kate (1989), *The Contested Castle: Gothic Novels and The Subversion of Domestic Ideology*, Urbana; Chicago: University of Illinois Press.

Ferguson Ellis, Kate (2001), 'Can You Forgive Her? The Gothic Heroine and Her Critics', in *A Companion to the Gothic*, ed. David Punter, Oxford: Blackwell, pp. 257–68.

Finlo, Rohrer (2009), 'How Do You Make Children's Films Appeal to Adults?' *BBC Magazine*, 16 December, <http://news.bbc.co.uk/1/hi/8415003.stm> (last accessed 16 March 2017).

Flint, David (2009), *Zombie Holocaust: How the Living Dead Devoured Pop Culture*, London: Plexus.

Flood, Alison (2014), 'Charlie Higson: "Kids Should Have Nightmares. They Should Be Scared of Things"', *The Guardian*, 13 December, <http://www.theguardian.com/books/2014/dec/13/charlie-higson-enemy-young-bond-interview> (last accessed 18 September 2016).

Fournier, Matt (2014), 'Lines of Flight', *TSQ: Transgender Studies Quarterly* 1 (1–2), 121–2.

Freud, Sigmund [1919] (1955) 'The uncanny', in *The Standard Edition of the Complete Psychological Works of Sigmund Freud XVII*, trans. James Strachey, Alix Strachey and Alan Tyson, London: The Hogarth Press, pp. 219–52.

Funk, Wolfgang, Florian Gross and Irmtraud Huber (2012), *The Aesthetics of Authenticity: Medial Constructions of the Real*, Bielefeld: Transcript.

Gaiman, Neil (1990), *The Doll's House (Sandman Collected Library)*, DC Comics.

Gaiman, Neil (2002), *Coraline*, London: Bloomsbury.

Gavin, Jamila (2000), *Coram Boy*, London: Mammoth.

Gavin, Jamila (2011), 'Coram Boy as History', *Jamila Gavin: News and Views*, 14 October, <https://jamilagavin.wordpress.com/history/coram-boy-as-history/> (last accessed 10 March 2017).

Gilbert, Sandra M. and Susan Gubar (2000), *The Madwoman in the Attic: The Woman Writer and the Nineteenth-Century Literary Imagination*, 2nd edn, New Haven: Yale University Press.

Gonzalez-Tennant, Edward (2013), 'Pedagogy, Engaged Anthropology, and Zombies', 5 December, <http://www.gonzaleztennant.net/2013/12/05/zombies_course/> (last accessed 20 February 2017).

Gooderham, David (2003), 'Fantasizing It As It Is: Religious Language in Philip Pullman's Trilogy, *His Dark Materials*', *Children's Literature*, 31, 155–75.

Gooding, Richard (2008), '"Something Very Old and Very Slow": *Coraline*, Uncanniness, and Narrative Form', *Children's Literature Association Quarterly*, 33 (4), 390–407.

Grazian, David (2005), *Blue Chicago: The Search for Authenticity in Urban Blues Clubs*, Chicago: University of Chicago Press.

Grazian, David (2010), 'Demystifying Authenticity in the Sociology of Culture', in *Handbook of Cultural Sociology*, ed. John R. Hall, Laura Grindstaff and Lo Ming-Cheng, New York: Routledge, pp. 191–200.

Greer, Germaine (2006), *The Female Eunuch*, London: Harper Perennial.

Grenby, Matthew (2014), 'Gothic and the Child Reader 1764–1840', in *The Gothic World*, ed. G. Byron and D. Townshend, London: Routledge, pp. 243–54.

Griffiths, Sarah Jane (2012) 'Tim Burton: "I've Never Made a Scary Movie"', *BBC*, 17 October, <http://www.bbc.co.uk/news/entertainment-arts-19923076> (last accessed 15 March 2017).

Halberstam, Jack (1998), *Female Masculinities*, Durham, NC: Duke University Press.

Hardinge, Frances (2015), *The Lie Tree*, London: Macmillan.

Harman, Graham (2008), 'On the Horror of Phenomenology: Lovecraft and Husserl', *Collapse*, IV, 332–65.

Harman, Graham (2012), *Weird Realism: Lovecraft and Philosophy*, Winchester: Zero Books.

Harries, Dan (2000), *Film Parody*, London: BFI.

Haynes, Natalie (2011), 'Night of the Living Metaphors', *The Independent*, <http://www.independent.co.uk/voices/commentators/natalie-haynes-night-of-the-living-metaphors-2300655.html> (last accessed 28 February 2017).

Heller, Jason (2009), 'Gateways To Geekery: H. P. Lovecraft', *The Onion – AV Club*, <http://www.avclub.com/article/hp-lovecraft-34737> (last accessed 22 March 2017).

Hendershot, Cyndy (1998), *The Animal Within. Masculinity and the Gothic*, Ann Arbor: The University of Michigan Press.

Hogle, Jerrold (2012), 'The Gothic Ghost of the Counterfeit and the Progress of Abjection', in *A New Companion to the Gothic*, ed. David Punter, London: Blackwell, pp. 497–509.

Höglund, Johan (2014), *The American Imperial Gothic: Popular Culture, Empire, Violence*, Farnham: Ashgate.

Holland, Eugene W. (2013), *Deleuze and Guattari's A Thousand Plateaus*, London: Bloomsbury.

Horowitz, Anthony (2005), *The Power of Five: Raven's Gate*, London: Walker.

Horowitz, Anthony (2006), *The Power of Five: Evil Star*, London: Walker.

Horowitz, Anthony (2007), *The Power of Five: Nightrise*, London: Walker.

Horowitz, Anthony (2009), *The Power of Five: Necropolis*, London: Walker.

Horowitz, Anthony (2011), 'Anthony Horowitz Q & A', Scholastic.com, <http://www.scholastic.com/teachers/article/anthony-horowitz-q> (last accessed 21 March 2017).

Horowitz, Anthony (2012), *The Power of Five: Oblivion*, London: Walker.

Houellebecq, Michel (2008), *H. P. Lovecraft: Against the World, Against Life*, London: Gollancz.

Hourihan, Margery (1997), *Deconstructing the Hero: Literary Theory and Children's Literature*, London: Routledge.

Howard, Jacqueline (1994), *Reading Gothic Fiction: A Bakhtinian Approach*, Oxford: Clarendon Press.

Hume, Robert D. (1969), 'Gothic Versus Romantic: A Revaluation of the Gothic Novel', *PMLA* 84: 2, 282–90.

Hunter, Nick (2013), *Popular Culture: 2000 and Beyond*, London: Raintree.

Hutcheon, Linda (1985), *A Theory of Parody: The Teachings of Twentieth-Century Art Forms*, New York: Methuen.

Hutcheon, Linda (2006), *A Theory of Adaptation*, London: Routledge.

Huyssen, Andreas (1986), *After the Great Divide: Modernism, Mass Culture, Postmodernism*, Bloomington: Indiana University Press.

Jackson, Rosemary (1981), *Fantasy: The Literature of Subversion*, London: Routledge.

Jackson, Anna, Karen Coats and Roderick McGillis (2008), 'Introduction', in *The Gothic in Children's Literature: Haunting the Borders*, New York: Routledge, pp. 1–14.

Jameson, Fredric (1991), *Postmodernism, Or, The Cultural Logic of Late Capitalism*, Durham, NC: Duke University Press.

Jenkins, Henry (2012), *Textual Poachers: Television Fans and Participatory Culture*, New York: Routledge.

Jenkins, Henry (2014), 'Textual Poachers', in *The Fan Fiction Studies Reader*, ed. Kristina Busse and Karen Hellekson, Iowa City: The University of Iowa Press, pp. 26–43.

Joshi, S. T (1990), *The Weird Tale*, Holicong, PA: Wildside Press.

Joshi, S. T. (2001), *The Modern Weird Tale*, Jefferson, NC: McFarland.

Joshi, S. T. (2004), *The Evolution of the Weird Tale*, New York: Hippocampus Press.

Kant, Immanuel [1781] (2007), *Critique of Pure Reason*, rev. edn, London: Penguin Classics.

Kidd, Kenneth B. (2011), *Freud in Oz – At the Intersections of Psycho-analysis and Children's Literature*, Minneapolis: University of Minnesota Press.

Kincaid, James (1994), *Child-Loving: The Erotic Child and Victorian Literature*, New York: Routledge.

Klosterman, Chuck (2010), 'How Modern Life Is Like a Zombie Onslaught', *The New York Times*, 3 December, <http://www.nytimes.com/2010/12/05/arts/television/05zombies.html> (last accessed 28 February 2017).

Kristeva, Julia (1980), *Desire in Language: A Semiotic Approach to Literature and Art*, ed. Leon S. Roudiez, trans. Thomas Gora, Alice Jardine and Leon S. Roudiez, New York: Columbia University Press.

Kutzer, Daphne (1986), 'I Won't Grow Up – Yet: Teen Formula Romance', *Children's Literature Association Quarterly*, 11:2, 90–5.

Landy, Derek (2007), *Skulduggery Pleasant*, London: Harper Collins.

Landy, Derek (2009), *The Faceless Ones*, London: Harper Collins.

Landy, Derek (2010), *Dark Days*, London: Harper Collins.

Landy, Derek (2011), *Death Bringer*, London: Harper Collins.

Landy, Derek (2013), *Kingdom of the Wicked*, London: Harper Collins.

Latham, Rob (2013), 'Tim Burton's Trash Cinema Roots: Ed Wood and Mars Attacks!' *The Works of Tim Burton: Margins to Mainstream*, ed. Jeffrey Andrew Weinstock, New York: Palgrave Macmillan, pp. 133–49.

Laws, Zach (2013), 'Writer/director Chris Butler on "True Hybrid" Oscar Contender *Paranorman*', *Goldderby.com*, 11 February, <http://www.goldderby.com/news/4034/paranorman-chris-butler-oscars-academy-awards-animated-feature-news-entertainment-13579086.html> (last accessed 16 March 2017).

Leith, Sam (2009), 'Do You Know What Today's Kids Need? Thumb Amputation, That's What', *The Guardian*, 1 November, <http://www.guardian.co.uk/books/2009/nov/01/sam-leith-childrens-films-books> (last accessed 18 September 2016).

Lesnik-Oberstein, Karín (1994), *Children's Literature: Criticism and the Fictional Child*, Oxford: Clarendon Press.

Lesnik-Oberstein, Karín (1998), 'Childhood and Textuality', in *Children in Culture*, ed. Karín Lesnik-Oberstein, London: Macmillan.

Lesnik-Oberstein, Karín (1999), 'What Is Children's Literature? What Is Childhood?' in *Understanding Children's Literature*, ed. Peter Hunt, London: Routledge, pp. 15–29.

Lesnik-Oberstein, Karín (2000), 'The Psychopathology of Everyday Children's Literature Criticism', *Cultural Critique*, 45, 222–42.

Lewis, Vanessa (2012), 'Preview of July Books', *Bookseller*, <http://www.annefine.co.uk/books/devilwalks.php> (last accessed 18 September 2016).

Lord, Beth (2010), *Spinoza's Ethics*, Edinburgh: Edinburgh University Press.

Lovecraft, H. P. (1927), 'Supernatural Horror in Literature', *HP Lovecraft.com*, <http://www.hplovecraft.com/writings/litcrit/shil.aspx> (last accessed 21 March 2017).

Lovecraft, H. P. (1963), *The Haunter of the Dark and Other Tales*, ed. August Derleth, London: Panther.

Lutz, Deborah (2006), *The Dangerous Lover: Gothic Villains, Byronism, and the Nineteenth-Century Seduction Narrative*, Columbus: Ohio State University Press.

McGowan, John (1991), *Postmodernism and Its Critics*, Ithaca, NY: Cornell University Press.

McHale, Brian (1987), *Postmodernist Fiction*, London: Methuen.

McIntosh, Shawn (2008), 'The Evolution of the Zombie: The Monster that keeps coming back', in *Zombie Culture: Autopsies of the Living Dead*, ed. Mark Leverette and Shawn McIntosh, Lanham, MD: Scarecrow Press, pp. 1–17.

Marcus, Steven (1984), *Freud and the Culture of Psychoanalysis: Studies in the Transition from Victorian Humanism to Modernity*, Boston: Allen & Unwin.

Massé, Michelle (2003), 'Constructing the Psychoanalytic Child', in *The American Child: A Cultural Studies Reader*, ed. Caroline Field Levander and Carol J. Singley, New Brunswick, NJ: Rutgers University Press, pp. 149–66.

Mecke, Jochen (2006), 'Der Prozess der Authentizitat: Strukturen, Paradoxien und Funktion einer zentralen Kategorie moderner Literatur', in *Authentizität: Diskussion eines ästhetischen Begriffs*, ed. Susanne Knaller and Harry Muller, München: Fink, pp. 82–114.

Meillassoux, Quentin (2009), *After Finitude: An Essay on the Necessity of Contingency*, London: Continuum.

Merritt, Stephanie (2008), 'What Lily Did on Her Holidays', *The Guardian*, 23 March, <http://www.theguardian.com/books/2008/mar/23/booksfor-childrenandteenagers.features1> (last accessed 15 March 2017).

Midgely, Nick (2008), 'The Courage to Be Afraid: Fearful Encounters in the Work of Neil Gaiman and Dave McKean', in *The Story and the Self: Children's Literature: Some Psychoanalytic Perspectives*, ed. Jenny Plastow, Hatfield: University of Hertfordshire Press, pp. 128–41.

Miéville, China (2005), 'Introduction', in H. P. Lovecraft, *At the Mountains of Madness: The Definitive Edition*, New York: The Modern Library, pp. xi–xxv.

Miéville, China (2008), 'M.R. James and the Quantum Vampire: Weird; Hauntological: Versus And/or and And/ or Or?' *Collapse*, IV, 105–28.

Miéville, China (2009), 'Weird Fiction', in *The Routledge Companion to Science Fiction*, ed. Mark Bould, Andrew Butler, Adam Roberts and Sherryl Vint, London: Routledge, pp. 510–17

Miles, Robert (2001), 'Abjection, Nationalism and the Gothic', in *The Gothic*, ed. Fred Botting, Woodbridge: Boydell & Brewer, pp. 47–70.

Modleski, Tania (2007), *Loving with a Vengeance: Mass Produced Fantasies for Women*, New York: Routledge.

Moers, Ellen [1978] (1985), *Literary Women: The Great Writers*, Oxford: Oxford University Press.

Moore, Alan and Melinda Gebbie (2006), *Lost Girls*, Top Shelf Productions.

Morgenstern, John (2002), 'The Fall into Literacy and the Rise of the Bourgeois Child', *Children's Literature Association Quarterly* 27 (3), 136–45.

Morris, Paula (2009), *Ruined*, New York: Scholastic.

Mulvey, Laura (2009), 'Visual Pleasure and Narrative Cinema', in *Film Theory & Criticism*, ed. Leo Braudy and Marshall Cohen, Oxford: Oxford University Press, pp. 803–17.

Murphy Selinger, Eric (2007) 'Rereading the Romance', *Contemporary Literature* 48:2, 307–24.

Nikolajeva, Maria (2010), 'The Identification Fallacy: Perspective and Subjectivity in Children's Literature', in *Telling Children's Stories: Narrative Theory and Children's Literature*, ed. Michael Cadden, Lincoln: University of Nebraska Press, pp. 187–208.

Olson, Danel (2010), 'The Longest Gothic Goodbye in the World: Lemony Snicket's *A Series of Unfortunate Events*', in *21st-Century Gothic: Great Gothic Novels Since 2000*, ed. Danel Olsen, Lanham, MD: Scarecrow Press, pp. 506–26.

Ottinger, Ken (2014), *Al Azif, The Cipher Manuscript known as 'Necronomicon'*, bibliotecapleyades.net <https://www.bibliotecapleyades.net/cienciareal/necronomicon/necronomicon_02.htm> (last accessed 28 March 2017).

Ouzounian, Richard (2009), 'Author Returns to First Girlfriend', *The Toronto Star*, 7 February, <http://www.thestar.com/entertainment/article/583129--author-returns-to-first-girlfriend> (last accessed 18 September 2016).

Oxberry, Victoria (2006), '"I Didn't Mean to Frighten You": The Disney Gothic', *The Film Journal,* 13, <http://www.thefilmjournal.com/issue13/disneygothic.html> (last accessed 15 March 2017).

Page, Edwin (2006), *Gothic Fantasy: The Films of Tim Burton*, London: Marion Boyars.

Pallant, Chris (2011), *Demystifying Disney: A History of Disney Feature Animation*, New York: Continuum.

Parker, Trey (2010), 'Mysterion Rises', *South Park*.

Parrish, Berta (1983), 'Put a Little Romantic Fiction into Your Reading Program', *Journal of Reading* 26 (7), 610–15.

Parsons, Elizabeth, Naarah Sawers, and Kate McInally (2008), 'The Other Mother: Neil Gaiman's Postfeminist Fairy tales', *Children's Literature Association Quarterly* 33 (4), 371–89.

Paul, William (1994), *Laughing, Screaming: Modern Hollywood Horror and Comedy*, New York: Columbia University Press.

Pearce, Lynne (2006), *Romance Writing*, Cambridge: Polity Press.

Phiddian, Robert (1997), 'Are Parody and Deconstruction Secretly the Same Thing?' *New Literary History* 28 (4), 673–96.

Platts, Todd K. (2013), 'Locating Zombies in the Sociology of Popular Culture', *Sociology Compass* 7, 547–60.

Pullman, Philip (2002), 'Review of *Coraline*', *The Guardian*, 31 August, <http://www.theguardian.com/books/2002/aug/31/booksforchildrenandteenagers.neilgaiman> (last accessed 18 September 2016).

Punter, David (1989), 'Narrative and Psychology', in *Gothic Fictions: Prohibition/ Transgression*, ed. Kenneth Wayne Graham, New York: AMS Press, pp. 1–27.

Radway, Janice (1991), *Reading the Romance: Women, Patriarchy, and Popular Literature*, Chapel Hill: The University of North Carolina Press.

Reeve, Clara [1785] (1930), *The Progress of Romance and The History of Charoba, Queen of Aegypt*, New York: The Facsimile Text Society, <http://catalog.hathitrust.org/Record/002041663> (last accessed 10 March 2017).

Reeve, Clara [1778] (2008), *The Old English Baron*, ed. James Trainer, Oxford: Oxford University Press.

Reynolds, Kimberley (2001), 'Introduction', in *Frightening Fiction*, ed. K. Reynolds, G. Brennan and K. McCarron, London: Continuum, pp. 1–18.

Richter, Virginia (2009), 'Authenticity – Why We Still Need It Although It Doesn't Exist', in *Transcultural English Studies: Theories, Fictions, Realities*, ed. Frank Schulze-Engler and Sissy Helff, New York: Rodopi.

Rollins, Lucy and Mark I. West (1999), *Psychoanalytical Responses to Children's Literature*, Jefferson, NC: McFarland & Co.

Rose, Jacqueline (1984), *The Case of Peter Pan: Or the Impossibility of Children's Fiction*, London: Macmillan.

Ross, Andrew (1999), *The Celebration Chronicles: Life, Liberty and the Pursuit of Property Value in Disney's New Town*, New York: Ballantine Books.

Rudd, David (2008), 'An Eye for an I: Neil Gaiman's *Coraline* and Questions of Identity', *Children's Literature in Education*, 39 (3), 159–68.

Rushdie, Salman (1990), *Haroun and the Sea of Stories*, London: Granta.

Russo, Mary (1994), *The Female Grotesque*, New York: Routledge.

Ruth, Greg (2014), 'Why Horror Is Good for You (and Even Better for Your Kids)', *Tor.com*, 29 May, <http://www.tor.com/2014/05/29/why-horror-is-good-for-you-and-even-better-for-your-kids/> (last accessed 18 September 2016).

Schickel, Richard [1968] (1997), *The Disney Version: The Life, Times, Art, and Commerce of Walt Disney*, 3rd edn, Chicago: Ivan R. Dee.

Schoene-Harwood, Berthold (1999), 'Dams Burst: Devolving Gender in Iain Banks's *The Wasp Factory*', *Ariel* 30 (1), 131–48.

Scott, A. O (2012), '*Frankenweenie*: Tim Burton's Homage to Horror Classics', *The New York Times*, 4 October, <http://www.nytimes.com/2012/10/05/movies/frankenweenie-tim-burtons-homage-to-horror-classics.html> (last accessed 15 March 2017).

Sedgwick, Eve Kosofsky (1981), 'The Character in the Veil: Imagery of the Surface in the Gothic Novel', *PMLA* 96 (2), 255–70.

Sedgwick, Eve Kosofsky (1986), *The Coherence of Gothic Conventions*, New York: Methuen.

Seelinger Trites, Roberta (2001), 'The Uncanny in Children's Literature', *Children's Literature Association Quarterly*, 26 (4), 162.

Seymenliyska, E. (2011), 'Children's Books: Fantasy 9–12', *The Telegraph*, 12 July, <http://www.telegraph.co.uk/culture/books/bookreviews/8623043/Childrens-Books-Fantasy-9-12.html> (last accessed 19 September 2016).

Shan, Darren (2012a), *Zom-B*, London: Simon & Schuster.

Shan, Darren (2012b), '*Zom-B*: Author Notes,' *Darren Shan: Master of Horror*, <http://www.darrenshan.com/books/details/zom-b/> (last accessed 25 September 2017).

Shan, Darren (2013a), *ZOM-B City*, London: Simon & Schuster.

Shan, Darren (2013b), *ZOM-B Underground*, London: Simon & Schuster.

Shan, Darren (2014a), *ZOM-B Baby*, London: Simon & Schuster.

Shan, Darren (2014b), *ZOM-B Circus*, London: Simon & Schuster.

Shan, Darren (2014c), 'Author Q+A: Darren Shan', *The Guardian*, 17 March, <http://www.theguardian.com/childrens-books-site/2014/mar/17/interview-darren-shan> (last accessed 25 February 2017).

Smith, Andrew, and Diana Wallace (2004), 'The Female Gothic: Then and Now', *Gothic Studies* 6 (1), 1–7.

Smith, David (2005), 'Potter's Magic Spell Turns Boys into Bookworms', *The Observer*, 10 July, <http://www.theguardian.com/uk/2005/jul/10/books.harrypotter> (last accessed 10 February 2017).

Snicket, Lemony [1999] (2007), *The Bad Beginning*, London: Harper Collins.

Snicket, Lemony [2006] (2012), *The End*, London: Egmont.

Soble, Alan (1990), *The Structure of Love*, New Haven: Yale University Press.

Spinoza, Benedict (1996), *Ethics*, ed. Stuart Hampshire, trans. Edwin Curley, London: Penguin Classics.

Spooner, Catherine (2006), *Contemporary Gothic*, London: Reaktion Books.

Spooner, Catherine (2013), 'Gove and the Gothic: Why are the Tories so troubled by Twilight?', *Lancaster University News & Blogs*, 27 September, <http://www.lancaster.ac.uk/news/blogs/catherine-spooner/gove-and-the-gothic-why-are-the-tories-so-troubled-by-twilight/> (last accessed 7 March 2017).

Springhall, John (1994), 'Pernicious Reading? The Penny Dreadful as Scapegoat for Late-Victorian Juvenile Crime', *Victorian Periodicals Review*, 27:4, 326–49.

Stephens, John (1992), *Language and Ideology in Children's Fiction*, Harlow: Longman.

Stirling Observer (2010), 'Review: The Lunatic's Curse', *The Stirling Observer*, <http://www.stirlingobserver.co.uk/lifestyle/arts-stirling/2010/07/09/book-review-the-lunatic-s-curse-by-fe-higgins-51226-26812686> (last accessed 7 April 2016).

Stommel, Jesse (2013), 'Toward a Zombie Pedagogy: Embodied Teaching and the Student 2.0', in *Zombies in the Academy: Living Death in*

Higher Education, ed. Ruth Walker, Andrew Whelan and Christopher Moore, Bristol: Intellect, pp. 265–76.

Summers, Montague (1964), *The Gothic Quest*, New York: Russell & Russell.

Swan, Susan Z (1999), 'Gothic Drama in Disney's Beauty and the Beast: Subverting Traditional Romance by Transcending the Animal-Human Paradox', *Critical Studies in Mass Communication* 16 (3), 350–69.

Tatar, Maria (1992), *Off With Their Heads!: Fairy Tales and the Culture of Childhood*, Princeton: Princeton University Press.

Tatar, Maria (2009), *Enchanted Hunters: The Power of Stories in Childhood*, New York: W. W. Norton.

The Telegraph (2009), 'Books for Children: Adventures to Enchanting Worlds', *The Telegraph,* 3 July, <http://www.telegraph.co.uk//culture/books/bookreviews/5720639/Summer-Reading-for-Children-Adventures-to-enchanting-worlds.html> (last accessed 18 September 2016).

Thomson, Philip (1972), *The Grotesque*, London: Methuen.

Thomson, Stephen (2004), 'The Child, the Family, the Relationship: Family, Storytelling, and Ideology in Philip Pullman's *His Dark Materials*', in *Children's Literature: New Approaches*, ed. Karín Lesnik-Oberstein, New York: Palgrave Macmillan, pp. 144–67.

Thornton, Sarah (1995), *Club Cultures: Music, Media and Subcultural Capital*, Cambridge: Polity Press.

Thurston, Carol (1987), *The Romance Revolution: Erotic Novels for Women and the Quest for a New Sexual Identity*, Urbana: University of Illinois Press.

Tichelaar, Thomas R. and Marie Mulvey-Roberts (2012), 'Foreword', *The Gothic Wanderer: From Transgression to Redemption. Gothic Literature from 1794–Present*, Ann Arbor, MI: Modern History Press.

Townshend, Dale (2008), 'The Haunted Nursery: 1764–1830', in *The Gothic in Children's Literature: Haunting the Borders*, ed. A. Jackson, K. Coats and R. McGillis, London: Routledge, pp. 15–38.

Trowbridge, Serena (2013), 'Why Harry Potter is Gothic and Twilight isn't', *blogs.bcu.ac.uk*, 4 July, <http://blogs.bcu.ac.uk/views/2013/07/04/why-harry-potter-is-gothic-and-twilight-isnt/> (last accessed 16 May 2017).

Tyler, Imogen (2008), '"Chav Mum, Chav Scum" – Class Disgust in Contemporary Britain', *Feminist Media Studies*, 8 (1), 17–34.

Tyler, Imogen (2013), *Revolting Subjects: Social Abjection and Resistance in Neoliberal Britain*, London: Zed.

Van Lente, Fred, and Steve Ellis (2000), *Why We're Here*, <http://www.fredvanlente.com/cthulhutract/> (last accessed 22 March 2017).

Vincent, Mal (2012), 'Disney Embraces Tim Burton's Taste for Dark and Quirky', *The Virginian Pilot*, 7 October, <http://hamptonroads.com/2012/10/disney-embraces-tim-burtons-taste-dark-and-quirky> (last accessed 15 March 2017).

Vološinov, V. N., and M. M. Bakhtin (1986), *Marxism and the Philosophy of Language*, trans. Matejka and I. R Titunik, Cambridge, MA: Harvard University Press.

Walpole, Horace [1764] (2014), *The Castle of Otranto: A Gothic Story*, ed. Nick Groom, Oxford: Oxford University Press.

Walz, Gene (1998), 'Charlie Thorson and the Temporary Disneyfication of Warner Bros. Cartoons', in *Reading the Rabbit: Explorations in Warner Bros. Animation*, ed. Kevin S. Sandler, New Brunswick, NJ: Rutgers University Press, pp. 49–66.

Warner, Marina (2000), *No Go the Bogeyman: Scaring, Lulling and Making Mock*, London: Vintage.

Warwick, Alexandra (2007), 'Feeling Gothicky?', *Gothic Studies*, 9:1, 5–19.

Wasko, Janet (2001), *Understanding Disney the Manufacture of Fantasy*, Cambridge: Polity Press.

Weinstock, Jeffrey (2013), 'Mainstream Outsider: Burton Adapts Burton', in *The Works of Tim Burton: Margins to Mainstream*, ed. J. Weinstock, New York: Palgrave Macmillan, pp. 1–28.

Wigutoff, Sharon, and Margaret Dodson (1983), 'Bait/Rebait: There's Nothing Dirty about a Good Clean Romance', *The English Journal* 72 (2), 16–19.

Young, Robert J. C. (1999), 'Freud's Secret: The Interpretation of Dreams Was a Gothic Novel', in *The Interpretation of Dreams: New Interdisciplinary Essays*, ed. Laura Marcus, Manchester: Manchester University Press, pp. 206–31.

Young, Robert J. C. (2013), 'Re: Freud's Secret', email, 15 February.

Zipes, Jack (1983), *Fairy Tales and the Art of Subversion: The Classical Genre for Children and the Process of Civilisation*, New York: Routledge.

Zipes, Jack (2002), *Sticks and Stones: The Troublesome Success of Children's Literature from Slovenly Peter to Harry Potter*, London: Routledge.

Žižek, Slavoj (1992), *Looking Awry*, Cambridge, MA: The MIT Press.

Index

Index